THE ROMAN REMAINS OF
SOUTHERN FRANCE

Frontispiece The Gallo-Roman officer from Vachères (see Avignon Museum, p. 154).

THE ROMAN
REMAINS OF
SOUTHERN FRANCE

A guidebook

James Bromwich

London and New York

First published 1993
by Routledge
11 New Fetter Lane, London EC4P 4EE

Simultaneously published in the USA and Canada
by Routledge
29 West 35th Street, New York, NY 10001

Typeset in 10 on 12 point Garamond Linotronic 300 by
Florencetype, Weston-Super-Mare, Avon

Printed in Great Britain by
Butler & Tanner Ltd, Frome and London

British Library Cataloguing in Publication Data
A catalogue record for this book is available from the British Library

Library of Congress Cataloging in Publication Data
Bromwich, James (James Stephen),
The Roman remains of southern France: a guide book/James Bromwich.
p. cm.
Includes bibliographical references and index.
1. France, Southern–Antiquities, Roman–Guidebooks. 2. Romans–
France, Southern–Guidebooks. 3. France, Southern–Maps, Tourist.
I. Title.
DC607.4.B76   1993
914.4′804839–dc20   92–14820

ISBN 0–415–00837–9

CONTENTS

FIGURES

PLATES

14 Gladiators fighting. The man on the left is a retiarius, on the right is a myrmillon. Medaillon de Cavillargues, Nîmes. Photograph: Musée Archéologique, Nîmes.

15 Arles. Amphitheatre external galleries showing how the flat stones that once separated the lower and upper passages have disappeared.

16 Arles. The surviving western side of a monumental entrance and staircase that once led up into the forum.

17 Arles. The exceptional exterior of the Baths of Constantine with the typical late Roman alternating brick and stonework.

18 Arles. Octavian, later to call himself Augustus, depicted here as a very young man with a thin, wispy beard. Photograph: Michel Lacanaud/ Musée d'Arles.

19 Arles. A rare marble copy, ordered by the Senate to be distributed round the Empire, of the golden shield given by the Senate to Augustus in gratitude for the peace he brought to the Roman world. Photograph: Michel Lacanaud/Musée d'Arles.

20 Avignon. Relief of a barge being pulled up a river. Probably from a tombstone dedicated to a boat-owner. Musée Lapidaire. Photograph: Musée Calvet, Avignon.

21 Barbégal. The great mill driven by sixteen water wheels. Note the cutting made through the rock to bring the water from the aqueduct. Photograph: Antoine Chenet, Centre Camille Jullian.

22 Carpentras. A German prisoner depicted on the triumphal arch.

23 Marseille. The Lacydon merchant ship being excavated in the horn of the silted Roman harbour. Photograph: Réveillac, Centre Camille Jullian.

24 Orange. Triumphal arch, looking at the south face.

25 Orange. The interior of the theatre looking down on to the stage. Note the size of the people and the Imperial statue on the stage building.

26 St Chamas. The twin memorial arches at each end of Le Pont Flavien Roman Bridge.

27 St Rémy-de-Provence. Glanum sits at the entrance to the Notre-Dame de Laval valley, one of the easier routes through the rugged Alpilles range. Photograph: Christian Hussy, Direction des Antiquités de Provence-Alpes-Côte d'Azur.

28 St Rémy-de-Provence. The arch and staircase down to the sacred spring in the sanctuary area of Glanum.

29 St Rémy-de-Provence. 'Les Antiques', the shrunken triumphal arch, attic removed, and the elegant, well-proportioned mausoleum.

30 St Rémy-de-Provence. This scene on the west relief depicts heroes fighting using a mix of Roman and foreign equipment.

31 St Rémy-de-Provence. A Gallo-Greek capital from the trapezoidal court in Glanum. The Gallic head of Apollo fills the space between the Corinthian volutes. Photograph: Réveillac, Centre Camille Jullian.

32 St Rémy-de-Provence. The high cheek-bones and formal bouffant hair-

PREFACE

The origins of this book lie in the bookshops and bars of southern France. Why was there so often that look of incomprehension, or shrug of the shoulders, if we asked for a guidebook that identified and described the major – and possibly some of the minor – Roman sites? After all, France had been part of the Roman Empire, and Roman civilisation had made an even deeper impact than in Britain. Yet there seemed to be nothing. There were general books, in both French and English; there were individual guides to a limited number of sites which were only available at or near the places they were describing; but no book that attempted to introduce the whole region to the interested traveller.

At first frustration simply led to another sip of wine, but the answer gradually emerged as we discussed the situation. Holidays became research events: discovering and visiting sites and museums, pursuing obscure references to books, articles, prints or photographs, and meeting people.

How do you find sites when there is no guidebook? Initially it seemed unlikely that there would be a problem; the general works on the Gallo-Roman era are distillations of knowledge drawing heavily on evidence from the remains. However, an important archaeological site has not necessarily left much to be seen, indeed some have left nothing at all. It was not always clear from the reading that the excavation which led to fascinating revelations was followed by the construction of a block of flats or that the site was afterwards abandoned and is now totally overgrown. My son, then 13, has never forgotten the tattered and dismal excavation remains of the 'second best villa' in France (not included in this book!).

It is, then, people on whom I have depended. The chance meeting at the roadside that led me to a Roman aqueduct hidden in the countryside; the assistance from museum curators, often so willing to help me with my awkward stumbling enquiries, and most of all, the archaeologists. The encouragement given by the enthusiastic replies of K. D. White on Roman olive mills and R. Agache on aerial photography were fundamental in the early stages. The kind help I received from the Regional Director and his assistants in Aix-en-Provence was vital. I would like to thank particularly

Chérine Gébara, the municipal archaeologist at Fréjus, who opened my eyes to what could be seen. Some of my most appalling Latin errors have been removed due to the generously given advice of Mark Hassall at University College, London. Librarians at the Institute of Archaeology (University College) and those of the Institute of Classical Studies have been consistently sympathetic. Without Tim Pooley (London Guildhall University) and his vital contributions, my written communications would have been dramatically poorer.

The drawings used to illustrate the text can rarely claim much originality, but I am responsible for the versions presented here. They embody what I have chosen to include – and exclude. However, they could not have been done without the crucial assistance of Edward Oliver and John Wilson, who actually drafted the majority of the maps and plans.

Lastly I would like to thank family, friends and colleagues. They have provided ideas, reassurance and tolerance for an increasingly one-track mind. Despite the 'second best villa', my son, Stephen, has collected map references, whilst my wife, Anne, has not only given me constant encouragement (amazing when I consider my obsessiveness), but also read everything I have written, pointed out faulty English, corrected many of my spelling errors and, perhaps most important of all, advised me when I seemed to be losing sight of the interested traveller.

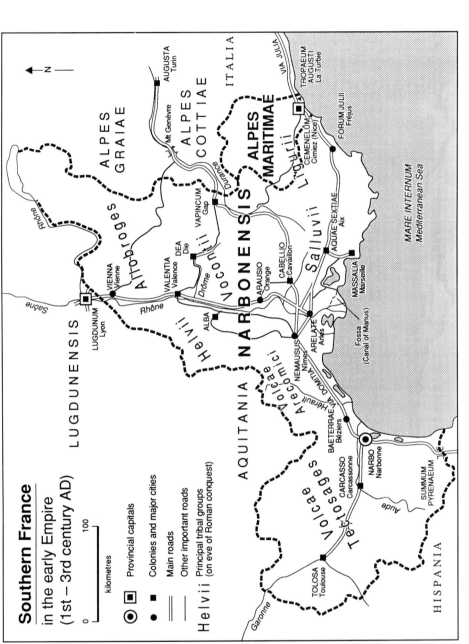

Southern France

in the early Empire
(1st – 3rd century AD)

kilometres

0   100

◉▣   Provincial capitals

■   Colonies and major cities

═══   Main roads

───   Other important roads

Helvii   Principal tribal groups
(on eve of Roman conquest)

← N ─

LUGDUNENSIS

ALPES
GRAIAE

AUGUSTA
Turin

Mt Genèvre

ALPES
COTTIAE

ITALIA

Allobroges

VIENNA
Vienne

Rhône

VAPINCUM
Gap

Durance

ALPES
MARITIMAE

VIA JULIA

TROPAEUM
AUGUSTI
La Turbie

CEMENELUM
Cimiez (Nice)

FORUM JULII
Fréjus

Ligurii

Saône

LUGDUNUM
Lyon

Rhône

Saône

DEA
Die

VALENTIA
Valence

Drôme

Voconii

ARAUSIO
Orange

CABELLIO
Cavaillon

Salluvii

AQUAE SEXTIAE
Aix

MASSALIA
Marseille

MARE INTERNUM
Mediterranean Sea

Helvii

ALBA

NARBONENSIS

NEMAUSUS
Nîmes

ARELATE
Arles

Fossa
(Canal of Marius)

AQUITANIA

Volcae
Arecomici

VIA DOMITIA

Hérault

BAETERRAE
Béziers

Volcae
Tectosages

CARCASSO
Carcassonne

NARBO
Narbonne

SUMMUM
PYRENAEUM

Aude

Garonne

TOLOSA
Toulouse

HISPANIA

Figure 1

INTRODUCTION

There is much pleasure to be found in the south of France: the blend of soft colours and powerful sun, the flowers and the twists of the olive trees, the vineyards and the stark rocks impart a warm glow to places like the Pont du Gard and help to create an immediate sense of the past – even more vividly in less visited sites like the temple ruins at Vernègues. I think though it is possible to get more. Only destruction, insensitive modern building and sometimes reconstruction can destroy our intuitive sense of the past; greater knowledge cannot. Just as a geologist can open our eyes to the physical environment, I hope I can add some meaning for visitors to the remains of what the French describe as 'la civilisation gallo-romaine'.

This guidebook is not an academic study, but it draws on what academics are doing. One of the excitements of visiting the amphitheatre at Arles is the possibility of understanding it in so many different ways: an awareness of the kind of activities that went on there; who sat in the seats and where, what made people want this kind of entertainment; the structural and architectural choices made by the builders; the changes that occurred during the Roman period and after; the different approaches adopted by archaeologists and the kinds of questions they ask themselves. Knowing more about these will not stop you sitting at the top and looking down into the arena and imagining the gladiators, nor will it stop you looking out across the river or to the more distant mountains, the same views experienced nearly 2,000 years ago; it can only enhance the imagination.

A guidebook is a personal choice, but in part driven by what we can see. In Britain, the major surviving features of romanisation are forts and villas rather than towns, in southern France romanisation is dominated by the city. This indicates a real difference – the southern Gallo-Roman world was certainly far more deeply urbanised – but it is also an aspect of the traditions of French archaeology where, until recently, interest has been concentrated on the major monuments and a desire to relate material discoveries directly to the sparse ancient written sources.

Today, there is far greater interest in the environment and economy of the south and a much more painstaking approach to archaeological research:

Christian Goudineau's work in Vaison-la-Romaine and J. L. Fiches's at Ambrussum on single houses are simply two examples of this changed attitude. However, much of this modern research does not produce dramatic new discoveries for people to see. Where Sautel, the original excavator, simply found a large Roman mansion, Goudineau's dig enabled him to give a history of the development of the site over three centuries: but to the visitor there is little overt difference between this and the next house that has not been re-excavated.

There is a wonderful variety in the Roman remains of the south. With the Maison Carrée (Nîmes), there is the shock of seeing a Roman temple virtually complete. There is the grandeur of the theatre at Orange, the amphitheatres at Nîmes and Arles or the triumphal monument at La Turbie. There is the surprise at finding a Roman milestone beside a road still in use (near Alba) and a perfect bridge still coping with car traffic (Le Pont Julien). At Vienne, it is admiration for the solution adopted to the damp problem of building houses beside the Rhône – an under-floor level of upside-down amphorae – that is as exciting as any of the more obvious remains. At Marseille, it is wonder at finding a ship preserved in a massive 'fish-tank' and pleasure at finding an archaeological garden in which a Roman quayside and a Greek city gate are preserved. Despite the lack of preserved villa sites and the absence of forts, there is the notable villa of Loupian and plentiful evidence of fortifications covering various periods, such as the ramparts of Fréjus or Carcassonne.

It is difficult to focus on the Roman period in southern France and fail to be aware of the Greek element. At last the 1960s excavations have given Marseille physical evidence of its hundreds of years as an independent Greek colony. A sub-colony has been revealed at Olbia (Hyères) and Greek influence is obvious at St Blaise and St Rémy (Glanum, the most complete of all Gallo-Roman cities of the south).

Equally, it would be wrong to ignore the indigenous element; without knowing anything about Gallic culture before romanisation it would be impossible to assess the nature of Gallo-Roman society. I have included the strikingly urban Entremont, just outside Aix-en-Provence, and the great hillfort site of Ensérune, the most fully excavated of the Languedoc sites and one with its own museum. It would be unforgivable to describe sites such as these without also pointing to the confident and sinister pre-Roman art (see Aix and Marseille museums particularly), and would give a very incomplete picture.

The south

The 'south' is a vague description. Here I have chosen it to mean all the departments in the Languedoc-Roussillon region and all those in Provence and the Côte d'Azur. In addition there are the three southern-most departments of the Rhône valley. These more or less cover the Roman provinces of Narbonensis and the Alpes Maritimae. The Romans included the Toulouse region in Narbonensis, more as a result of early expansion to control the route to the Garonne than as a natural part of this province. It seems to me it is better treated along with the rest of the Midi-Pyrénées and western France. Narbonensis also covered more of the alpine area while the Alpes Maritimae extended into what is now Italy.

The rationale for my choice comes with a notion of Mediterranean France. Travelling down the Rhône valley, it is at Vienne that the atmosphere seems to become southern. In fact the border the Romans chose for Narbonensis is just north of the city and approximates as well to the limits of Mediterranean soil and vegetation types, including olive cultivation. France here is characterised by a distinct climate; not only hot summers, short winters with rain in between, but also high winds. Above all, there is the openness to the sea. Even though there are differences in this part of the Mediterranean zone, limited to the east by the alpine frontier and to the west by the Pyrénées, the environment in which both indigenous peoples and Greek and Roman intruders developed was a common one: in this sense it is not surprising that romanisation was so successful here.

Sites and other sites

The importance of the majority of sites described here is obvious. Some sites that I have relegated to the summary 'Other sites' could easily have been given fuller treatment. The Gallic site of Martigues or the Gallo-Roman bridge sites in the lower Rhône region certainly made me hesitate, but a guidebook is ultimately a personal choice – governed finally by the need to avoid making it too heavy!

Maps and site plans

My own outline maps are designed to help you find sites, but should be used in conjunction with good published maps.

Each site is referenced to the relevant sheet number in the Michelin 1:200,000 and the IGN 1:100,000 series. The Michelin yellow series are cheap, ubiquitous and also use a fold number; the IGN products cover wider areas and are the nearest equivalent to the British Ordnance Survey maps.

Grid cross-references are also provided. Current Michelin maps use standard latitude and longitude degrees. On IGN maps and older Michelin maps, a gr(id) system based on Paris is used.

Detailed maps: many Gallo-Roman sites are covered by modern towns and there will be no problems in finding them. However, in some cases, such as the Fréjus aqueduct, the IGN Carte Topographique Bleu

1:25,000 or Orange 1:50,000 series, available in local tourist shops, should be used.

Site plans: these are all based on published plans in archaeological books and journals. They are frequently simplified to help you to identify the most important features.

Opening times of museums and sites

Despite misgivings, I have included times. Entry prices I ignore: they change even more often. The local tourist office is the best resource for the current position.

Books

There are now two modern books in English which provide excellent academic foundations for further research; my debt to them, and their bibliographies, should be clear. A. L. F. Rivet's *Gallia Narbonensis* (London, 1988) is a companion volume in a series on the provinces of the Roman Empire. It includes the Alpes Maritimae, although rather briefly. There is a detailed history of the development of the whole region followed by separate chapters on the cities and their territories. Each is a survey of the evidence in constructing history with an administrative bias; Rivet's main interest is structural growth and change. Anthony King's book, *Roman Gaul and Germany* (London, 1990), obviously takes in a much wider area, but it is also more broadly based, covering the ways in which archaeology has affected our notions of economic activity, the experience of town and country life and Romano-Celtic religions. Much of the evidence is drawn from southern France.

Two other books are stimulating. Barry Cunliffe's *Greeks, Romans and Barbarians* (London, 1988) brilliantly brings together recent research to provide a synthesis explaining the interaction of trade, influence, imperialism and assimilation. The changing position of southern France is a regular theme. Paul MacKendrick's *Roman France* (London, 1971) is interestingly organised to combine a straightforward history with case studies of particular sites and, though dated, is beautifully written.

Major French works are provided in the main bibliography, but many French newsagents stock *Les Dossiers d'archéologie* and less frequently *Archéologia*, two really excellent popularising journals that frequently have articles on sites in the south of France.

HISTORICAL DEVELOPMENT

Pre-Roman southern France

The traditional term used for the later prehistoric period in Europe is the Iron Age (*c.* 650–100 BC). Despite the apparent technological foundation for the term, based on the change of the material used to manufacture tools and weapons from bronze to the more widespread iron, for many years the term was primarily used to signify 'cultural' meanings: rather than metallurgy it implied weapon designs and distinctive pottery types. However, this approach no longer gives an adequate understanding of what was going on, particularly in southern France. It is now felt that the major features are not the gradual or sudden emergence of new 'cultures', but the trend to large settlements with signs of communal planning, the intensification of resource exploitation and the appearance of foreign goods. French authors often write of this period as 'la Protohistoire'.

650–450 BC

In the later seventh century BC, pottery from Punic Carthage, Etruscan Italy and the Greek world began to appear in significant amounts, much of it to be used to carry or consume wine. The process of dealing with such trade stimulated change. Production of salt along the Languedoc shore could be increased, metal ores could be mined in some parts of the more mountainous hinterlands, to find products the foreigners would want, exchange with peoples living inland could be sought out. Economic expansion was encouraged and centres to channel the activity developed. Large settlements, known today as oppida, with rectangular stone-built houses emerged on hilltops (e.g., Ensérune) and less frequently on the plains (e.g., Lattes).

By the sixth century these large settlements are clearly in competition with one another: they have walls and even towers. Perhaps the terraced streets and tower defences were simply a Mediterranean-wide phenomenon, more likely they were the result of the impact made by Greek colonisers. The most important were those from Phocea with foundations at Marseille, Agde, Antibes and Nice. By the later sixth century BC Marseille – the Greek Massalia – had become the major focus for trade, first up the Rhône, then throughout the region.

450–120s BC

From the mid-fifth century this pattern became less stable without undermining the position of the Greek colonies or upsetting the trend towards large indigenous towns. Celtic migrations from central Europe *c.* 450 BC–

150 BC helped create new tribes and tribal confederations in southern France, and their art forms, social and religious ideas permeated the region. It becomes possible to talk of an overall identity, the Gauls, with less integrated groups on the periphery: Ligurians on the mountainous eastern coastline and Iberians in the Roussillon plain.

Another large-scale change taking place in the west Mediterranean as a whole was to affect southern Gaul. Etruria never recovered from Celtic attacks while the Greek city states of the west were plagued by wars. Massalia became a territorial power in her own right, expanding inland and establishing her own sub-colonies like Olbia (by Hyères). But the main change was the steady rise of Rome. This had both an economic and a political impact.

There was an upsurge in trade with central Italy: amphorae and ceramics, particularly a black ware called Campanian, pour in. Other products, including slaves, are increasingly exported. The Gallic towns have more regular streets, grow larger and the walls around them are more impressive. They began to make stone sculpture and, another sign of the local Greek cultural impact, start to use Greek script.

Political change was equally significant. By the third century there were only two major powers: Rome and Carthage. In the series of wars fought between them (the Punic Wars of 261–244, 219–202 and 149–146 BC), southern Gaul became a buffer area between Roman power in Italy and the Carthaginians in Spain. Roman victory over Carthage did not change the situation as by then she had become embroiled in the conquest of Spain. Roman armies marching through Gaul became a common experience and Massalia a reliable ally of the Romans.

The origin of the Roman provinces 120s-20s BC

The decisive step in transforming southern Gaul came in the 120s. The Salluvii, a large tribal confederation, attacked the Massaliotes, who turned to Rome for help. The climax of the campaigns that followed was the establishment of Roman colonies at Aix and Narbonne and the consolidation of the road that ran from the Rhône to the Le Perthus pass into Spain, called the Via Domitia after Domitius Ahenobarbus, the founder of Narbo (Narbonne). Massalia was encouraged to take over control of much of central Provence, but it was always as Rome's subsidiary partner. In the early first century BC, southern Gaul was known as 'Provincia Gallia Transalpina' and Narbo had become a significant Roman town. Invaders were fought off, revolts put down and trade was intense, but there are few signs of major change amongst the inhabitants. The Gallic hilltop towns continue to be occupied, although now there was the occasional house built in the Roman manner.

From the 70s both Rome and Gaul underwent major transformations.

Pompey undertook significant recruitment of southern Gauls into the Roman army. In 62 BC the last tribe to rise against the Romans in the south, the Allobroges, was crushed. In 59 BC the first Triumvirate of Crassus, Pompey and Caesar was formed, an uneasy alliance of the leading men of Rome to control the Empire, which left the Roman Senate almost powerless. It allowed **C. Julius Caesar** to carry out the conquest of all northern Gaul (58–50 BC). The 'province' was no longer on the borders of the Empire.

When the Triumvirate collapsed (49 BC) and civil war broke out, Caesar immediately began to consolidate his power in southern Gaul. Having chosen to support Pompey, Marseille was besieged and subsequently lost most of its territory. It retained a semi-independent status which became increasingly meaningless. Fréjus was perhaps established as a military base in this period, Arles was made a veteran colony and probably Vienne too. Elsewhere Caesar encouraged much wider romanisation, made easier because he too had recruited widely in the region. Many of these veterans had been granted citizenship and absorbed a Roman lifestyle (see St Rémy, p. 201).

The murder of Caesar in 44 BC was ultimately followed by the accession to power of his adopted son **Octavian**. During the period of civil war that marked the years up to 31 BC (when Octavian became sole ruler) he and his right-hand man, Agrippa, obtained control of Gaul early on and they visited 'the province' in 39 BC. Veterans were settled in colonies at Béziers, Orange and Nîmes. Octavian **took the title of Augustus** in 27 BC when consolidating his position as **Emperor**. Reorganisation of the Empire soon followed: in 22 BC the Senate was allowed to appoint the governors of 'the province', now named '**Narbonensis**' after its leading city Narbonne. No legions were based here, a sure sign that it was considered securely romanised. Shortly after, when the Alps were finally conquered, the province of '**Alpes Maritimae**' emerged under a governor appointed directly by Augustus.

Southern Gallic society in the first century BC had many features that helped make romanisation relatively easy. Greek influence had paved the way and people were long accustomed to living in large settlements. Their economies were tied in with the Italian and they had already begun to cultivate both the vine and olive. There was an aristocracy, 'high spirited and quick for battle' (Strabo). Their aggression could be channelled into providing commanders of auxiliary troops, their love of display into an appreciation of the grand house. Communal decision-making occurred in large assemblies, but the nobility took the lead; it was a system easily modified to the Roman method of local government through a council of the privileged. They were accustomed to having numerous dependants, not significantly different from the Roman 'client' system. Where the traditional reward for followers might have been a feast it could become an amphitheatre performance. The most obvious Gallic survival was in religious belief. Even though the Druids were suppressed, at a deeper level romanisation was only a veneer. The awkward portrayals of gods use the conventions of classical sculpture, but embody a very different spirit.

The early Empire 20s BC–AD 270s

Romanisation above all meant towns. Early colonies had led the way and in the 40s BC indigenous towns were already copying the Roman model. However it was under Augustus that the massive upsurge in public building took place. There were the forums with their basilicas and temples (particularly linked to the cult of the Imperial family), creating administrative, ceremonial and social centres; theatres and then amphitheatres were to extend this social function; wells and springs gave way to piped water provided by aqueducts, supplying fountains, public baths and increasingly grand private houses. At the same time underground conduits were created to carry away sewage. Some cities had ramparts and triumphal arches to demonstrate their status. By AD 43, Pomponius Mela, a Roman geographer, felt justified in using the word 'opulent' to describe many of the major cities.

Most of the old oppida were abandoned, but not all. Sites like Ambrussum in Languedoc evolved into country towns, glorified farming villages. The great landowners, no doubt mostly descendants of the Gallic nobility, began to build large country houses with farming and residential sections that became increasingly luxurious. They were centres for the agricultural production of oil, wine, cereals and wool; for mining in the hinterland of Languedoc or the Estérel; and for fish-based industries on the coast. Rural sanctuaries equipped themselves with Roman-style temples and precincts. The old Gallic roads were modernised, bridges built and milestones put in place.

The details of economic history remain obscure. As site research has become more sophisticated, the development of specific places can be traced, but how much new building means regional prosperity and to what extent a fire is evidence of barbarian marauders is more difficult to say. Certainly the first two centuries AD were prosperous when compared with the troubled third century: a period racked by inflation, civil war and barbarian disturbances that may have reached southern Gaul as well.

There is little directly relevant political history. Whilst many leading men achieved senatorial status and a few became consuls, the pinnacle of a public career, they rarely became leading figures in Roman affairs. **Agricola**, born in Fréjus and educated in Marseille, was a notable exception. Few major events took place in this apparently peaceful province.

Significant disturbances were few. A revolt in central Gaul (AD 21) led by the Gallic nobles Florus and Sacrovir seemed threatening, but the population of Narbonensis ignored it; indeed the Orange triumphal arch probably records its suppression. In the short violent civil war that followed the death of Nero in AD 68, troops were raised in Narbonensis and a battle was fought somewhere near Fréjus. Following the murder of Commodus in AD 192, who like Nero, had chosen to indulge mad fantasies in power, much of Gaul was controlled by Clodius Albinus. Defeated in 197 by Severus, the aftermath was a period of Imperial distrust of Gallic administrators, including those of the south. However, the restoration of peace brought a major phase of public building.

When the last distant heir of Severus was deposed and killed in AD 235, the effect was very different: it marked the beginning of fifty years of political instability as one general after another created a short-lived regime. Roman armies fought one another; barbarian raids became common; debased coinage generated inflation and economic instability. Though Narbonensis and the Alpes Maritimae were not at the centre of any of the conflicts, the general impact is clear: urban renewal stops, whole town districts are abandoned and in the 270s widespread fires suggest further breakdown.

Southern France in late Antiquity AD 270s–470s

There is no precise date for the beginning of the late Roman Empire, but despite the recognition that the origins of the new structure lie earlier, the major figures in creating the very different Empire of the fourth century are still considered to be **Diocletian** (284–305) and **Constantine** (306–37). They created a new administrative system, adopted a new approach to defence, imposed a tough taxation system to support both and ensured that the very nature of religious belief would be transformed.

The provinces were reorganised on a two-tier basis. Whilst Alpes Maritimae only underwent boundary changes, Narbonensis was split into three new provinces: Narbonensis I in the west with its metropolis at Narbonne; Viennensis covering the lower Rhône and much of central Provence; and Narbonensis II east–central Provence. These four were combined with three new provinces created from Aquitania. The whole diocese was known as the Septem Provinciae, or Viennensis, as its *vicarius* or governor had his residence in Vienne (perhaps because it was of greater strategic importance than Narbonne).

Throughout the fourth century, Narbonne and Marseille remained important, but Vienne and Arles were the leading cities. Arles was able to compete with Vienne for prominence as it was chosen as an Imperial residence and, when Trier (Rhineland) was abandoned as a capital at the end of the fourth century, Arles became the main Imperial centre for Gaul. Most

Figure 2

cities were characterised by the construction of massive walls, but they generally enclosed only tiny areas: they were little more than bastions for the administrators, church and perhaps surrounding population. Old hilltop oppida were also reoccupied, yet for most of the fourth century southern Gaul had security. Though city life experienced this widespread decline, many of the elite spent massively on their villas. It was not them, but their peasants who carried the weight of Imperial taxes to pay for the new mobile army and the increasing numbers of barbarian soldiers who were taken in as ready-made forces.

When the Rhine froze in 406 and barbarian armies poured across, the uncertainties of ravaging armies were added to the constrictions of life imposed by the Imperial authorities. Faith in the revival of the Empire drained away, symbolised perhaps by the last known Roman milestone erected in the 430s.

The **Visigoths** were the most important barbarian group in the south. During the 420s, they were granted permission to settle in Aquitaine and soon took Toulouse and Carcassonne. When Narbonne fell to them in 462 the rest of Languedoc quickly followed. Arles finally capitulated in the 470s, thus opening the whole of Provence to them, although their control here was subsequently disputed by the Ostrogoths from Italy. The **Burgundians**, meanwhile, had occupied Vienne and the lower Rhône.

As the letters of Sidonius Apollinaris (*c.* 430–80) show, it was still possible in the 460s to commend the good life in Arles and to enjoy a Roman life on the estate, but it was best to make your peace with the local administrators (Roman or barbarian) or to become a bishop, preferably both: Sidonius did. Certainly, for the Gallo-Roman aristocracy the Emperor had become an irrelevancy, and when in 474 the last western Emperor was deposed and not replaced, it was hardly noticed.

How much land was taken by the barbarians is obscure; the evidence for their occupation is thin. It seems likely Gallic peasants still tilled the land, and largely for the same landowners. Barbarian administrators rarely wished to destroy Roman life and culture, they simply wanted their share: they had educated men at their courts, Latin was used and Roman law was maintained, barbarian law being adapted to it. International trade continued, even if at reduced levels. The roads remained open, as the letters of Sidonius reveal.

The most important element in late Antiquity was Christianity. Previously a minority sect, Constantine provided state backing and began the destruction of temples. Even so, it is only gradually through the fourth and fifth centuries that the bishops of southern Gaul are recorded, often through the councils they held. Roman paganism could accommodate both local Gallic gods and traditions and the many diverse eastern religions introduced, but Christianity could not. The process of absorption was slow but the transformation fundamental. Archaeology is demonstrating that by the fifth century the only significant monumental building going on is of churches, baptisteries and episcopal palaces. The main features of the medieval world were born in late Antiquity: the centrality of the church, the landowner and his dependent peasants, the insignificance of town life and the military power of the local ruler; only the Empire died.

CHRONOLOGY

BEFORE THE EMPIRE
c. 650–100 BC	Iron Age in southern France
600 BC	Marseille founded
510	Roman Republic established
c. 450	Celtic migrations
390	Celtic Gauls sack Rome
218	Hannibal leads Carthaginian army across Provence and the Alps into Italy
120s	Transalpine Gaul defined
122	Aix-en-Provence fort established
118	Narbonne colony founded
60	First Triumvirate (Pompey, Crassus and Caesar)
57–50	Gallic Wars Caesar conquers northern Gaul
49–45	Civil war
49	Siege and capture of Marseille
44	Victory of Caesar
	Murder of Caesar
43–31	Second Triumvirate (Antony, Lepidus and Octavian) and Civil War
31	Octavian triumphs at battle of Actium

Julius Caesar (100–44BC)

EARLY EMPIRE
27 BC	Octavian proclaimed **Augustus**
22	Gallia Transalpina renamed **Narbonensis**
	Alpes Maritimae area finally conquered
AD 14	Augustus dies
AD 14–68	*Julio-Claudians* (descendants of Augustus)
14–37	**Tiberius**

Strabo (Greek, born 64 BC)

37–42	Gaius, known as **Caligula**	
42–54	**Claudius**	
54–68	**Nero**	**Lucan** (AD 39–65)
68–9	*Civil War* (**Galba, Otho, Vitellius, Vespasian**)	
AD 69–96	*Flavians* (Vespasian and his family)	
69–79	**Vespasian**	**Pliny the Elder** (AD 23/4–79)
79–81	**Titus**	
81–96	**Domitian**	
AD 96–192	*The adoptives*	
96–8	**Nerva**	**Frontinus** (c. AD 30–104?)
98–117	**Trajan**	**Suetonius** (AD 70–130s?)
117–38	**Hadrian**	
138–61	**Antoninus Pius**	} known as *the Antonines*
161–80	**Marcus Aurelius** (with **Lucius Verus** 161–9)	
		Tacitus (c. AD 56–120s?)
180–92	**Commodus**	
192–4	**Civil war**	
AD 193–235	*The Severans* (Severus and his heirs)	
193–211	**Septimus Severus**	
211–17	**Caracalla**	
217–35	*Later Severans*	
AD 235–84	*The military men*	
	Frequent civil war and short-lived Emperors	

LATER EMPIRE

AD 284–305	**Diocletian**	
	Creation of smaller provinces in southern France	
306–37	**Constantine**	
395–423	**Honorius**	
476	**Romulus Augustulus** last Emperor	**Sidonius Apollinaris** (AD 432–80?)
	Deposed and spared	

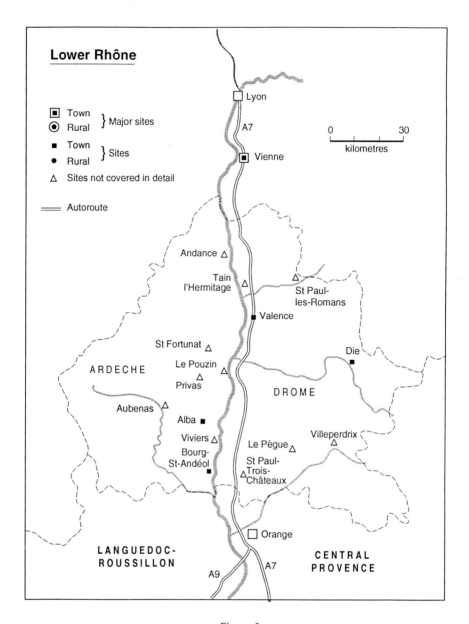

Figure 3

1

THE SITES OF THE LOWER RHONE

ALBA, Ardèche

Michelin 80–9
IGN 59–A8
2,52/49,50gr
4°36/44°34

Town site.

The remains are on both sides of the D107, Viviers to Aubenas road, 1 km north of Alba village.

Gentle bare hills, whose peaks form a rim round a rich agricultural basin, are the sedimentary and volcanic backdrop to the decline of the former chief city of the Helvii people. The small village of Aps, renamed Alba in 1903, is to all appearances a medieval village of tiny streets and gritty limestone and basalt houses with a market, restaurants and a good local information office.

Little is known about the Helvii before the Roman conquest. The isolated exploration of the lower levels shows that the Alba area was occupied in the second century BC but that urbanisation only took place after Caesar's conquest of the rest of Gaul and the introduction of the vine during the first century AD was probably the key to the city's economic growth in the early Empire. The prosperity, though, was shortlived: Alba, outside the main lines of communication, never recovered from the collapse experienced throughout the lower Rhône in the later third century. The replanting of vineyards has inspired the present professional archaeological activity as it has revealed, and threatens to destroy, the extensive ruins just below the surface. Sadly for the visitor, more could be done to keep the exposed remains clear of undergrowth.

The main north–south road

A 10–15 m stretch of the main *cardo* has been excavated on the northern side of a cutting for the D107. The easiest approach is to walk up the track

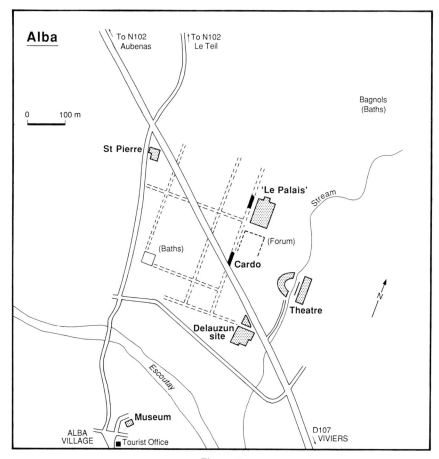

Alba

To N102
Aubenas

To N102
Le Teil

Bagnols
(Baths)

0   100 m

St Pierre

'Le Palais'

Stream

(Forum)

(Baths)

Cardo

N

Theatre

Delauzun
site

Escoutay

Museum

ALBA
VILLAGE

Tourist Office

D107
VIVIERS

Figure 4

50 m to the west. A wall marks the eastern side and a pavement the western.

The Le Palais/'forum' site

The *cardo* runs on through fields and vineyards. It has been recently suggested that the porticoed buildings still hidden here could include the forum. The next exposed section is reached by walking *c.* 150 m from the modern road in a north-north-west direction, roughly parallel to the *cardo*. It is partially surrounded by bushes, trees and fencing but is still accessible. This is the site that has traditionally been known as 'Le Palais'.

The buildings excavated here are now interpreted as a temple complex with five shops facing the road, probably selling gifts for visiting worshippers. The precinct portico was surrounded by a wall with *exedras* and rectangular recesses.

The theatre

This is the only properly consolidated site in Alba and is signposted from the D107.

It is a curious and rather disappointing place. It still seems dilapidated even after considerable restoration. Despite its discovery in 1821, the three-stage development of the theatre was only finally determined in the early 1980s. Originally an Augustan polygonal *cavea* was built with wooden seats using the natural sides of a valley, expanded during AD 30–45 and then massively strengthened in the later second century. This final modification gave it a semi-circular shape, a new upper section constructed over vomitoria and a balcony whose vaulted base is still visible. The real surprise is that the river has not changed course but seems to have been present in Antiquity, passing under the *pulpitum*! It was the abandonment of maintenance that led to its destructive role (see model in the museum).

Delauzun site

Almost entirely hidden by grass are traces of two houses and a road.

St Pierre site

At the junction of the D107 and the side road to Alba village, an unidentified Gallo-Roman building, indicated by the *petit appareil* walling, was found under the remains of two early Christian churches. The remains still confuse professional archaeologists.

The museum

Rue de Chabrol.
Hours: Monday–Saturday 2.00–6.00 p.m.

An attractive traditional stone house contains the current museum. It is also the excavation centre and there is therefore only limited, though interesting, material on display.

The finest exhibit is the **fish mosaic**. It is only part of a much larger mosaic, 12 × 8 m, taken from a dining room, judging by the subject matter and position, in the northern *domus* on the Delauzun site. The line and colouring of the carp and perch are particularly delicate.

There is a **model of the theatre** and pictorial displays of the latest excavation work. It is to be hoped that space will be found for showing more

Alba

MILESTONE

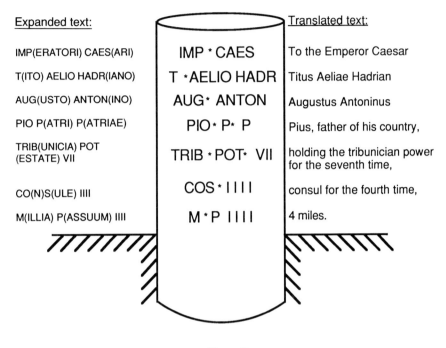

Expanded text:		Translated text:
IMP(ERATORI) CAES(ARI)	IMP * CAES	To the Emperor Caesar
T(ITO) AELIO HADR(IANO)	T *AELIO HADR	Titus Aeliae Hadrian
AUG(USTO) ANTON(INO)	AUG* ANTON	Augustus Antoninus
PIO P(ATRI) P(ATRIAE)	PIO* P* P	Pius, father of his country,
TRIB(UNICIA) POT (ESTATE) VII	TRIB * POT* VII	holding the tribunician power for the seventh time,
CO(N)S(ULE) IIII	COS * I I I I	consul for the fourth time,
M(ILLIA) P(ASSUUM) IIII	M *P I I I I	4 miles.

Figure 5

of the finds to the public. Especially interesting is an inscription describing a financial endowment for the *centonarii, fabri, utricularii* and *dendrophori* of Alba: the cloth merchants, woodworkers, boatmen and woodcutters. Perhaps we have here a patron not just supporting four leading corporations or guilds, but a fire service as they are known to have been grouped together for this purpose in other Roman towns.

Milestone

On the northern side of the N102 in the twisting bends of the Montée des Combes, about 6 km from Roman Alba down the Frayol valley towards Le Teil.

This well preserved milestone dating from the second century is one of more than twenty that survived on the road up from Nîmes to Alba and down to the Rhône at Le Teil, finishing near Le Pouzin. They represent the town at its most prosperous when it could attract travellers away from the direct north–south Rhône route. The engraver has cut deep into the hard

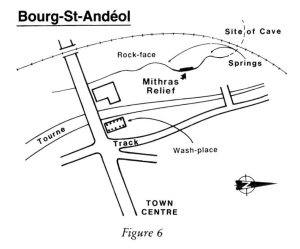

Figure 6

limestone; his inscription records that it is 4 Roman miles from Alba and was put up in AD 145, using the fourth consulship of Antoninus Pius to give the year. The apparently inaccurate holding of the tribunician power ('trib.-pot.' on the milestone) – it should be VIII not VII – occurs on some others as well. Perhaps no one noticed the engraver's inaccuracy before his batch went out to the road.

BOURG-SAINT-ANDEOL, Ardèche

Michelin 80–10
IGN 59–B8/9
2,55/49,30gr
4°38/44°23

Mithras bas-relief.

In the town, signposted from *centre ville* (Place de Mars); about 200 m via Boulevard Jean Jaurès and Avenue de Tourne.

Over 500 Mithraic bull-slaying scenes have been found throughout the Roman Empire; the example at Bourg-St-Andéol is the only one in France to be carved in a rock face. The bas-relief is set in a small, enclosed valley through which the brook, created by two springs, wanders round the back of the town to the Rhône. The railway viaduct has destroyed the cave that lay next to the springs.

An old communal wash-house, the gentle water, the little footbridge, the silence, make it an attractive place for children to play. That they have done so in the past is suggested by the bas-relief itself: it is damaged not just by weather but by stone throwing. Despite this it is well worth visiting, both for what can still be made out and to help understand the context of a Roman mystery religion.

The bas-relief

Now about 2.3 m above ground level, it is thought considerable clearing has artificially raised it. A niche roughly 2 m × 2 m was cut deeply into the sloping rock. Above there was once some sort of façade, however, no detail is recognisable.

Although the relief is cut between the springs, recalling the miraculous birth of Mithras from such a rock, the scene portrayed is Mithras in his classic pose; leaning, knee placed on the bull's back, pulling back its head with his left hand in the animal's nostrils. The left arm is damaged, but less so than the right which has disappeared; undoubtedly this held a sword plunged into the bull's shoulder. The cloak blows out to the left from his shoulders, but his Phrygian hat (conical with a bobble on top) is broken. In the top left-hand corner the sun god Sol has a radiate 'crown' of eleven rays, though some observers claim a twelfth. The parallel moon goddess Luna with her crescent crown is much more difficult to make out, top right-hand side. Around the bull are various animals associated with the scene: a dog on the right leaps forward; a snake wriggles along the ground; a scorpion clutches at the bull's genitals. A crater and lion are known on other reliefs and are usually between the bull's bent front legs and the extended right leg of Mithras, a curve carved on the bottom right could be a lion's back. From the bull's tail an ear of wheat grows. Above the cloak, near Mithras' head, but not very clear, is a bird, normally identified as a raven. In the bottom right-hand corner a panel contains an inscription.

Interpreting the bull-slaying scene

The large number of known portrayals and the central position of the scenes in most Mithraic places of worship clearly define it as the crucial image of Mithraism. Unfortunately we are dealing with a mystery cult which kept its secret rites well: its theology is a matter of interpretation and these vary considerably.

Mithras himself and the names of the ranks of the faithful are Iranian and the 'Mysteries' arrived in Rome from the east, probably via south-eastern Anatolia. Traditionally, turning to Persian Zoroastrian sources, the scene has been taken to show the climax of the mythical life of Mithras: receiving an order from heaven brought by the raven, he kills the bull. Although unhappy at this destruction he finds that renewed life comes from it, shown by the burst of corn from the tail. The blood-letting symbolises the struggle of good and evil. The scorpion attacks the bull's seed, the snake is fought off by the dog. The snake, together with the crater and lion, form symbols of earth, water and fire, the basic creative elements of the cosmos.

The weaknesses in this explanation are evident in the relief. The snake squirms along the ground; he is not attacking the bull and the dog is nowhere near him. This has led some to see the scene as an embodiment of the continuity of life: as the bull dies his blood is drunk by the dog and both snakes and scorpions were identified with fertility. Mithras is then firmly in the Graeco-Roman tradition of sacrificing a bull.

A recent and totally different approach has stressed the astrological element. All the animals and obviously the sun and moon can be seen as signs of the cosmos. The scene then becomes a map reading of the various constellations. Perhaps it represents the supposed astral 'death' of Taurus after the spring equinox. It is interesting that the relief faces east, and the best time to see it is with glancing light, achieved most effectively at the time of the equinoxes.

The worshippers

The three-line inscription is now virtually unreadable and there is no agreed transcription. The most attractive reading is that it was a dedication by Greek traders working in the Rhône valley, providing a small sanctuary for believers in the area.

Above the niche there are two grooves, which are taken to be evidence of a roof covering a small, say 3 m long, temple. Nothing of this structure survives. Descriptions of other temples suggest holes in the roof to create lighting effects (e.g., at the equinox?) on the relief, helped by glass and special paints. Some contemporaries suggested these holes were also used for astrological observations. Outlandishly clothed officials of the different ranks, complex rituals, a 'secret' society suggest freemasonry as much as anything else: socially exclusive, using extensive symbolism and providing dramatic participatory theatre. The cave that once existed would have provided a splendid environment for initiation rites.

DIE, Drôme

Michelin 77–13
IGN 52–C8
3,37/49,73gr
5°26/44°45

Late Roman walls.

The 2,000 m high mountain ridge to the west and the green meadows by the Drôme give the attractive small town of Die an almost alpine feel, yet it is little more than 50 km from the Rhône. Modern expansion has been sharply

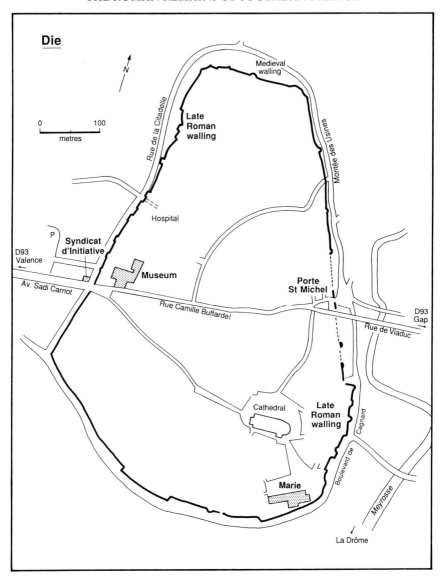

Figure 7

separated from the narrow streets, tiled roofs and unpretentious stone buildings of the old town. It is a quiet and gentle place. Medieval development took place within the framework of the late Roman walls, though in the process apparently removing virtually all evidence of the Roman city.

During the later Iron Age the Diois region formed part of the Vocontii territory, whose main centre lay to the south at VAISON. In the early Roman period, Luc-en-Diois was the leading northern settlement of the tribe (see the magnificent mosaic at VALENCE, p. 28). The limited evidence available and the few modern excavations suggest Dea Augusta Vocontiorum superseded Luc in the second or third century AD. Though nothing is visible, excavations have revealed the existence of two aqueducts and the remains of public baths. An inscription points to an amphitheatre. Fragments in the museum suggest other grandiose public buildings.

The fortification of Die perhaps indicates its value in fourth-century Roman strategy, securing a major link between Gaul and Italy. The fifth-century Burgundian conquest signalled its ultimate failure and marked Die's decline into obscurity, despite its status as an episcopal see. (The wonderful twelfth-century naive mosaic in the Chapelle St Nicholas, in the Marie building, should not be missed.)

The late Roman walls

The kilometre-long circuit is still sharply defined either by its surviving stretches or by the roads that ring the old town. The late Roman walling is typical: stone blockage cemented core, facing foundations of *grand appareil* with a particularly large amount of reused material, *petit appareil* work in the upper courses with the occasional use of bricks. The towers are a mix of rectangular, semi-circular and polygonal. In some places the rampart is entirely replaced by medium *appareil* medieval walling.

North-east section

Rue de la Citadelle, by the Syndicat d'Initiative. Parking available nearby.

30 m after the hospital entrance, the base of the rectangular tower has late Roman foundations. As the road rises steeply, the striking feature is the use of column drums and other architectural elements in the curtain wall and the next towers. Half hidden by bushes, cave-like holes show the removal of finer stonework. As the rampart reaches the top of the hill, medieval work supplants Roman.

Porte St Michel: the exterior structure is late Roman with an arched, single gate entrance guarded by semi-circular towers. Above the gate, medieval rebuilding is apparent and there is much patching elsewhere. Hidden from the exterior is an earlier triumphal arch. Battered floral relief survives on the vaulting. The interior face of the gate is decorated with a keystone shaped as the front of a bull and the remains of a triton, or merman, in the western spandrel.

Southern section

After the gate the wall is lost in buildings for a time, though a semi-circular tower provides an incongruous attic room for one house. However, the **Boulevard du Cagnard** has the best evidence of late Roman construction in both curtain walls and towers, especially the polygonal tower where foundations, facing stones and brickcourses are visible.

The museum

Rue Camille Buffardel.
Open: 15 June–15 September. For hours contact Syndicat d'Initiative, Rue de la Citadelle.

Housed in an attractive old town mansion with patterned polished floors, the museum has a large Gallo-Roman collection, most of it sculptured or inscribed stonework taken from the ramparts. The curator is happy to explain exhibits.

Room 5 draws together the signs of the official city, Dea Augusta. A great base of Greek marble and a Corinthian capital suggest a large temple. A colossal statue is evoked by one surviving foot, a battered Venus suggests the Roman pantheon, whilst the dedication to Andarta emphasises Gallic divinities. There are a large number of altars recording the Taurobolium ceremony of sacrifice (when a bull dedicated to the Cybele mother goddess was slaughtered) which are decorated with various ritual instruments. Only a single bust recalls the Imperial cult. With its Augustan hairstyle (locks lying across the forehead) it could be Germanicus, the adopted son of Tiberius who died in his 20s (AD 19).

Room 4 is dominated by tombs and tombstones. Epitaphs record not just the town elite, but also slaves and freedmen. Amongst them is a *secutor* or 'pursuer', one of the many differently armed gladiators. He belonged to the troop of Valerius Proculus, which must have appeared in the city's amphitheatre. As usual, the most moving are those of parents recording the loss of their children.

VALENCE, Drôme

Michelin 77–12
IGN 52–C4/5
2,85/49,92gr
4°54/44°56

Mosaics in museum.

Rhône valley, 70 km south of Vienne by N7 or A7.

The main Gallo-Roman attractions of Valence are the excellent mosaics in the small and sensitively lit museum. Only one comes from Valence itself. This is perhaps surprising because in Antiquity Valentia was a large town of perhaps 30 ha. Typical of the major Rhône valley sites, it combines good local and regional characteristics. The flat plateau, sharply sloping down to the Rhône, was well supplied with springs. Goods and people travelling by river, or on the north–south road built by Agrippa, could take the major route south-east to DIE (Dea) or cross the river for the rich agricultural land of the Mialan on the slopes of the eastern Massif Central and the road south to ALBA. Yet there are virtually no visible remains. Nothing of the excavations on the main *cardo* or the walls and southern gate has been left exposed; evidence of a theatre in the St Ursula area is only known from foundation remains in local cellars. The existence of other public or religious buildings is based on educated supposition and even less is known of dwellings and commercial structures.

Musée de Valence

4, Place des Ormeaux. In the old Palais Episcopal next to Cathédrale Saint-Apollinaire.
Hours: Wednesday, Saturday, Sunday   9.00 a.m.–noon, 2.00–6.00 p.m.
          Monday, Tuesday, Thursday, Friday   2.00–6.00 p.m.

The very good **Labours of Hercules** mosaic was found 27 km away in a villa outside St Paul-les-Romans, north-east of Romans-sur-Izère. Although known since at least 1900, the mosaic and the villa were only excavated after 1964. However, this ensured that the mosaic could be investigated in context. It, like the Orpheus mosaic, was in a room overlooking a garden with an ornamental pool. Its large border area, with space for couches, suggests that it decorated the floor of a triclinium. The border design and some Antonine coinage suggest a second-century workshop in Lyon.

Most of the scenes are damaged, but only four really badly. The best is possibly the third down on the left side. Here Hercules struggles with the horses of Diomedes. They were war horses fed on human flesh and Hercules had been commanded to bring them back to Argos. He dragged them from their stable, killed Diomedes with his club and when the horses ate the king's body they became tame and he led them away.

This type of mosaic is rare and was probably a special order; perhaps the central figure is the villa owner. More likely is that it is either King Eurystheus, who ordered the Labours, or Hades, symbolising the eternal life gained by Hercules through his labours.

The **Orpheus** mosaic, also found in the St Paul-les-Romans villa, is more seriously battered than the Labours of Hercules. The marble repair work indicates that it was first damaged in Antiquity; it has suffered since as well, and was left exposed but unprotected for a time after excavation in 1964. Orpheus holding his lyre captivates not only a dog before him and birds in the trees, but also a collection of animals set in twelve surrounding panels. It is a format similar to that originally designed for the VIENNE Orpheus mosaic and may be a product of the workshop there.

The **Luc-en-Diois** mosaic is incomplete but of high quality. Since its discovery in 1892, 83 km the other side of Die in what was the Roman town of Lucus, it has been restored twice; originally it had a surface four times the size.

Purely decorative, the main panel was surrounded with delicate polychrome fig-leaf foliage. Four *bucrania* are in turn enclosed by medallions filled with flowers, leaves, small animals and birds with beaks poised above grasshoppers. One medallion is particularly unusual as it has the only known builder's signature in the Roman world: Q(uintus) Amiteius 'architect' has thus achieved his hoped for immortality, whether for constructing the mosaic or the house in which it lay.

The final example on view, in the gallery next to the main room, is the local **baptistery** mosaic. The excavator, André Blanc, identified it as early Christian, probably sixth-century (though others have seen it as Romanesque). The deer from the octagon has been interpreted as a convert drinking at the River Jordan – represented by the running water brought to the baptistery. The hares and lambs being attacked by evil crows are also converts defended by the eagles of regeneration and faith given by baptism.

VIENNE, Isère

Michelin 74–1
IGN 51–C4
2,83/50,58gr
4°53/45°33

Major city site.

The northern frontier of Narbonensis was marked by the city of Vienna, capital of the Allobroges. The petty antagonisms with Lugdunum, only 30 km to the north, are clearly long over. While modern Lyon has experienced dynamic expansion, Vienne survives as a quiet, pleasant and relatively small town. Perhaps Martial's compliment for its beauty is as much based on the already famous Rhône wine as its fine buildings or setting, but undoubtedly during the first and second centuries it became one of the largest and most prosperous cities in Gaul. Traces of the Augustan walls suggest they were

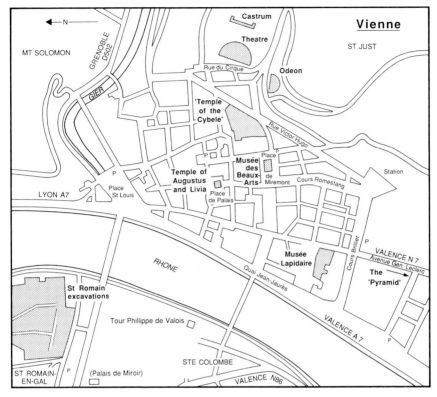

Figure 8

over 7 km long and enclosed an area of around 300 ha. There were major
suburbs and eleven aqueducts supplied the population with clean water.

The Allobroges had been a powerful tribe ruling a territory stretching as
far as Geneva, but there is little evidence of pre-Roman urbanisation.
Though finds of Greek pottery show that Vienne was a Rhône trading stop,
before the conquest in 121 BC and for many years after both Strabo and the
archaeological material so far uncovered suggest Vienne was a relatively
minor site. Excavation on Ste Blondine hill behind Mt Pipet has shown a late
Iron Age settlement (see Musée des Beaux Arts, p. 35).

The Allobroges' unsuccessful rejection of Roman rule in 62–61 BC and
Julius Caesar's subsequent wars of conquest (throughout which they
remained loyal) led to a rapid expansion of Vienne. This was probably
helped by the establishment of a veteran colony here. Already known as
Colonia Julia Viennensium by the 30s BC, it was possibly a foundation of
Caesar himself.

Vienne developed at a key river crossing. The Rhône itself provided the
major route north and south, but for anyone travelling by land up the river

valley, it was essential here to cross from the east to west bank to avoid the marsh terraces between Vienne and Lyon. Also, to the west is the narrowest point between the Rhône and Loire valleys with an easy link via the Gier; to the east lay routes into the Alps to both Grenoble and Geneva. Surrounded by small hills, the city developed on the river terraces below Mt Pipet. Across the river, the suburbs of Ste Colombe and St Romain spread themselves on the lowest terrace of the river's sweeping turn south-west. A bridge crossed the Rhône: wooden piles on the western side, which were exposed in 1938, are now thought to be part of the river docks, but the stone bridge that stood by the Philippe de Valois tower till the 1600s was undoubtedly Roman and known as the 'pont de Trajan'.

Vienne's economic decline began early in the third century as the right bank was increasingly abandoned. No obvious explanation has been found for this but the civil wars and barbarian invasions can only have made the situation worse. Typically new walls only 2 km long were constructed enclosing a much smaller area and Mt Pipet was turned into a *castrum* strongpoint whose massive foundation stones are still visible. It emerged from Diocletian's reforms as a diocesan capital, a major centre superseding Lyon as the key Rhône city, a metropolis in charge of seventeen provinces (380–430). Emperors such as Constantine and Julian used Vienne as a major staging post to Trier. No remains of their accommodation have been recognised. The remnants of 'Roman' status ended with Vienne's absorption by the Burgundian state in 468.

Temple of Augustus and Livia

Place du Palais.

Originally surrounded by the open space of the forum, which it must have dominated, the temple is now hidden away from the rest of the town in a small square; it gives the building a striking if awkward sense of size.

The temple has survived as one of the best preserved in France because, like the Maison Carrée (see NIMES, pp. 95–7), it has a continuous history of use. Converted into a church before the sixth century it briefly became 'a temple of Reason' in 1792, a market-place, then a museum (1815); the major restoration took place on Prosper Mérimée's orders in the 1850s with further repair work in the 1980s.

Broadly similar to the Maison Carrée in size, it is a less balanced building, but has a more grandiose impact, probably caused by the decision to give the façade more prominence. The elevation of the temple is also emphasized by the typically Roman high podium (2.75 m) on which the *cella* covers the whole width only at the very back, leaving six free-standing Corinthian columns on each side. The heavy pediment may be the result of rebuilding rather than original.

Different approaches to the treatment of the capitals suggest reconstruction early in the building's history. The pilasters and three southern column capitals are typical of Glanum Corinthian *c.* 30 BC; the rest are like those on the Maison Carrée. Pelletier suggests a date of 27–25 BC to coincide with Augustus' first visit to Vienne, with a major rebuild fifteen to twenty years later.

The god for whom the temple was intended was originally proclaimed on the frieze with metal letters, now only the holes survive. Using these, it has been possible to identify the original inscription and its subsequent modifications. It must have been one of the first temples dedicated to the Imperial cult in Gaul, initially linking Augustus with Rome, then adding the divine Augusta (his wife Livia) and finally dropping Rome and extending the dedication to all divine Emperors.

We also know something about how the temple functioned in the city and the role it served for Vienne. Inscriptions found in Vienne (see Musée Lapidaire, p. 34) and elsewhere commemorate '*flamines*', '*flaminicae*' and '*seviri*'. They were appointed by the town council (*ordo*) to serve the cult, the *flamines* and *flaminicae* as 'sacrificers' and the *seviri* as a priestly association. They might lead ceremonies or hold banquets, but were not the staff of the temple: those were too unimportant to record. Rich patrons through their expenditure on the temple could court Imperial favour and win prestige for Vienne (the city in return granted them privileged seats in the theatre).

'Temple of the Cybele'

Rue Victor Hugo.

Between 1945 and 1968, Formigé, then Pelletier, excavated this large, heterogeneous site. The lowest part to the north was the best preserved and most easily identified. Behind a good section of road, is part of a grand portico. Through the arch to the east up the hillside are exposed remains of a small section of public baths.

The rest of the site has been identified by the excavators as a *metroon* or cult centre of the mother goddess Cybele. A massive six-sectioned wall in front of the portico has been identified by Pelletier as the buttress wall of a narrow and rather unconventional theatre used for Cybeline ceremonies. A podium by the road below could be a temple and re-erected pillars help to give this impression. The building behind the temple had a series of pools that could have been ritual baths belonging to the guardian priests.

Equally convincingly the walling has been interpreted as a support for a monumental staircase up the hill and the building behind as a typical Vienne *domus*, its pools much like those in St Romain-en-Gal (see p. 37).

As the visitor can see, the ruins themselves give little help in resolving the debate.

31

Vienne

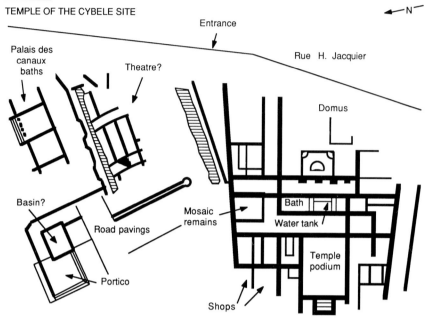

Figure 9

The theatre

Rue du Cirque.
Hours: 1 April–15 October   open 9.00 a.m.–noon, 2.00–6.30 p.m.,
                              closed Tuesday
        16 October–31 March   open 10.00 a.m.–noon, 2.00–5.00 p.m.,
                              closed Monday, Tuesday, Sunday morning

The town is dominated by its great theatre, using the Pipet hillside in a way more Greek than Roman to provide the audience with a splendid view out over the Rhône valley. It is the second largest in Gaul with a capacity of *c.* 13,500; only Autun is bigger. The excavations were completed in 1938, and Formigé's thorough restoration has ensured that it can be used again for all kinds of shows.

The grand entrances on each side of the theatre have been destroyed, but the northern lobby is still used as the way in; the beautifully cut shining white limestone masonry, although broken and disconnected, suggests the magnificence of the decoration. Originally the lobby allowed access to the upper levels by covered stairs (now collapsed) and to the passage circling the orchestra on which patches of chevron-patterned pink and yellow marble survive. The four rows of honour made of white marble, with seats 5 cm

32

wider than the rest, were entered through a *balteus* or balustrade of green marble, which separated both them and the orchestra from the rest of the *cavea*.

The *cavea* above is divided into two sections marked by a passage. The lower section has twelve, the upper thirty rows. Access is from a mix of stairs cut through the seats and vomitoria from two vaulted tunnels joining the side stairs. The top of the *cavea* has a passage with a single entrance down into these steeper seats – perhaps the poorest were expected to clamber over each other. Nothing remains of the porticoed terrace that once stood above the passage. Channels cut in the rock carry rainwater and seepage down into a special drain constructed above the first vaulted access tunnel.

The large stage is frequently covered by a modern platform. When exposed, note the restored foundations of the *pulpitum*, the holes for the rising curtain counterweights (see Lyon Musée for a reconstruction of the workings) and two lonely caryatids from the stage building.

Stratigraphic evidence for the date of construction is totally absent: it could be Augustan or even second century. During the late Empire it was plundered, later still it was covered by gardens.

The odeon

Montée Beaumur. (No access to the interior of the building.)

Perhaps even more illustrative of the high level of classical culture in Vienne is the existence of an odeon. From the upper tier of the theatre, it can be seen set in the St Just hillside. With a diameter of over 70 m and potential seating for an estimated 3,000 people, it is comparable to the odeon in Lyon, but considerably more dilapidated. The external surrounding wall is the most impressive element. It is made of *petit appareil* and was once covered with stucco.

The 'pyramid'

Boulevard de la Pyramide.

South of Vienne on the N7, and 50 m to the right off the Avenue Général Leclerc, is a strange obelisk standing on a four-way arcaded arch. It is the one surviving feature of a massive circus that stood outside Roman Vienne. Chariot-racing demanded considerable space and examples of stone circuses are rare in Gaul (see also ARLES, pp. 148–9). Although there has been very little excavation here, enough is known to estimate a total length of over 450 m and a width of nearly 120 m, which would be suitable for a twelve chariot start. A small excavation in the 1900s in Rue Vermaine revealed the substructure of metre-thick walling used to support the seats.

Running down the centre of the circus and dividing the track were a series of pools and walls linking the turning posts at each end (the *metae*). This was called the *euripus*, later known as the *spina*. The 'pyramid' and its base stood at the centre, copying the Egyptian obelisk brought to Rome from Heliopolis: the cost for a provincial city of a genuine obelisk must have been prohibitive. Still impressive, it rises 15.5 m on top of the arch, itself 7.25 m high. The best picture of how the *euripus* might have appeared is the magnificent circus mosaic in Lyon (in the Musée de la Civilisation Gallo-Romaine).

Dating evidence is minimal, but the circus is unlikely to be earlier than the second century and the obelisk may well be late Roman. Major games are likely to have been held here when the Emperors Julian and later Valentinian II stayed at Vienne during the fourth century.

Musée Lapidaire

Place St Pierre.

Hours: 1 April–15 October   open 9.00 a.m.–noon, 2.00–6.30 p.m., closed Tuesday

16 October–31 March   open 10.00 a.m.–noon, 2.00–5.00 p.m., closed Monday, Tuesday, Sunday morning

The material described below may be displayed in the new museum at St Romain-en-Gal, but whilst it remains in this deconsecrated church the overriding impression is likely to be of darkness, dust and neglect. Control these feelings because it houses some outstanding evidence of the high level of Roman civilisation achieved in this provincial city. Over 200 mosaics have been found in Vienne, more than in any other Gallo-Roman city. Three are exceptional, indicating the high standards achieved by local craftsmen in the late second century. Sadly none are exactly as they should be.

The **Orpheus mosaic** was found in 1859, one of twelve pavements in a peristyle *domus* and probably part of the bath suite. The mosaic was cut into pieces, damaged parts thrown away, and it was reassembled in a new pattern with some sections left out. Orpheus, not the duck, should be at the centre. This is a popular subject, well-known in Britain as well, personifying the power of music with Orpheus charming the animals with the beauty of his lyre-playing. They surround him in hexagons and squares. The polychrome waves around the god's head give a rare three-dimensional effect, more often found in Rome and Greece. Note the similarity of the twisted rope and opposed chalice patterns here and on the Athletes' mosaic.

The **Lycurgus mosaic** was found in Ste Colombe in 1900 and treated in equally arbitrary fashion. Happily, though at considerable cost, it has been restored again. The reclining figures and semi-circular apse form suggest it decorated a dining room.

Dionysus was the god of fertility, particularly associated with wine. In the myth Dionysus and his followers were thrown out of Thrace by its king, Lycurgus. Driven mad by Dionysus, the king killed his son, mistaking him for a vine, and was himself then torn apart by his subjects.

In the centre of the rectangle, a small Lycurgus brandishing his axe is dominated by the swirling vines on the deep green base. Birds are hidden in the foliage. Unknown elsewhere in Gaul, the design may have been copied from a textile by an outstanding mosaicist. The apse figures are damaged and inferior in quality with their long legs, poorly drawn feet and hair (the work of assistants or another workshop?). They originally formed three pairs of figures celebrating the god's power. Dionysus appears in a leopard skin carrying his cone-topped staff wreathed in vines, and drinking from a crater of red wine. A bacchant plays a lyre for him. The second pair are so ruined they are not displayed. The last two are Pan (recognisable from his goat's feet) holding a jar from which wine gushes, and a headless bacchante perhaps pointing out the agony of Lycurgus.

The **Athletes' mosaic** was found, in 1966, in Place St Pierre in a house containing ten pavements. A rectangle encloses a circular field. The four spandrels each had a season, but only 'winter' is undamaged. The circle is divided into geometrical shapes with Hercules taking the central octagon, strangling the lion in his first Labour. Around him in squares are theatre masks, mainly from comedy sources. Of the athletes in their octagons, the best preserved are the tense-faced pugilist in his leather skullcap, the discus-thrower and the runner with the victory palm. The least trouble seems to have been taken with the outer ring of ocean masks. Pelletier thinks it might have decorated the banquet room of a young men's club.

Amongst the other material, the finest is the **head of Magnentius** (350–3) treated in typical military style: a square head, staring eyes and double chin. A usurper, first proclaimed in Gaul, he committed suicide in Lyon after defeat in battle. There is also a reconstruction of the *metroon* site. From the *pulpitum* in the theatre come damaged elements of the frieze showings dogs and bulls.

Musée des Beaux-Arts et d'Archéologie

Place de Miremont.
Hours: see Musée Lapidaire

The Musée des Beaux-Arts is a typical provincial nineteenth-century museum. Unlabelled material fills dark wooden cases and covers the walls. Set amongst the small Egyptian, Celtic, Etruscan and Roman collections are the Ste Blondine Iron Age finds and an attractive 1984 hoard of Roman silver from the Place Camille Jouffrey.

The full-size **bronze statue of C. Julius Pacatianus** is the most important Roman object in the museum. In fact it is made up of three elements. The body in its swirling toga is probably first-century and even made in Italy; when found it was smashed and has been painstakingly put together again. The head and inscription are of the third-century Severan careerist, Pacatianus. Clearly a money-saving recycling of an earlier figure! The inscription shows him to have had a career ranging the Empire. Posts of increasing importance took him to Dacia (Romania), Mesopotamia, the Alps, Mauritania (Africa) and back again to Mesopotamia. He managed to select Severus as the winner in the civil wars of the 190s and lasted as an imperial 'comes' or companion even under Severus' malevolent son Caracalla. Like Talleyrand in the Revolution, he survived.

Ste Colombe: Rue Garon

On the west bank of the Rhône, there are the remains of large public baths, called the Palais du Miroir, but these are private and closed to visitors. However, a Gallo-Roman domestic dwelling has been restored *in situ* and recently opened.

St Romain-en-Gal

The other major suburb on the west bank of the Rhône, to the north of N86 road bridge, next to the lycée.
Hours: 1 April–30 September   9.00 a.m.–12.30, 2.30–7.00 p.m.
        1 October–31 March   9.00 a.m.–noon, 2.00–5.00 p.m.

In 1967, 6 ha in St Romain became available to the state and excavations – still continuing – began to expose this massive site. The guidebook, summary sheet (available in English) and small museum are all good. A whole district is on display and from the central mound it is possible to distinguish the roads and *insula*, the houses, warehouses, shops, workshops, baths and public lavatories; they are the remains of the last rebuildings made at the end of the second and beginning of the third centuries.

Perhaps most interesting is that the city's underside is revealed: water was clearly both a resource and a problem on this low river terrace. Remains of piping show how water was used everywhere: fountains, decorative pools, industrial basins, flushing lavatories; stone drains that carried waste to the main disposal system under the streets. The fine **Via II** covers a deep central sewer with limestone access points set in the granite flagstones. A parallel drain runs under the road's high pavement. Upturned amphorae demonstrate a unique way of tackling a moist subsoil.

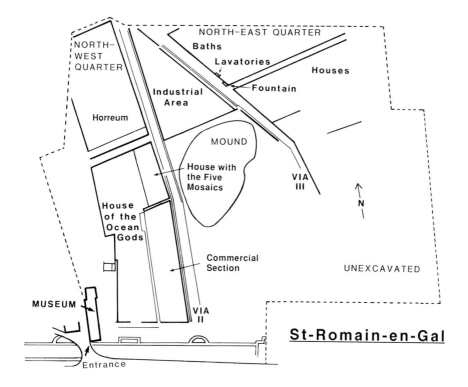

Figure 10

The Grand Portico

The portico stretching *c.* 200 m marks off a public area that possibly included the Palais du Miroir baths (see p. 36).

The residential quarter

Of the ten *domus* houses known, two major examples are represented on Insula 1; they suggest life for Vienne's wealthy bore comparison with the Pompeian elite.

House of the Ocean Gods

Named after the mosaic found in the vestibule (not on view here), this grand *domus* covered 2,500 sq. m in the final form restored here. It had gone through at least three rebuildings following its original smaller Augustan

37

construction. Characteristic of Vienne design are the 'U'-shaped pools spread throughout the house. The portico in the rear, with its kiosks used perhaps for summer parties, was probably a late addition as the orientation differs from the rest of the building.

Vienne

ST ROMAIN-EN-GAL

House of the Ocean Gods

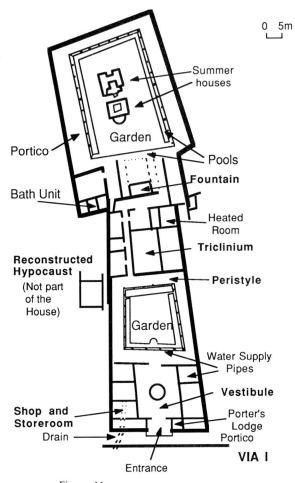

Figure 11

House with the Five Mosaics

The entrance led to a fine peristyle round which the main rooms are distributed. The house may have been joined to the Ocean Gods house in its final phase. Again the mosaics have been removed.

38

Vienne

ST ROMAIN-EN-GAL

House with the Five Mosaics

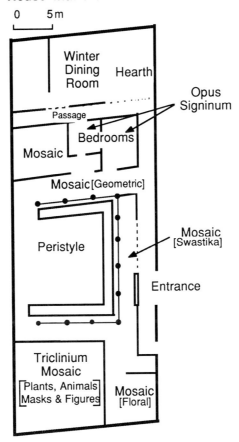

Figure 12

Commercial section

Beside the House of the Ocean Gods is a small workshop and home, probably that of a dyer. Little remains of the frontage, but jars of colourings and the two basins draining direct into the sewer running under Via II suggest his craft. The most interesting features here are the resurrected doorway, showing the massive stone frame and lintels used, and the floor completely covered with upturned amphorae to capture the rising damp before it could damage any perishable stock.

Vienne

ST ROMAIN-EN-GAL
Commercial Section

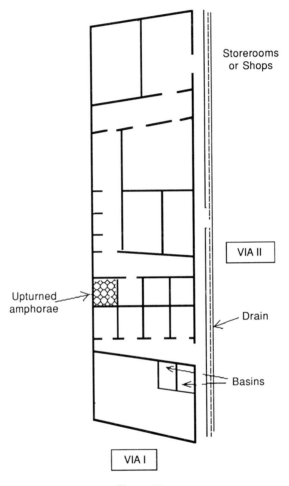

Figure 13

The north-east quarter

Insulae 4 and 5 are not yet open to the public; the houses and shops, even a fish-pond, are excavated but not restored. In the northern corner beside Via III, there is a bath unit and a public lavatory using piped water and washing into the drain running under the road.

The north-west quarter

The Horreum

Insula 2 is filled with a large warehouse (3,000 sq. m) of which only the deep and thick foundations survive. Built in the second half of the first century AD it is of a standard corridor courtyard design. Although probably constructed

Vienne

ST ROMAIN-EN-GAL
The Horreum

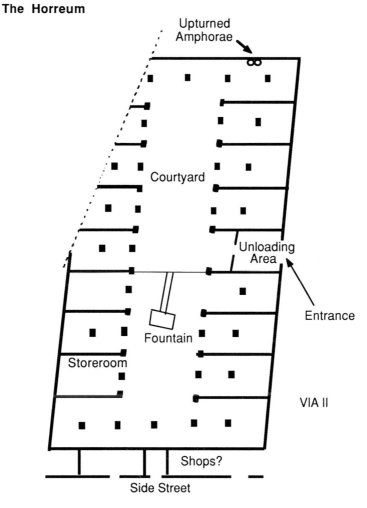

Figure 14

on Imperial initiative, it is likely at that time that it was sub-contracted to a private businessman or 'conductor'. He would run it with his *horrearii* or warehousemen, leasing out space to the merchants and traders storing wine, cloth, grain and all the other cargo that moved up and down the river and inland from here. Carts would carry the goods to and from the riverside wharfs to the gateway where porters – *saccarii* – would unload and carry them inside to the long courtyard dividing the rows of rectangular store-rooms. Grain may have been carried to a second floor, suggested by the central pillars dividing the entrances, although the ground floors were insulated from the damp with upturned amphorae; two have been left by the building's north wall.

A small statue of Hercules was found in the courtyard near the fountain. Often considered by merchants as a protecting god, it may also represent Imperial ownership. The merchants using the facility would naturally be amongst the wealthy freedmen supporting the Imperial cult temple in Vienne.

The industrial area

The triangular-shaped Insula 3, formed by the junction of the porticoed Vias II and III, is filled with tiny workrooms, separated into three groups by solid dividing walls, probably used for cloth- or leather-working. The northern group has not been identified.

The middle group is a workshop complex round a courtyard. It is dominated by basins. Similar designs in Pompeii are *fullonicae*, that is fullers' workshops where the grease and dirt was removed from wool with a mixture of soap and urine, followed by heavy rinsing; they could also operate as laundries. Passers-by were often asked to urinate into roadside amphorae, but perhaps this one got its supplies from the public lavatory on Via III (and even paid the appropriate tax!). The last group of workrooms line a rectangular courtyard reminiscent of a *macellum* or market. Most were likely to be for dyeing or leather tanning: the courtyard has hearths for heating cauldrons, a stone block in each room – perhaps for laying out materials – and a gutter for carrying away the dirty liquid. The fountain in Via III was an easy source of water supply.

Site museum

The small site museum contains a few finds. The new museum will enable the curators to present both material from the St Romain-en-Gal excavations and from the old Musée Lapidaire (see p. 34–5).

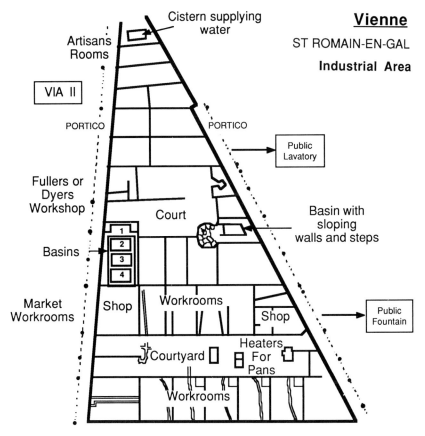

Figure 15

* * *

OTHER SITES IN THE LOWER RHONE

Andance, Ardèche

Michelin 76–10 or IGN 52–A4
2,74/50,27gr or 4°48/45°14

At Cueil, 1½ km south of Andance, there are a 14 m wall and two towers, which were probably part of a rural villa. At La Sarrasinière, 3 km south of Andance, a large funeral monument stands beside the road.

Aubenas, Ardèche

Michelin 76–19 or IGN 59–A7
2,24/49,55gr or 4°24/44°36

In the St Pierre-le-Vieux area (champs des colonnes) there are villa remains. At **Jastres**, there are two major oppidum sites on the hill. Jastres North has Iron Age walls and towers, and was occupied during early the Gallo-Roman period and again in the late Roman era.

Le Pègue, Drôme

Michelin 81–2 or IGN 60–A2
3,02/49,36gr or 5°04/44°26

12 km north of Nyons, there is an oppidum on *colline* St Marcel. Hillfort of Iron Age with evidence of limited early and late Gallo-Roman occupation. Site museum.

Le Pouzin, Ardèche

Michelin 76–20 or IGN 59–A9
2,68/49,72gr or 4°50/44°45

A single-arch Roman bridge crossing the Ouvèze, a tributary of the Rhône. 25 km south of Valence by the N86 and 500 m west on the N104. The construction design resembles that at Viviers (see p. 45) for the same west bank Roman road.

St Fortunat-sur-Eyrieux, Ardèche

Michelin 76–20 or IGN 52–C3
2,60/49,81gr or 4°41/44°50

At Pontpierre in the gorges of Eyrieux are the remains of a single-arch Roman bridge. There is no arch, but a massive 25 m high masonry abutment and pier on the right bank.

St Paul-les-Romans, Drôme

Michelin 77–3 or IGN 52–B6
3,10/50,08gr or 5°08/45°04

Small Gallo-Roman collection in the regional museum.

St Paul-Trois-Châteaux, Drôme

Michelin 81–1 or IGN 59–C9/10
2,71/49,28gr or 4°47/44°22

Capital of the small Tricastini tribe. Poor excavation and subsequent rebuilding have left virtually no material exposed *in situ*. The museum has Gallo-Roman stonework, bas-reliefs, altars, artefacts.

Tain L'Hermitage, Drôme

Michelin 77–2 or IGN 52–B4
2,78/50,08gr or 4°52/45°05

Opposite Tournon by the Rhône. An inscribed *taurobolium* altar found in the eighteenth century stands in the Place du Taurobole.

Villeperdrix, Drôme

Michelin 81–3 or IGN 60–A3
3,28/49,38gr or 5°17/44°27

To the west of the village, 500 m from the junction with the Eygues River, 8.5 m and 4 m high bridge abutments survive over a tributary torrent.

Viviers, Ardèche

Michelin 80–10 or IGN 59–B9
2,63/49,43gr or 4°42/44°29

North of Viviers on the N86, take the D107 road for Alba and Aubenas. A Roman bridge crosses the River Escoutay outside the town. Nine of the arches are semi-circular and despite obvious repairs are Gallo-Roman with similar design features to Le Pouzin (see p. 44). The town has a Roman background.

THE THEATRE: ENTERTAINMENT AND RELIGION

Theatre buildings

The theatre is one of the most overt signs of romanisation in Gaul. There are over seventy examples, almost as many as in Italy. The earliest and finest are in southern France. A Greek theatre certainly existed in Marseille and there could have been temporary wooden theatres during the first century BC, but virtually all of these distinctive structures were erected in the great phase of public building during the early Empire, promoted by Imperial visions of what constituted a city.

Though inspired by Roman concepts, theatres were built on the initiative of the Gallic nobility, either acting as individuals or as *civitas* magistrates. They paid for their construction not simply as an embodiment of city life, but also as a sign of commitment to Roman forms amongst the rural population as well. More than half the theatres have been found at sanctuary sites, though these are rare in the south.

Building enabled the aristocracy to enhance their status within the wider Roman world and the local community. Like Pompey, when in 55 BC he ordered the construction of his magnificent theatre in Rome, by joining theatre with temple, so the nobles' patronage linked them with the sanctity of the local god. Seating also reinforced the hierarchy: dignitaries sat on display in the orchestra, the first tier was for lesser local figures such as leaders of corporations, the second tier for the plebeians, whilst the third tier was for the disreputable. Slaves could attend, but were not supposed to sit.

A typical theatre of the grand type is illustrated in Figure 16. The stage embodied a street, the wing doors representing the way into and out of town. The *scaenae* were seen as a set of three houses, each with its own door. The front or *frons scaenae* became a highly decorated, permanent backcloth of columns, statues and altars, to which cloth and wooden scenery could be added; most have been robbed and ruined. However, ORANGE has a *scaena* to its full height with fragments of the *frons scaenae* and ARLES, VIENNE and VAISON have well-preserved *caveae* or seating areas. In the theatres of the countryside the *scaena* was simply a wall, possibly lacking even the specified three doors in the *scaenae* and the two wing doors. Here, *caveae* were frequently built on earth mounds with only the best seats made of stone.

Theatre performances

Very little is known about how theatres in France were actually used in the Gallo-Roman period. Hints are provided by the existence of artefacts with theatrical references such as the mask motifs used in stonework decoration and found most widely on funerary monuments (see VAISON museum), or

46

A Typical Roman Theatre

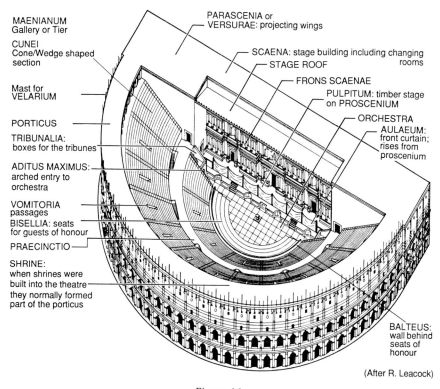

MAENIANUM
Gallery or Tier

CUNEI
Cone/Wedge shaped
section

Mast for
VELARIUM

PORTICUS

TRIBUNALIA:
boxes for the tribunes

ADITUS MAXIMUS:
arched entry to
orchestra

VOMITORIA
passages

BISELLIA: seats
for guests of honour

PRAECINCTIO

SHRINE:
when shrines were
built into the theatre
they normally formed
part of the porticus

PARASCENIA or
VERSURAE: projecting wings

SCAENA: stage building including changing
STAGE ROOF   rooms

FRONS SCAENAE

PULPITUM: timber stage
on PROSCENIUM

ORCHESTRA

AULAEUM:
front curtain;
rises from
proscenium

BALTEUS:
wall behind
seats of
honour

(After R. Leacock)

Figure 16

on the moulded masks found on the faces and handles of clay lamps. An ivory statuette (in Paris) of an angry old woman has not only the exaggerated pose of a tragic actor, but also the high wooden stilt shoes and agonised mask derived from Greek models.

A less formal theatre is implied by the burlesque cupids and mythological figures on the appliqué medallions produced in the lower Rhône valley and the dancing girl statues found in Arles. An enigmatic epitaph found in ANTIBES refers to a 12-year-old boy's death, having danced pleasingly in the theatre for two days.

Literary evidence from elsewhere, particularly from Rome itself, suggests that during the early as well as the late Empire classical drama existed simply in the form of occasional revivals and the presentation of great scenes or speeches. The flowering of Roman plays took place in the second century BC, based on the forms, story-lines and costumes of Greek drama. But, in both tragedy, *fabula crepidata*, and in the even better comedy or *fabula palliata*, there were virtually no successors to the great Plautus or Terence.

47

Even the specifically Roman historical plays, never particularly successful, became more a written form. Seneca's 'plays' of the AD 60s were designed at best to be read in the small odeon theatres. By the end of the Republic, the playwright was a despised and inferior person, while the producer of spectacular effects was rather more valued.

Tragic acting took two paths, both stressing performance rather than coherent drama. While some actors went for rhetorical and emotional effects in their moralising recitations (accompanied by musicians), others developed 'pantomime'. Emerging in the Augustan period, it involved an actor miming tragedy or mythological stories accompanied by musicians and a chorus hidden behind the scenery. Being wordless, a closed mouth mask became typical of pantomime. As an art form it lay between masque and ballet. Good sets and costumes were seen as enhancing the range of emotional effects.

Stage comedy in southern Gaul would have owed most to the closely related Italian models of *fabula atellana* and *fabula togata*. Both of these specialised in farce. The former featured traditional characters from Campania wearing masks, such as Bucco 'the fool', Pappus or 'grand-dad', always seen as an old dotard, and Manducus or Maccus, the champion chewer with his chattering teeth, 'the guzzler'. His name entered French as *manger*. They were partially written down with titles like 'Hog's sick' or 'Maccus the Maiden', but also involved a great deal of ad lib dialogue.

The *fabula togata* used native Italian clothes and dispensed with the mask. Based on the stock scenes of Palliatan comedy, they depicted adultery, lost children, the pampered or overweaning slave and the manipulating lady's maid. The social range depicted appears to have been wider but unfortunately little has survived. During the Imperial era, these were increasingly replaced by 'mime', cruder farce appealing to a mass audience. They mixed mimicry, prose and verse, the crudest obscenity and moralising and, like Atellanan farce, had distinctive costumes including the patchwork jacket and tights that later evolved as Punch and another with a huge phallus. In both pantomime and mime 'shameless' women appeared.

Actors, dancers and musicians formed small troupes, each member of which could play a range of parts; they were often slaves under the leadership of a freedman *dominus* (master), no doubt the leading actor/singer. A key member was the piper who accompanied much of the performance and who could signal different characters with certain tunes. Inscriptions found in NIMES show that during the second and early third centuries the troupes in the city were organised in an artists' corporation with its own president (*archierius*) and members divided between *sympiaci* or musicians, and *symmeleini* or singers – a word used interchangeably with actor. Some of the inscriptions are in Greek, suggesting that in southern France as elsewhere in the Empire, there were still Greek stage performers.

Members of the Nîmes corporation had appeared in a number of competitive '*ludi*' and taken the prizes. 'Games' such as these must have taken place in many of the cities in the south, and like those in Rome retained their religious context as well, the entertainments being associated with either Dionysus or the local god(s). Certainly most theatres must have contained altars similar to that found in ARLES. It may even be that theatres, especially in rather isolated and small communities, were used more frequently for ritualised ceremony rather than true theatrical entertainment, in some ways perhaps more like the temporary theatres of early Republican Rome. However, it is a comment on the depth of romanisation amongst the elite of southern Gaul that an anonymous play based on the work of Plautus should have been written in the fourth or fifth centuries AD!

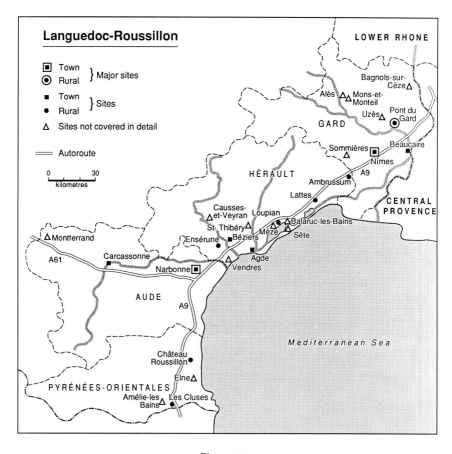

Languedoc-Roussillon

LOWER RHONE

Legend:
- ▣ Town ⊙ Rural } Major sites
- ▪ Town ● Rural } Sites
- △ Sites not covered in detail
- ═══ Autoroute

0 — 30 kilometres

Bagnols-sur-Cèze△

Alès ▪△ Mons-et-Monteil

Uzès△ Pont du Gard ⊙

GARD

Sommières ▣ Béaucaire ▪

△ Nîmes

CENTRAL PROVENCE

HÉRAULT

Ambrussum ● A9

Lattes ●

Causses-et-Veyran △ Loupian

St. Thibéry △ △ Balaruc-les-Bains

Ensérune ▪ Béziers ▪ Mèze Sète

△ Montferrand

A61 Carcassonne ▪ Agde △

Narbonne ▣ Vendres ●

AUDE

A9

Mediterranean Sea

Château Roussillon ●

Elne △

PYRÉNÉES-ORIENTALES

Amélie-les-Bains ● Les Cluses △

Figure 17

2

THE SITES OF LANGUEDOC-ROUSSILLON

AGDE, Hérault

Michelin 83–16
IGN 65–D8
1,28/48,12gr
3°28/43°17

Museum of underwater archaeology.

Cap d'Agde was once the sign for sailors in the ancient world that they had reached the mouth of the Hérault and the safety of the port of Agde. 4 km inland, Agde has been swamped by the growth of mass tourism, though its narrow streets preserve something of the traditional coastal town. Yet in this transformation of the old Languedoc, one of the finest underwater archaeology museums in France has been created.

Agde derives its name from the Greek Agatha, yet despite this obvious sign of Antiquity, serious archaeological research in the area is a very recent phenomenon. Aris and Clautres carried out limited excavations in 1938–9, their work providing the first concrete confirmation of Greek and Roman activity at Agde, subsequently supported by Nickels's 1970s excavations. The most exciting discoveries have arisen from the postwar sub-aqua exploration carried out by teams from Béziers and Agde, led respectively by A. Bouscaras and D. Fonquerle. Loss at sea was common throughout Antiquity, not simply on the rocks of Cap d'Agde, the Ile de Brescou and Rochelongue, but also in the Hérault itself; and many of the finds are now on display in the new museum.

Development

With such thin archaeological evidence from Agde itself it is difficult to be confident about its early history. Indisputably, the Hérault River area was being opened up by Mediterranean merchants from the seventh century BC, as both Greek and Etruscan finds show. This merchant activity intensified in the sixth century. The local Iron Age oppidum of La Monédière at Bessan,

6 km up the Hérault, has enough sixth-century Greek material to imply that some Greeks may have settled there, while the material discovered at Agde supports the literary evidence for a colony here. It is possible that this was originally an independent Phocaean foundation like Marseille, as a late source states, but both Strabo and Pliny claim it was actually founded by Massalia (Marseille), and some recent writers have suggested a 'second foundation' or takeover. There is no dispute that Agde was a Massaliote dependency in the fourth century BC when the earliest ramparts have been dated and when it is likely that the classic Greek grid-iron town was laid out (which is still reflected in the streets of the old quarter).

A more surprising development has been linked to the town plan: the land division of the surrounding region (shown up in aerial photographs) as far as the Heraklean Way/Via Domitia (see BEAUCAIRE, p. 59) is aligned to the street blocks of Agde. This Greek 'chora' or territory seems to have persisted into the Gallo-Roman period and beyond: the later church diocese covers the same area. Perhaps the presence of Greek farmer-settlers explains the survival of the Greek city name as well and might explain why the local inhabitants abandoned the Bessan oppidum.

Agde's importance throughout Antiquity must have remained essentially dependent on her position as a port. Goods, primarily wine in the period of Massaliote control, were unloaded here for carrying inland by river craft. The products obtained from the Gallic world were no doubt a very similar selection to those carried from Narbonne and elsewhere in Languedoc: metals and slaves from the interior, cereals, shellfish and salt, but with the addition of the distinctive local dark hard stone, basalt, found only in this Hérault delta zone. It was exported in semi-manufactured form as millstones; local masons would complete the work. They have been found widely in the western Mediterranean, including the fellow Greek colony of Ampurias (Spain).

In the Gallo-Roman period, Agde became part of the territory of BEZIERS, but remained a significant port. Despite evidence of quays and a bridge, virtually nothing has survived of this phase.

Musée d'Archéologie Sous-marine

Mas de la Clape.
Hours: 15 April–30 September 9.00 a.m.–noon, 2.00–7.00 p.m.
        1 October–14 April   9.00 a.m.–noon, 3.00–6.00 p.m., closed
                               Monday

The museum, opened in 1982, has a light, relaxed feel and successfully reflects the calm professionalism necessary in the sub-aqua archaeologist. Nearly all the material found in the sea, river and *étangs* (mainly the Thau) is from Antiquity, and it is the world of Greek and Roman mariners and their trade that comes across most vividly.

Ships (Room 4)

The **model Roman merchant ship**, based on the Portus bas-relief in Rome, highlights their typical features. It embodies two masts, one amidships, carrying a large main sail and a triangular topsail, another forward mast at an angle carrying a steering sail. Heavy extra timbers, wales, have been added to the planking to give the upper part extra rigidity. Two large oars, not a rudder, are used for steering. The poop deck has a galley for the crew (generally roofed with tiles). Behind it rears the sternpost carved in the form of a swan.

Amongst the paraphernalia of ancient sailing, such as the lead sounding stones and pumping gear, are the many **anchors**. The triangular three-holed stone types were once secured to the ship by rope and gripped soft seabeds with the help of double wooden spikes. Wealthier masters and the large ship-owners would have used lead-stock anchors. Made with a wooden stem and two wooden spikes, they were held together by a lead assembly section and weighed down by a lead cross piece to hold the anchor rigid on the sea floor.

Goods (Rooms 4 and 5)

Basalt millstones, found in a ship wrecked on the Ile de Brescou, were rough-cut in the quarry of Embonne, situated in the hill of la Clape, site of the museum itself. The **ingots** represent the major metals used in Antiquity. Most are copper or lead, but one rarity is the tube-like lump of tin nodules, shaped by the sackcloth they filled. The copper discs came in various sizes and thicknesses, the lead pigs were shaped like fish – the earliest type – or loaves of bread, with the producer's name stamped on the top. The main source for these metals is Spain. Eleven pigs have the Cartagenian Planii company stamp, a name also known in Narbonensis – suggesting a classical multinational enterprise.

The major containers used were, of course, the **amphorae**. These varied over time, between different national and cultural groups and for different products (e.g., oil or wine). Agde's collection is one of the finest and in itself demonstrates the changing trade links of the Hérault region. A major feature of the first- to third-century AD transit trade from Spain to Rome was that in *garum*, a hideously smelly but apparently delicious fish paste, carried in the fat globular amphorae displayed here.

Works of Art (Room 6)

The prize possession of the museum is the so-called **Ephèbe**. The young man is naked, apart from a short cloak over the right shoulder and arm. His hair is dishevelled, but he has the stance of a proud aristocrat, leading to his initial identification as one of the Athenian elite military college youths (epheboi). The slender figure, proportions and sense of a moment caught, seems to reflect the style of the great Lysippus. This led Charbonneaux to argue that he is really a Hellenistic prince: the hair and pose are loosely modelled on Alexander and were fashionable *c*. 200 BC, the cloak is that of a Thessaly prince and he wears a diadem or band of cloth to hold his hair. De Santerre considers it a Roman copy: if so – and despite the pitted and corroded surface – it is a version which retains much of the balance and vitality of an original. This river-bed discovery (1964) provided no clues as to its origins.

Agde Museum (Musée 'Escolo dau Sarret')

5, rue de la Fraternité.
Hours: 10.00 a.m.–noon, 2.00–6.00 p.m. (closed Tuesday)

The municipal museum in the old town of Agde is a charming jumble of 'folklorique'. The archaeological finds include more millstones from Embonne and a fourth- or third-century BC helmeted figure, crudely carved and very un-Greek, found in the workings along with local pottery, helping to confirm that the basalt quarrymen were indigenous and not colonists.

The rampart

By Agde central post office on the Esplanade round the town, there is a section of large, vaguely polygonal basalt blocks. Broadly similar to Greek walling at ST BLAISE (see p. 200), they must have presented a grim vision in Antiquity.

AMBRUSSUM, Hérault

Michelin 83–8
IGN 66–C4/5
2,02/48,56gr
4°09/43°53

Gallo-Roman oppidum and bridge.

Today, Ambrussum is hidden between two major road arteries (A9 and N113) and can only be approached easily from Villetelle village to the north, where the minor road to the site is signposted. Known for many years from classical sources as a stopping point on the Via Domitia, milestone finds have confirmed the route and made clear that the Domitia crossed the River Vidourle by the 'Pont Ambroix'.

Jean-Luc Fiches's careful excavations, between 1968 and 1984, have demonstrated that it was first occupied in the Neolithic period and became a

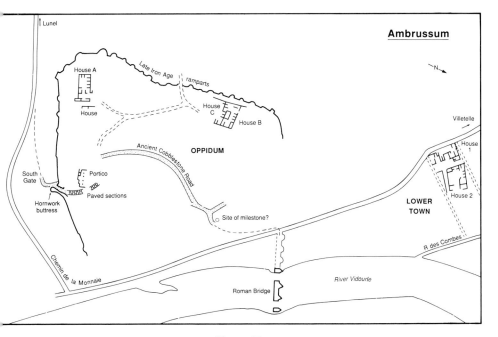

Figure 18

defended oppidum in the Iron Age. More surprisingly perhaps, he has
shown that although only the lower town was occupied into the later third
century AD, houses in the upper town were still fully used at the end of the
first century AD. Until recently it has been assumed that all hilltop sites were
abandoned by the time of Augustus, a century earlier.

The bridge

The leaning trees, swaying canes and vast water lilies conceal the volatile
nature of the river. There is only one arch left of at least nine constructed by
the Romans. Flooding has swept the rest away, most recently in 1933 when a
neighbouring arch was reduced to a pier. As usual the lower courses are
massive blocks. The piers are strengthened upstream with cutwaters and
provided with rectangular storm apertures in the spandrels. Projecting
corbels show where the wooden scaffolding rested before the arch was
completed. The design was severely functional with a single convex moulding, though the lost parapet may have had more decoration. The bridge was
used well into the Middle Ages, long after the Roman road surface had gone,
as the ruts in the arch stones show.

The road

100 m south of the bridge, climbing up through the gorse and dwarf oaks, is one of the best preserved ancient roads in southern France. Oblong cobble-stones form a surface 3 m wide, neatly marked at the edge by stones set at right angles. In places there are deep ruts, probably used as tracks to steer cartwheels. A 1984 aerial survey using infra-red techniques suggests a much more extensive system, though the excavated example could be the Via Domitia itself as a roadside hole has been interpreted as one dug for a milestone. Subsequently, the road skirted the foot of the oppidum.

The portico and southern gate

The first-century BC road has been traced for about 300 m to a small plateau looking south-east. A building with one long open side and internal columns set at 4 m intervals suggests its public nature. The rooms at the back could be shops.

The southern gate, with its hornwork extension creating the corridor entrance, represents the final rampart modification undertaken at the start of the first century BC. Sections of paving in front of the portico and down to the gate suggest an effort to create a more typically Roman appearance. The gate door socket has survived. The cobblestone road resumes in the corridor and has been traced for a short distance beyond.

The ramparts

The walls and towers on the west are the best preserved. Like the even more imposing defences less than a dozen kilometres away at Nages (see NIMES, p. 109), they are built with thin rectangular blocks with new interior facings added after the initial construction (250–175 BC or earlier), making them very thick in places. Most of the towers are semi-circular, with one excep-tionally massive example at the highest point on the site: this 'watch-tower', like those at Nîmes and Nages, may well have had some symbolic meaning for the inhabitants.

The houses

Excavations have shown housing which evolved to the same basic courtyard design by the later first century AD: the Roman veneer to a simple farming household given by a tile roof and a portico.

House A provides the clearest picture. Rather than adopting a classical atrium or peristyle design, a portico has been added to the courtyard. On two sides are the owner's quarters. Room 5 clearly adopts the Roman form: a large room looking out through the portico over what must have been a

Ambrussum

HOUSE A

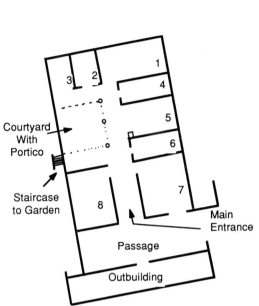

Key

1 Storeroom ?

2,3,6 Bedrooms ?

4 Dining Room

5 Reception Room

7 Farm Workshop Room

8 Domestic Living Room

Figure 19

low wall into a garden and across to the rampart – probably partially pulled down in the first century AD. A possible couch base lends support to its identification as a reception room. But on the third side room 8, equipped with a central hearth, was filled with a wide variety of domestic finds, both pots and personal ornaments. Here was the traditional general room, where lesser members of the household still lived. Room 7 was their workroom: the floor was covered with fragments of *dolia*, amphorae and farm tools.

Houses B and C are very similar courtyard houses, though in poor condition.

Lower town

Two houses have been excavated in Le Sables, though they are sadly dilapidated now. This area, on the plain between the hill and river, was occupied from the second century BC. They are again courtyard houses and are unlikely to have been the '*mutatio*' mentioned in later classical sources: the stopping place for road travellers to change horses must have been nearer the bridge.

BEAUCAIRE, Gard

Michelin 80–20
IGN 66–B8
2,56/48,52gr
4°37/43°48

Local museum and Via Domitia.

As a bridgehead site, Beaucaire has always depended on the traffic generated by the river crossing and the Rhône itself. Today the crossings at Avignon and Arles are more important, but commercial and tourist traffic still uses the bridge passing by what appears to be a rather run-down and even seedy town, a view helped by the main road by-passing the old town. It is deceptive because it obscures the quiet, narrow, inward-looking medieval streets, an impressive château hill with Roman remains, an attractive local museum and the opportunity to walk along the Via Domitia in peaceful countryside.

La Redoute or Castle Hill on the north of the town has produced Bronze Age material, and by the Iron Age had become an oppidum. Extensive seventh-century BC Greek finds confirm the early development of the Rhône as an international waterway. Excavation has been rare and little is known about the emergence of Ugernum, the Gallo-Roman town below the hill, though it was possibly established to protect the crossing when the Via Domitia was created; material in Marronniers necropolis on the western side of the town suggests that significant romanisation had certainly taken place by the start of the first century BC. Ugernum was probably at its peak in the first and second centuries AD before the east–west route via Arles began seriously to undermine the town's role. In late Antiquity, Castle Hill was reoccupied, probably as a fortress or *castrum*.

The château

The grounds cover the whole hill and include both the excavated Gallo-Roman remains and the local museum.

Hours: 1 April–30 September   10.00 a.m.–noon, 2.15–6.45 p.m.
1 October–31 March   10.15 a.m.–noon, 2.00–5.15 p.m.
Closed Tuesdays

Temple(?) foundations

On the rim of the south face of the hill, seven semi-circular buttresses constructed of *petit appareil* survive 3–4 m high. They could have supported the podium or enclosure wall of a temple. The building technique is reminiscent of the Tour Magne (see NIMES, p. 100).

Musée de la Vignasse

This is a diminutive municipal museum without pretensions, but the two-room collection is interesting and well displayed. The most important discovery has been the remnants of a massive mausoleum. Some of the blocks and the statues that stood on the base survived work on the Ile de Comte in the Rhône because of the sharp eyes of the engineer in charge. The reconstruction suggests a monument comparable to that at Les Antiques (see ST REMY, p. 217).

Via Domitia

Those planning this 11 km walk (one way) should use IGN Série Bleu map 2942 est 1:25,000.

The Via Domitia is the oldest Roman road in Narbonensis, created by Cn Domitius Ahenobarbus when he had completed the conquest of Languedoc-Roussillon in 118 BC (see NARBONNE, pp. 84, 90). It replaced the older prehistoric 'Heraklean Way', providing a modern route for the rapid movement of troops from the Rhône and friendly Massalian territory to Rome's Spanish province. Eighty-four milestones have been found along the route from Beaucaire via Nîmes, Béziers, Elne and the Le Perthus pass across the Pyrénées into Spain.

The main feature of this short section is the large number of **milestones in situ**. Perhaps surprisingly, some sites have more than one. The erection of milestones was a relatively cheap means of demonstrating local loyalty to the new Emperor or it could be done under Imperial command to link the current Emperor with his godly predecessors; in some cases it could also have had a local function in defining land divisions – a new milestone would reassert old boundaries. The miles are measured from Nîmes. The measurement was the *passus* or double step, a thousand in the Roman mile (MP) = 1,481.5 m.

The Roman road took a straighter and more direct route to Nîmes than the modern D999. Only the part in Beaucaire is on a modern road, the rest is track, marked as 'Chemin Romain' before it joins the D999.

From the Place Jaurès, take the D38 in the direction of the station, but turn right for Marronniers cemetery.

Rouanesse crossroads: XV MP. There are two Claudian milestones at this junction by the edge of the Marronniers necropolis, marked by a large sarcophagus nearby. Continue on roads passing the Halle des Sports and under the railway.

Clos de Melettes/'Colonnes de Cesar': XIII MP. Four milestones, the earliest of which is Augustan and the latest Antonine. In 1962 three were known, one fallen. It was decided to put this upright and in the process a fourth was found!

Enclos d'Argent: X MP. At the junction with a track, the chemin de Duvez, which may have been a minor Roman road. Two milestones of Augustan date, one of which is broken.

Les Pradas/'Peire di Novi': VIIII MP. One milestone of Tiberius. After the farm it still marks the commune boundary and was once used as a site for local marriages.

2 km further west the Domitia joins the D999, just south of Redessan. The main road then follows the Roman route to Nîmes.

BEZIERS, Hérault

Michelin 83–15
IGN 65–D6
0,97/48,15gr
3°14/43°22

Museum and fragmentary remains.

Béziers stands on a dark rocky promontory, dominating the Orb River crossing where the Via Domitia meets a significant north–south route from the mountains to the port of Agde. The area had rich agricultural resources and Baeterrae, as a colony, was a city of high status in the Roman Empire. Yet the surviving remains are extremely scanty and the museum collection, whilst worth seeing, is rather less impressive than that in Narbonne.

Development

Avienus, writing in the fourth century AD, has been supposed to have used a sixth-century BC source in which Béziers features as a great settlement, though recently declined. However, the existence of his presumed source has been seriously doubted, which makes the archaeological evidence more central. Of the two major excavations in the 1970s and 1980s, the St Nazaire site seems to support an early settlement, but the La Madeleine site does not; this would at least imply the hill was not extensively occupied. Fifth- and fourth-century BC evidence confirms brick houses, a rampart and the usual Greek links, but third- and early second-century material is so thin it has been possible to suggest the site was actually abandoned until Roman political and trading interests stimulated new development. Perhaps ENSERUNE (see p. 71), only 10 km away, really was the major regional centre.

In 36–35 BC the local population was joined by veterans of the VII Legion and the town became Urbs Julia Baeterrae Septimanorum. Following a land survey the new colonists at last received what they had long wanted – release from the army and the security of their own holdings. Octavian's decision no doubt encouraged their lasting loyalty to the future Emperor and his family (note the splendid Imperial portraits of the Julio-Claudians removed to Toulouse in 1844). Other major public buildings are unknown, but the amphitheatre is the second smallest in Narbonensis. The number of inscriptions that have survived might be revealing: they total only 100+; Nîmes has over 2000. Only one man is known for his career outside Béziers. The overriding impression is not of lost grandeur, but of staid conservatism.

Even less is known of the late Roman city. Silver treasure found in the countryside to the north shows that there were still rich and classically cultured men living in the surrounding villas. As Sidonius Apollinaris' writing illustrates, this was equally true in the sixth century when Béziers belonged to the Septimania province of the Visigoth kingdom.

Musée d'Archéologie

Hours: 9.00 a.m.–noon, 2.00–6.00 p.m., closed Monday

Most of the following should be on display in the new museum.

Inscriptions

The town elite are recorded in their official *civitas* capacities, but only **L. Aponius** is of more than local interest. His early career indicates his (relatively) close contact with the family of Augustus. He was the first priest appointed to the municipal Imperial cult. When Caius Caesar (see NIMES, p. 95) was made honorary magistrate in Baeterrae, L. Aponius did the work for him. He undertook a military career that culminated as a staff officer (tribune) in the VII Legion – the local connection? – and XXII Legion in Egypt. The inscription finishes there, but Tacitus describes a loyal and reliable *eques* L. Aponius helping in the dangerous dealings with mutineers just after Tiberius succeeded Augustus in AD 14. Unless he died soon after, he must have gone on to the procuratorial posts suitable to a man of his status; nothing has survived to tell us his fate.

Sculpture

The best is a fine head of **Silenus**. This wise but alcoholic tutor to the god Bacchus is depicted with a grotesque mouth, fat high cheek-bones, dishevelled hair and beard and a skullcap secured by a knot on his forehead. Bacchus himself also appears, both as a young man, graceful and feminine, and as an old Greek philosopher type, the latter head found at the villa of Puissalicon. This site also produced a striking **Julio-Claudian portrait**. The thrusting jaw, prominent cheek-bones and strained forehead stress the vigour and determination of an aristocratic man, his hair cut in classic early Imperial style. Perhaps it came from the home of a leading family as it accompanied the head of Faustina the Younger, Empress (AD 161–76) and wife of Marcus Aurelius.

Small finds

The imported fourth-century **silver plate** is outstanding. The two large plates and one bowl were found in 1983, placed/hidden? in the storage chamber of a late Roman villa near Béziers. They were worn from domestic or cult use; if the latter, the most likely would seem to be by followers of Bacchus.

The larger plate has a central medallion with an ecstatic male Bacchant or satyr dancing in front of an altar. Attributes of Bacchus decorate the scene: the fawn's skin, the thyrsus or wand and the pipes. The rim is equally filled with Dionysic symbols as well as animals and other gods like Mercury and Luna. The slightly smaller plate has a gilded medallion, in this case a female figure seated on a throne, probably a goddess. The medallion in the deep bowl depicts a 'good shepherd' scene, given perspective by using incised and relief work, some gilded; the rim decor has more Bacchic icons.

Amphitheatre

La Rue des Anciennes Arènes.

Buildings still curve round the hollow dug in the hillside to create the early style segmented ellipse shape. Foundations have been observed in cellars and garage walls but nothing is presently visible.

La Madeleine church

The west wall has traces of a late Roman rampart just over a metre high.

St Aphrodise church

A simple Aquitanian-style sarcophagus has been used as a side-door lintel. Inside the church, the tomb of the saint is another late Roman sarcophagus. Decorated with a hunting scene of horsemen and lions, it has no obvious Christian associations.

Pépézut statue

Place de l'Hôtel de Ville.

The battered, draped body of an Imperial figure. His head was removed and lost in the sixteenth century and guesses on identity range from Augustus to Tetricus. He symbolised the freedom of the city in the Middle Ages.

Pont Vieux

The foundations of arches 11 and 12 have been identified as Roman, but the earliest visible structure is unlikely to be anything but medieval or later.

CARCASSONNE, Aude

Michelin 83–11
IGN 72–B1
0,03/48,03gr
2°10/43°13

Late Roman walls.

'La Cité' of Carcassonne is a dazzling sight. Approached from any direction, there, sitting on the top of a hill, is a perfect medieval city. Surrounded by not just one, but two walls with great towers capped by pointed pepper-pot roofs, it seems a vision from medieval romance, whether based on the Duc de Berry's *Book of Hours* or Hollywood re-creations of King Arthur's mythical kingdom.

Development

The citadel, on a last outcrop of the Razès, looks down to the Aude, dominating the valley where the river turns east to create a gap between the Montagne Noire and the Corbières. From prehistoric times it was crucial in the control of the major route from the Mediterranean to the plains of Gascony and the port of Bordeaux.

Chance finds and modern excavations have confirmed occupation by Iberian-influenced people from the sixth century BC, but inevitably with the high concentration of medieval building within the ramparts the evidence is isolated for the existence of both Iron Age and Roman Carcaso. The most impressive finds have been the monochrome mosaics discovered under basement flooring in the Château Comtal in the 1920s. In the fourth century the Bordeaux–Jerusalem Itinerary lists a 'Castellum Carcassone'. However, the general collapse of central Roman power in Gaul in the fifth century led to Carcassonne being taken by the Visigoths in 436 when it became, for the next three centuries, the major bulwark of their French province, Septimania.

The ramparts

The walls and towers that surround the city have a complex history, but there are three main phases of development. It is impossible to begin making sense of the Roman elements without first understanding how the ramparts evolved.

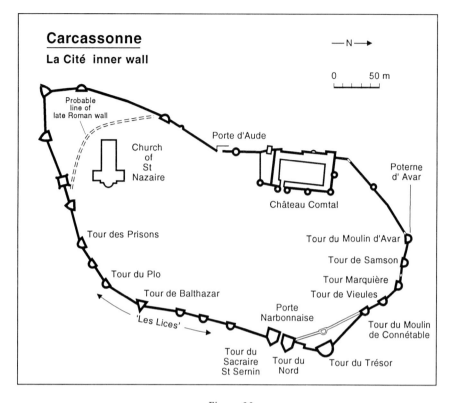

Figure 20

Late Roman features

It is now accepted that the line of the inner rampart with about thirty towers was of late Roman construction. The medievalist perspective of earlier writers on the town led them to assume it was Visigoth, despite the absence of any specific supporting evidence. In fact the ramparts embody many typical late Roman features: large blockwork foundations, small square blockwork and rubble core about 3 m thick for the main structure, the use of tile bricks as bonding courses, a rampart walk level of 6–7 m and 'U'-shaped towers that sit astride the wall, only their semi-circular fronts projecting beyond the rampart face. Similar fortifications were being constructed all over Gaul after the later third-century invasions; their construction here would certainly justify the Itinerary calling the place a *castellum*.

The medieval modifications

A second phase of major building took place in the thirteenth century when the town became a royal fortress city after being surrendered by the Cathars to the Albigensian 'Crusaders'. The ground level was lowered to create a flat

Carcassonne

RAMPART STRUCTURE

A Schematic Presentation

(Not to Scale)

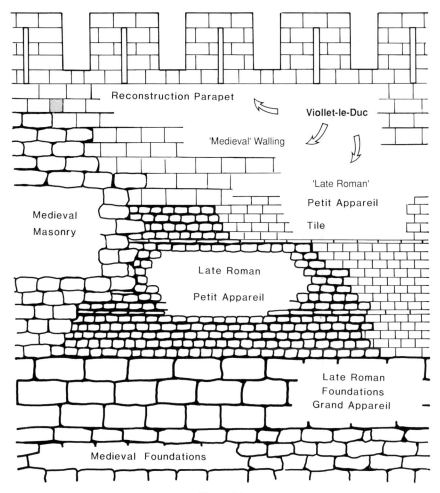

Figure 21

65

zone outside the rampart ('Les Lices'), and a new lower, outer wall was added. New towers were built, some on the inner wall replacing the originals, but by no means all. The medieval-designed towers are much larger and extend further out from the walls than the late Roman type and have sometimes been given a pointed front. Massive new gates replaced the older ones at the Porte Narbonnaise and the Porte d'Aude and a castle was built into the western side of the inner ramparts. In two places the alignment of the inner rampart was changed, slightly extending the area enclosed.

Restoration

Though the army retained a residual control, by the nineteenth century it was clear the ramparts' military role was well past. The walls were burrowed into, either to make hovels or for the ready-made building stone; crenellations were easily knocked down and towers above rampart walk level disappeared. A 'quartier des Lices' was created between the walls, made up of lean-to houses shared by the poor and their animals.

An Inspector of Historic Monuments, Cros-Mayrevieille, first voiced serious concern, reporting his worries to Mérimée, the Chief Inspector, and carrying out the first detailed study of the ramparts. Viollet-le-Duc, an architect fascinated by the medieval, was called in by Mérimée to plan the preservation of Carcassonne. As he was later to explain: 'to restore a building is not just to preserve it, to repair it, and to remodel it, it is to reinstate it in a complete state such as it may never have been at any given moment' (*Dictionnaire d'architecture*, VIII, 14 (1866)).

The work was still going on when Viollet-le-Duc died in 1879 and was only finished in the early twentieth century. First the ramparts and gates were restored to their full height, and where necessary walls were underpinned and facings recovered. Using fragmentary remains for models, the rampart walk crenellations were completely rebuilt and the towers given two-storey rooms above rampart height and capped with new roofs of slate. The houses inside began converting themselves into restaurants and tourist shops. As Viollet-le-Duc pointed out, 'the City of Carcassonne, scarcely visited formerly, has become a resort for all travellers'.

Major sections of late Roman work

Most of the visible late Roman work is on the north-eastern side of the citadel.

North of the Porte Narbonnaise

The Gate Tour du Nord and the Tour du Trésor, the rampart linking them and the rampart to the Tour de Moulin du Connétable are thirteenth-century. However, from 1971 intermittent excavations began that confirmed the original late Roman perimeter ran just behind this section. Probably the section from the Tour du Moulin de Connétable to Poterne d'Avar has the most surviving Roman work. Both rampart sections and towers show neat ancient small blockwork divided by single, double and treble courses of tiles (though frequently below, above or beside the larger, longer medieval work and the smoother restoration examples of both).

Tour de Vieules: Roman foundation work is visible on top of medieval underpinning where the tower has collapsed dangerously outwards. Above are Viollet-le-Duc's reconstructed tower rooms, with 'medieval' arrow slits, now more appropriately capped with a low tile roof, rather than his anachronistic northern French slate pepper-pot.

Tour Marquière: three Roman window arches with double tiles indicate where the ballistae stood guarding the ramparts; the central window shows the space needed to manoeuvre the bulky frames. The side windows have been converted to arrow slits; the medieval soldier was better protected but used a less powerful weapon.

Tour de Samson and Tour du Moulin d'Avar: square and semi-circular medieval foundations support Roman work that meshes quickly with re-created tower rooms, windows and roofs.

Poterne d'Avar: a classic Roman small gate. The lintel and door jambs are made of large stone blocks. Above, there is a relieving arch of tiles. Typically the door is close to a tower to provide flanking fire if attacked. The lowering of the ground level is obvious here.

South of the Porte Narbonnaise

Between the Porte and the thirteenth-century Tour des Prisons, there is a long stretch of basically late Roman walling and towers (except the Tour de Balthazar). However, the evidence of heavy restoration is equally apparent.

Tour du Sacraire St Sernin: between the medieval underpinning and the chapel windows, in addition to the course of large blocks, the tiles are laid in a simple decorative pattern.

Tour du Plo: the remains of five courses of large blocks are visible.

Musée Lapidaire, Château Comtal

Hours: Tourist season   9.00 a.m.–6.30 p.m. daily
        Out of season   9.30 a.m.–12.30, 2.00–5.00 p.m. daily

Room 1 contains the limited Carcaso material and room 3 has a collection of ninteenth-century photographs of restoration work in Carcassonne. Eventually the mosaics found in the castle cellars should be put on view.

CHATEAU-ROUSSILLON, Pyrénées-Orientales

Michelin 86–19
IGN 72–G3
0,68/47,46gr
2°56/42°44

Early Empire town of Ruscino.

5.5 km east of Perpignan by the D617, turn right on to the C7 for Cabestany and Château-Roussillon Centre Commercial; fork to right under the D617; *c.* 200 m to site.

Polybius and Strabo both mention 'Ruscino' as the capital of the Sordones tribe, identified as Château-Roussillon from its position on the Domitia road. It stands on a low plateau, overlooking the Tet River from which it could control trade inland, the whole of the Roussillon plain being visible from here.

However, the visual remains and most of our knowledge concerning the site focus on a very narrow period. The public buildings and the excavated living area are almost entirely Julio-Claudian remains. Though known to have been occupied since the eighth century, work on Ruscino's early evolution has been limited, whilst the post first-century AD development is puzzling, and not simply because the Roman levels have been badly cut into by medieval occupation and modern farming.

There are no obvious explanations for the apparent lacuna in second- and third-century AD material. The Domitia was still being used and Ruscino is mentioned in the Itineraries. Certainly a lower town might have existed near the Tet crossing (as at AMBRUSSUM, p. 57), and this would have been covered by the sea's incursion during the fourth century. However, the area between river and hill appears to have been too narrow to contain enough development to justify the abandonment of the older city centre. This nevertheless seems a more convincing reason than the reuse of stone in the construction of Perpignan; no definite examples of Roman masonry have been found there and no evidence suggests it is anything but a medieval creation.

The forum

Perfectly orientated north–south, the general design is broadly similar to the forum at Glanum (see ST REMY, p. 211) and other contemporary examples in Italy. Stratigraphically dated to 20–25 BC, Ruscino's forum/basilica typifies many of the changing concepts of town centre planning at the beginning of the Empire. The forum was traditionally an open area for people to meet, yet Ruscino's square is small. Large stone bases suggest it was dominated by equestrian statues and whilst excavating the porticoes, forty dedications to

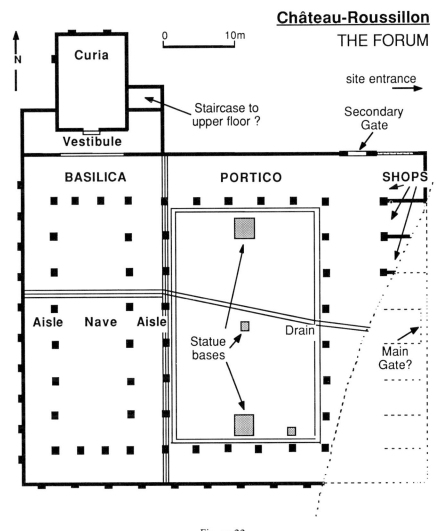

Figure 22

the Emperor, his family, provincial officials and civic leaders were found. This forum was not a centre for people to express their will but a place where the state demonstrated its power in the community.

The three aisles of the **basilica** are clearly defined by the pillar bases to the west of the forum and its separate identity is emphasised by the steps up from both square and porticoes. The central nave would probably have carried a second floor. Traditionally, basilicas had a dual function: on a daily basis they were the place for businessmen to meet and talk while less frequently and more formally, they were the law courts. The walls of the

Château-Roussillon
LIVING AREA

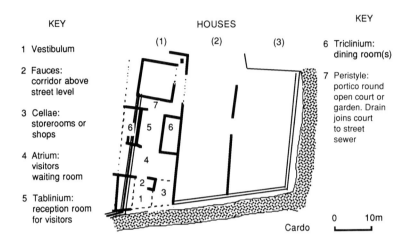

KEY

1 Vestibulum

2 Fauces:
  corridor above
  street level

3 Cellae:
  storerooms or
  shops

4 Atrium:
  visitors
  waiting room

5 Tablinium:
  reception room
  for visitors

HOUSES

(1)   (2)   (3)

KEY

6 Triclinium:
  dining room(s)

7 Peristyle:
  portico round
  open court or
  garden. Drain
  joins court
  to street
  sewer

Cardo

0   10m

Figure 23

annexe indicate three rooms. The largest is considered to be a curia or meeting-place for the council. The vestibule might have served as the magistrate's tribunal or place for his ceremonial chair. The small room could have contained a staircase to a second floor where the town archives were usually kept, listing privileges, recording legal decisions and defining the duties of local government. One is clearly visible on the site: the **great sewer** that cuts across the forum/basilica, draining into the valley.

The forum's commercial role is represented by the partially excavated **row of shops**.

Living area

East of road; open summer months during excavations.

Barruol and Marichal's recent work has revealed three early Julio-Claudian houses. The best-preserved foundations are those of house 1. However, due to the medieval intrusions, the plan has had to be reconstructed using surviving elements drawn from the other two houses. A surprisingly Pompeian atrium house emerges, very inward looking, its entrance between two possible shops, its main rooms surrounding a rear garden. Thousands of fragments of painted wall plaster from house 3 have been reconstructed to reveal architectural features, theatre masks, candelabra, etc.

Museum

It is hoped to have an on-site museum opened by 1993.

Medieval tower

A small promenade at the northern edge of the promontory next to the tower provides a fine view over the plain.

ENSERUNE, Hérault

Michelin 83–14
IGN 65–D6
0,87/48,12gr
3°06/43°18

Oppidum site.

The Ensérune ridge rises over 100 m above the coastal plain 3 km north of the N9 between Béziers and Narbonne; the D62E is signposted for the oppidum. In addition to the excavations, there are a national museum dedicated to the site and a marvellous view. A car park is situated near the top of the hill.

The earliest evidence found for the permanent occupation of this commanding site is sixth-century BC; it is easy to see why it was chosen. Typical of the more important Languedoc Iron Age settlements, it combined local resources and security with the potential for more long distance contacts. Sharp slopes mark the north, east and west of the ridge and even the south is a steep climb. The extraordinary spoked wheel drainage pattern of the Etang de Montady, created in the Middle Ages, indicates one of the many former lagoons that then covered the plain, no doubt providing an added sense of security.

Ensérune was not isolated though. Set back from the coast, it overlooked the prehistoric Heraklean road to Spain, but was near enough to the Aude estuary to engage in the traffic utilising the Carcassonne Gap and Garonne route linking the Mediterranean to the Atlantic. The finds demonstrate with great clarity the inevitable cultural mix and it is surprisingly hard to get a clear sense of indigenous identity. The local coarse ware is undistinguished and the fine ware all seems to be imported. The largest known collection of Iberian inscriptions has been found here, but Greek script was also extensive. Local development is divided on the basis of external trade contacts and influences, rather than any obvious cultural breaks.

In **Phase I**, rectangular mud-brick houses with storage silos were constructed on the eastern spur. A perennial spring on the northern slope provided some water, but from early on it cannot have been sufficient.

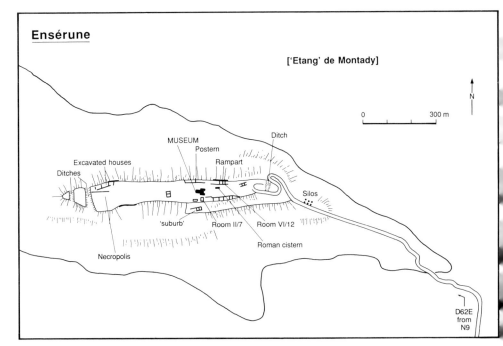

Figure 24

Certainly during **phase II**, from *c.* 425 BC, round silo-shaped cisterns were being used. This phase is marked by the expansion of the settlement, the construction of a rampart and a necropolis on the western ridge. The houses now had drystone foundations, some stone walls, others mud-brick, with timber and earth roofs. In the third century BC, growth continued; there could have been 10,000 inhabitants. Greek influence is apparent in the simple east–west grid pattern of roads, and the new terraced houses covered earlier buildings on the south face where crudely carved capitals decorated pillars in some buildings. *Dolia* were replacing silos in houses and a simple reservoir was created by linking forty-five silos on the south side; it could contain an estimated million litres.

Phase III, from the late third century BC, saw the settlement reach its largest extent with suburbs beyond the walls, the old necropolis covered with building (no new graveyard is known) and the rebuilding of the ramparts three times. It is possible that these mark the appearance of the Volcae (a local Celtic-led tribe), Hannibal on his way through to Italy and finally the Romans. Celtic influence shows most in the metalwork, though little else changes until the first century BC when multi-room Roman-influenced houses began to appear. However, there is little evidence of distinctive public buildings, even of the simplest religious type. This period of occupation has been seriously damaged by subsequent farming, but it is clear that early in the first century AD Ensérune was abandoned. The Roman peace, competition from the new cities of Béziers and Narbonne and its own water problems presumably removed the rationale for its existence.

The site

Hours: Tourist season   9.30 a.m.–7.00 p.m., closed Tuesday
        Out of season   10.00 a.m.–12.30, 2.00–6.00 p.m.

Ensérune could be an easier site for the visitor. Signs are infrequent and rarely informative: the best is a horizon orientation table! The excavators divided the site into *insulae*, but no attempt has been made to use this to help the visitor find specific features.

Silo terrace

Below the car park, the road embankment reveals sections of pits, some over 2 m deep, cut into the yellow tufa hillside. Seventy-six were excavated during 1966–7 by de Santerre. Linking channels and ceramic linings in some suggest water cisterns. However, they were filled with third- to first-century BC material with no real stratigraphy, implying that during the last phase they were a rubbish dump. They even contained some stele and skeleton remains, perhaps the bodies of 'outsiders' (possibly murderers?) denied the privilege of normal cremation.

Roman cisterns

There are a number of first-century BC 'Roman' circular, rectangular and, most distinctively, apse-shaped cisterns. An example of the latter type can be seen on the left-hand side of the path to the museum.

South-facing slope

Single-room third-century BC terraced housing along the east–west roads is clear in some places, in others, rebuilding has left a confusing muddle to the visitor. One typical 5 × 6 m house (Insula II, house 7) has remains of a Roman period plaster dado, painted with simple decorative motifs.

Northern slope

A line of houses has been excavated along the rim of the hill looking inland. Below them runs a road with some evidence of paving. House 12 in Insula VI has a central column with a simple capital roughly shaped as twin corbels (others are amongst the earliest Ionic- or Doric-inspired in Gaul). The silo in the corner would have been covered with a paving stone. *Dolia* in the next house are protected from rain damage by a modern tile roof. Below the road (and difficult to see) are remains of the rampart, surviving six to seven courses.

Museum

Despite interesting individual cases, the museum still embodies a staid and traditional approach. The curators have recognised the need for wide-ranging revision and the audio-visual presentation is a valuable help, if the grandiose music is ignored.

Ground floor

The multiplicity of external influences is demonstrated by the ceramics, metalwork and coinage. From the sixth to the fourth centuries BC, the Greek world dominates. Probably the Ionian bowls and Attic vases came via Marseille, a suggestion supported by the large number of Massalian coins. Campanian craters, bowls and plates indicate how south Italy came to dominate ceramic trade from the third century onwards, until, in the first century, Arretine then south Gaul sigillata arrived. A Punic ritual vase hints at more tenuous contacts with the Carthaginians.

Upstairs

The necropolis finds are gathered here. The best cases reproduce the crema-tion burials and their associated finds, mainly from the fifth to third century BC. The most interesting offerings are the eggs, thought to have been left as symbols of resurrection; one ossuary had three eggs and the bones of three children. At last a distinctive Ensérune personality emerges, but sadly, only in death.

LATTES, Hérault

Michelin 83–7
IGN 66–C3
1,75/48,42gr
3°54/43°34

Museum and excavations.

5 km south of Montpellier is the village of Lattes. The museum, set in the modernised farmhouse of St Saveur, is half a kilometre from the village on the D132 to Pérols. It is a flat and featureless area. In Antiquity the now

separate *étangs* of Pérols and Mauguio were one large *étang* and the marsh-land was far more extensive. Pliny describes how in his time the fishermen who lived in this 'stagnum Latera' caught mullet with the help of local dolphins. On the day when the fish tried to go out to the open sea through a channel in the sand bar, the dolphins frightened many of the fish into nets and ate the ones that escaped. 'As they are aware that they have had too strenuous a task for only a single day's pay, they wait till the next day and are given a feed of bread mash dipped in wine.'(!)

In the 1960s it became clear that ancient Lattes was much more than the fishing village implied by Pliny. A group from Montpellier, inspired by H. Prades, carried out a whole series of small-scale excavations which by the 1970s had established the importance of the settlement: at least 12 ha of buildings, forming a mound 5 m high, were located by the farm. In 1984, a new team including M. Py (see NIMES, p. 109) and J.-L. Fiches (see AMBRUSSUM, p. 54) began their work. The museum opened two years later.

The site

Prades discovered a major port. Ancient ships with their shallow draft and the existence of channels through the sand bar made lagoon rather than shoreline sites a possibility. In the early sixth century BC it was no more than a landing stage, but it quickly evolved into a focus for Etruscan, Punic and Greek traders. The latter, especially those from Marseille, became the dominant influence. Typically for Languedoc, this influence was first challenged in the third century BC, then superseded in the second by the arrival of Italian traders with their Campanian and central Italian wines. No doubt, as elsewhere in the region, they were seeking the metals and slaves of the interior. This change in the economic balance was followed by integration in the Roman province. Its commercial role stopped abruptly at the end of the second century AD when silt and a rising water level made continued habitation impossible.

Despite the discovery of a planned town organised in blocks along a main road, the actual excavations make little visual impact. It is still very much an archaeologist's site and the general visitor is restricted to a view from the museum.

The museum

Hours: 15 June–15 September   10.00 a.m.–noon, 3.00–6.30 p.m.
　　　　16 September–14 June   10.00 a.m.–noon, 2.00–5.30 p.m.

The museum's role as a regional research and study centre has two particular advantages for the visitor: important temporary exhibitions are shown here and the permanent displays can be changed rapidly to integrate new discoveries. A minor disadvantage is that this need for adaptability has somehow produced a rather anaemic setting.

Gallo-Roman Lattes

First floor: 'household' goods are well presented. The large collection of high quality unbroken glass, found in the waterlogged necropolis, is outstanding. The wall charts are particularly helpful.

Mezzanine floor: the stonework section is well-lit, but the statuary found so far uninspired. Amongst the tombstones, thirty inscribed examples are from the necropolis, the best a marble plaque, probably second century AD, recording Titus Troccius Masclinus' dedication to Marcianus, his 'educator' or foster-father. Most moving is the uninscribed relief of a family group, the father's hand delicately resting on the child's head.

Top floor: as well as the altar to Mercury, metal artefacts and an excellent coin collection including 3,000 Massaliote obols, there is the most important single find made in Lattes: the dedication to Mars by a Sevir Augustalis. Titus Eppilius Astrapton was probably a freedman of Greek origin, whose wealth had enabled him to achieve the status of priest of the Imperial cult in Nîmes, the territory to which Lattes belonged. He was probably the patron (the corner of the plaque is broken where this would be specified) of the craftsmen and boatmen of Lattara. It is the only inscription that specifies the name of the town.

Entrance: four milestones stand in the portico. The best is an Augustan example of 3 BC, recovered from the Via Domitia.

LES CLUSES/LE PERTHUS, Pyrénées-Orientales

Michelin 86–19
IGN 72–J3
0,55/47,21gr
2°50/42°29

Late Roman fortress.

The N9 takes the traveller from France to Spain over the pass of Le Perthus. Looking up westwards from the lay-by at the 100 m marker 49.8 km, the ruins of Castell dels Moros cling to the rocks above the Rom, seemingly just another gaunt and abandoned mountain castle. Recent investigation has shown that this was a Roman fortification deliberately built to guard a major route, a type known as '*cluserae*' – a term echoed by the name of the local hamlet.

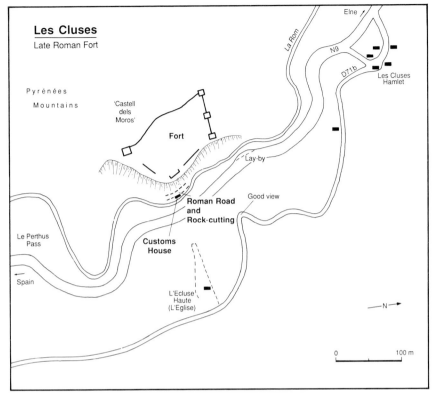

Figure 25

The Roman road

The Via Domitia, following the prehistoric Heraklean Way, split after Elne and reached Spain either by the coast road through Port-Vendres (Portus Veneris) or went over the low and relatively easy Col du Perthus – the Summum Pyrenaeum. It followed the path of the River Rom more closely than the heavily embanked modern road. Below the south-east corner of the fort, where the Rom ran near to the sloping rock face, a laboriously made cutting has survived, leaving a pillar of rock beside the winter torrent.

A customs office

Besides the cutting are a few courses of Roman building stone. Some is *grand appareil*, well cut and not local, possibly from an earlier structure. The smaller blockwork is of the same type as the fort. The likely explanation is that these are the remains of a customs office. The Pyrénées formed one limit of the Gallic customs union. Trade in and out of this group of provinces involved payment of the Quadragesima Galliorum, a fortieth or 2 per cent of the value of the goods. It was not a heavy tax, and probably as important in the insecure conditions of the later Empire was the desire to check and control movement.

The fort

Military posts guarding the civilian tax-collection office had been normal since the beginnings of Empire, but the fort constructed here is a major strongpoint. Brigandage was certainly worse in the third and fourth centuries, whilst barbarian incursions into Gaul and Spain at times reached the Pyrénées and added to the overall insecurity.

The fort covers nearly a hectare, forming a rough quadrilateral rising very steeply to the tower on the south-west tip. This seems to have been massive, but is now only a lump of solid masonry. The eastern walling, of which only parts survive – or perhaps they were never built as the rock-face is so precipitous – overlooks the Roman road. Guardposts survive at each end. The northern wall facing down the valley covers the weakest point, the slope here 'only' has a gradient of about 25 per cent. Three square towers sit astride the wall in typical late Roman fashion. This section is well preserved with staircases to the rampart walkway and the main gateway marked by its threshold and door sockets. The western wall has an intact postern gate.

The road would have been unusable without the permission of the fort's soldiers. They were secure from any ordinary attack and armed with ballistae, the 300–400 m range heavy arrow firing machines, mounted on the towers or sited on the sloping enclosure would have made movement anywhere in the valley hazardous.

Only the remains of the eastern wall and the north-east tower are visible from the N9 lay-by. To reach the other side of the Rom and the Domitia road cutting is not difficult in the summer. The Rom is a trickle and it is possible to use the rocks as stepping stones, but the climb up to the fort is extremely arduous, very time-consuming and can be dangerous. An alternative is to take the turning for Les Cluses (Marie), and then follow the D71b, signposted for L'Eglise and Col de L'Ouillat. Much more of the fort can be seen from L'Ecluse Haute, about a kilometre up the road, where there is a Romanesque chapel and a farmhouse standing on walling that may also be part of late Roman fortification.

LOUPIAN, Hérault

Michelin 83–16
IGN 65–D9
1,44/48,28gr
3°37/43°27

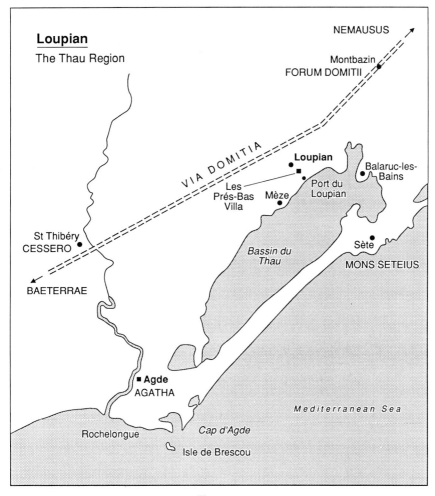

Figure 26

Villa and mosaics.

800 m to the north of the Thau basin is the site of Les Prés-Bas, just south of Loupian. It is the finest Roman villa in Mediterranean France. Found in 1962, Les Prés-Bas is still being excavated and clearly there is much more to be discovered. Loupian owns the site and is justifiably proud of it, planning, when they have raised the money, to construct the museum and protective roofing that it deserves. Until this is created, they are providing guides. Tickets are obtained from Loupian town hall in the 'château', a fine sixteenth-century fortified house.

Villa development

The villa remains suggest two major construction phases. When established in the **early first century**, Les Prés-Bas was on a significantly grander scale than a simple farmhouse or 'villa rustica'. Its 'villa urbana', the living quarters of the owners, were equipped with monochrome mosaic and marble decorated rooms and a bath system.

Coinage finds suggest continuous occupation into the fifth century, with the largest concentration in the **fourth century** when the house was remodelled: an external portico was added on the northern side and the house was refocused round a new central peristyle garden with a marble pool, its lead piping still in place today. However, it is the number of splendid polychrome mosaics that makes the villa an epitome of the luxury of the great landowners of the period. Their style suggests craftsmen were brought in both from the neighbouring province of Aquitaine and from Syria. Expensive marble decoration was also used and no doubt the best artists were employed for wall-painting, though unfortunately only tiny fragments of plaster have been found so far. The south and east of the site are still being excavated.

Early in the fifth century, rather than repair worn floors, many were covered with a mix of concrete and broken tile, less prosperous perhaps, but certainly more functional. Later in the century it fell into ruin, though squatters may have occupied some rooms.

Main rooms and mosaics

Room A–A'

Two older rooms have been combined to create an impressive reception room. The semi-circular alcove A has a mosaic mixing geometric and floral decor, whilst the mosaic in main room A', though predominantly patterned, has panels in each corner embodying the four seasons. Unusually, the top ones are larger and had complete figures while the bottom had busts only. The autumn and winter panels on the right are the best preserved.

Rooms G, B and C

At the side of room A' a passage leads to two other rooms with mosaics, both of fourth-century geometric design (on top of simple concrete first-century floors). Perhaps the threshold in the north wall of room C was the main entrance to the house.

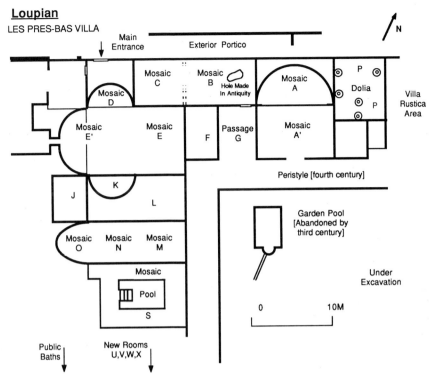

Figure 27

Rooms E–E', D and K

Here the fourth-century builders created a magnificent triple-apsed room. This could have been a grandiose winter dining-room. The top semi-circle E', where the owner and his most important guests would have had their couches, was supplied with underfloor heating. Room E has an enormous carpet mosaic consisting of arcades of short, fat columns and vases with stylised foliage. In apse room D, the mosaic is almost intact; a beautiful Greek key design using twisted rope and diamonds is surrounded by a swastika maze pattern.

Rooms J, K, L and M, N, O

This area was more badly damaged by cultivation than others, but room N has six medallions including a repetition of the four seasons. Apse room O has a black and white design with vines and tendrils that is entirely exposed to view.

Immediately next to room A–A', room P marks the 'villa rustica' section.

Here five storage *dolia* are embedded in the floor and in the basin next to this room a decanting cup was found. As well as its vineyards there would have been fields of wheat, hunting in the marshland and the exploitation of the shallow waters of the Thau basin, not only for fish but, as today, for oysters. They were an expensive delicacy. Examples have been found at the villa, but they must have been a significant export. The Thau was then open to the sea and in a clump of trees by the water are the remains of the villa's own port. A large buttressed building, probably a warehouse, was discovered surrounded with the remains of Gallic amphorae.

Loupian museum

Church of St Hippolyte, next to the town hall. Opened by guide.

The deconsecrated Romanesque church with its attractive capitals is being used as a simple museum for the small finds collection.

Other sites

In Antiquity the Thau basin was surrounded by settlements exploiting the local resources.

Mèze

A small port stood on the hill to the south of Loupian. There are no visible remains, but there is a local museum.

Balaruc-les-Bains

The construction of a new school gave the opportunity to excavate the foundations of a Gallo-Roman building and create a garden round the consolidated remains. Uncertainly identified as a temple, possibly to Neptune. It is well-labelled and in the town centre.

Sète

A dramatic hill, recorded by most ancient geographers as Mons Setius. A fish processing plant, together with baths, were found by the shore of the Le Barrou promontory. This is now covered by water; the Musée Paul Valéry on the outskirts of Sète has a single case of the finds made here.

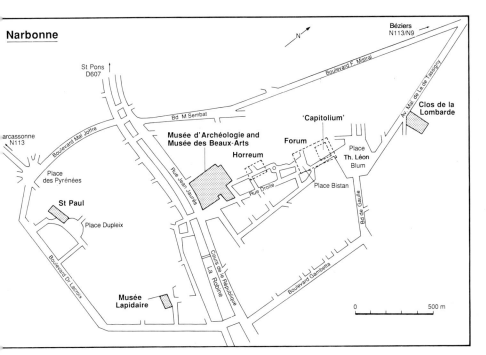

Figure 28

NARBONNE, Aude

Michelin 83–14
IGN 72–C4
0,75/47,95gr
3°00/43°12

Museum and urban remains.

In 118 BC the Romans founded Narbo Martius, their first successful over-seas colony. By the time of Augustus, Strabo, the famous geographer of the period, could describe Narbo as 'the greatest of emporiums in this country [the Midi]'. Martial, in one of his epigrams composed in the later first century, wrote of 'pulcherrima Narbo'. Sadly, that 'most lovely Narbo' is no more. While the city's underground galleries, the Horreum, hint at Narbo's commercial pre-eminence, only the material gathered together in her museums suggests something of the grandeur of the provincial capital.

The admiration of Renaissance rampart-builders led them to use the ancient material as decorative elements; nineteenth-century determination to sweep away the old has given the city its enormous collection of Roman inscriptions and architectural elements. Recent restoration techniques have given Narbonne the finest Roman wall-paintings on display in France.

Development

When Domitius Ahenobarbus secured the Languedoc area for Rome, he set about creating a road for rapid troop movement between the Rhône (and friendly Greek Massalian territory) and Spain, where Roman forces were steadily extending their empire. The key site for a colony was the junction of the Via Domitia and the road inland by the Aude valley to Aquitaine and the Atlantic: Roman trading interests were already substantial in this direction. The surrounding area was carefully divided into plots of land that avoided coming too close to the local oppidum, 4 km away at Montlaurès. These plots, it has been estimated, were enough for as many as 4,000 plus colonists and their families. Probably not all were taken up as, many years later, Julius Caesar decided to settle his battered Legion X veterans here.

The site itself was on a low sandstone platform by a branch of the River Aude, now the canalised Robin, which then drained into a vast inlet covering a much larger area than the Etang de Bages et de Sigean. Even then it was silting up and sand bars forming, but it remained possible for boats to sail up to Narbo, though La Nautique and other minor sites increasingly took over the role of ports for the city.

Very little is known of Republican Narbonne after its foundation in 118 BC, but it clearly prospered. Narbo retained its leading position in Transalpine Gaul and by the 70s BC had become the capital. Narbo gave its name to the province when Augustus, four years after his visit to the city in 27 BC, granted the Senate the task of appointing governors in peaceful regions. Its grateful people happily raised altars and temples to the Emperor.

From inscriptions, a list of buildings that impressed the fifth-century writer Sidonius Apollinaris and fragmentary archaeological finds, it seems that there were two forums and their associated buildings; the largest amphitheatre in the province, found in 1838, but badly excavated, poorly drawn and then built over; a large public baths next to the amphitheatre and probably a Flavian provincial cult centre; a theatre, though its site is totally unknown; and a number of temples. There were also fine houses, as wall paintings and mosaics indicate. M. Gayraud in his major work on the city suggests it extended over 100 ha and had a population of 35,000.

In the 150s AD there was a great fire in the city. Inscriptions record how Emperor Antoninus Pius helped in the reconstruction of a number of public buildings. However, suburban development seems to decline; possibly the effort was too much when Arles and Nîmes were challenging for leadership in the province as the economic axis moved more to the Rhône: certainly contraction seems to have begun before the first barbarian attacks. The late Roman walls, believed to be third-century, are estimated to have enclosed no more than 16 ha. Still the capital of the reduced province of Narbonensis Prima, it was Christianised early, but again struggled to fight the challenge of Arles for metropolitan status. Under the Visigoths from 462 it became capital of the renamed and further contracted province of Septimania, no more than the fringe of a Spanish kingdom; its conquest by the Franks in 759 merely put it on the borders of a northern-based French state.

The Horreum

14, Rue Rouget de Lisle.

| Hours: | Summer | 10.00–11.50 a.m. 2.00–6.00 p.m. |
| | Winter | Closed Mondays and at 5.15pm |

Approached by Rue Deymes it is signposted for walking from the Place d'Hôtel de Ville. 3 m below ancient ground level (now 5 m), covering an area 51 × 38 m, were constructed three, or perhaps four, galleries with central vaulted passages and cells alongside around a solid core of earth. The north and west galleries have been cleared and the beginnings of a south gallery noted; an eastern gallery is probable but not certain. The modern entrance descends into the north gallery.

The northern gallery

The cell vaulting is at right angles to the central passage so that the vaults rest on the dividing walls. Each room has a narrow entrance with a large lintel; there is no sign of door jambs or locks – there cannot have been any regular doors. In the Middle Ages the first cell on the southern side was provided with a vertical opening for a hoist. Curiously, the southern cells are larger than those on the north. The stonework is excellent: either rectangular *petit appareil* or square blocks laid at an angle, a design that the Romans called *opus reticulatum*, and which was popular in the first century BC. *Grand appareil* is used as strengthening. In the north-west corner are six extra cells, along a southern side passage. At the end of this passage six arch stones outline what was an entrance in Roman times but was filled in during the Middle Ages. The stonework is especially good in this part. At the corner junction of the two galleries a cell extends out to the north – it is possible that the gallery system once extended further in this direction.

The western gallery

The vaulting that once covered the cells is here parallel to the passage and the vaulting rests on the passage walls. In the Middle Ages the cell dividing walls were removed as they played no structural role. Old entrances were filled in

Narbonne

THE HORREUM

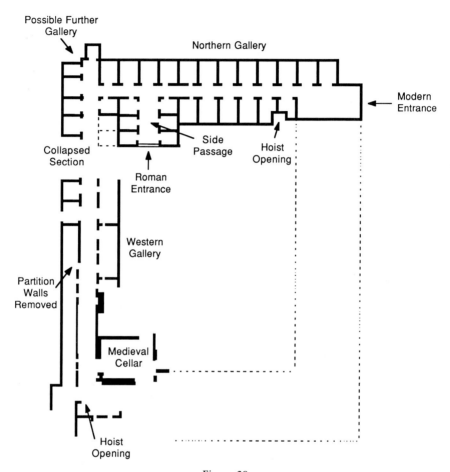

Figure 29

and new ones cut. At the end of the western passage there is another medieval vertical shaft for a hoist. In the south-west corner, replacing the extra gallery of the north-west, is a single, large, purely medieval cellar.

The first explorers in 1838 saw the galleries as a prison or slave workshop. The lack of doors and the awkwardness of the setting make these possibilities unlikely. Nor does it look like a *cryptoporticus*; it has cells and there were no light or air shafts in the original Roman structure (cf. ARLES, pp. 145–6). A warehouse or *horreum* seems the most likely use. The cells were lined with plaster limiting damp and the floor mortar mix is particularly water resistant. The lack of air-holes would limit temperature changes. A further function for the system could have been as structural foundations for a building above, implied by the fine-fluted column found in the western gallery – a food market or an early forum have been suggested.

Exhibits

The northern gallery contains a small collection suggestive of the lost sites of Narbo Martius; none of them found in the Horreum. The most interesting and mysterious piece is a small incised picture illustrating **bears in an amphitheatre**. One is held in a cage, whilst two others appear to be separately attacking two men in tubs. Are the bears being made to look stupid by the men prodding them, as the great analyst of bas-reliefs, Espérandieu, claimed, or are the men the victims helplessly secured in the tubs? Has the bear in the foreground been attracted by some food on the man's head?

Forum and *capitolium*

Place Bistan.

In the corner of the square, a few decorative blocks and broken columns and pilasters have been pulled together and a scene painted on the walls behind to illustrate the surveyors and masons at work constructing public buildings.

During the nineteenth century the area was poorly excavated and then badly recorded. A great rectangular enclosure was discovered and, on the northern side, a massive podium divided into three sections. It has been interpreted as a classic *capitolium* or a Hadrianic Imperial shrine.

Clos de la Lombarde

(Projected opening to the public.)

Immediately south of the modern cemetery de la Cité at the junction of the Avenue de Lattre de Tassigny and Rue Chanzy.

An area of urban development on the limits of Narbo. Excavations have been carried out since the 1970s. It was residential from the 40s BC until the later third century, followed in the fourth century by a short-lived church.

House of the Porticoes

The plaster fragments recovered here led to the superb restored wall-paintings currently in the Musée d'Archéologie, but on-site display is planned.

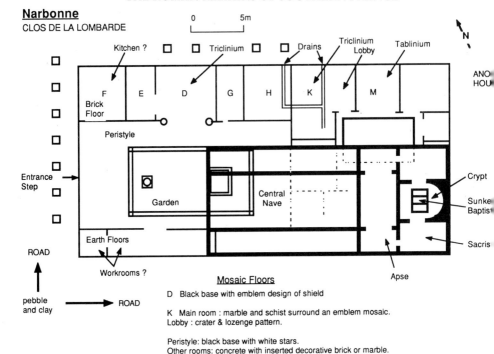

Narbonne
CLOS DE LA LOMBARDE

Mosaic Floors

D Black base with emblem design of shield

K Main room : marble and schist surround an emblem mosaic.
Lobby : crater & lozenge pattern.

Peristyle: black base with white stars.
Other rooms: concrete with inserted decorative brick or marble.

Figure 30

The early church

The foundations overlap the south-west section of the house. Despite the fragmentary state of these remains, they show a church more familiar in Africa and Syria than southern Gaul. The three naves are extended behind the side apses to provide sacristies beside the central apse. In the fifth century the church became a burial place. By the sixth century it was completely abandoned.

St Paul's church

Place Dupleix.

A Romanesque and Gothic church with a late fourth-century cellar. It contains seven sarcophagi and two children buried, as was usual, in amphorae. Once thought to have contained the third-century bishop St Paul's own tomb, it is now believed that it belonged to a rich family, and was subsequently opened up for other coffins, largely destroying the covering mosaic floor.

88

Ramparts

7, Boulevard Dr Lacroix.

A short 24 m section of sixteenth-century rampart, next to the Ecole de Montmorency. The upper levels of the wall still have examples of Gallo-Roman inscribed and sculptured material.

Montlaurès

Oppidum 4 km north-north-west of Narbonne.

Take D607 signposted for St Pons; about a kilometre from town turn right into the Rue Simon Castan, immediately after the railway bridge over the main road. The Rue Castan divides: take Chemin Communal No. 8 de Bougna on the right. The road finally becomes the Chemin Communal No. 148 Montlaurès and ends on the north face of the hill.

Montlaurès is only 56 m high but even so overlooks the surrounding plain. From at least the sixth century BC, it was a centre of urban development. One of the many sites occupied by the indigenous Elisyces tribe, even when overrun by the Volcae, Montlaurès quickly recovered its prosperity. For a time it benefited from the upsurge in regional trade associated with Roman penetration, but finally at the end of the first century BC it was abandoned, its rationale lost due to the growth of Narbonne. Still visible on the north-east hillside are rock-cut hut foundations that once lined an oppidum road. Some houses were cut 3 m deep into the rock with walling only used on the frontage.

In summer the hill is covered in flowers, butterflies and the smell of thyme. If it is too hot or windy to picnic and admire the view, then the pine woods are equally relaxing.

Musée d'Archéologie

Hôtel de Ville, Place d'Hôtel de Ville.
Hours: Summer   10.00–11.50 a.m., 2.00–6.00 p.m. daily
           Winter   10.00–11.50 a.m., 2.00–5.00 p.m., closed Monday

The medieval Archbishop's Palace has been the municipal museum since 1975. It houses an exceptional collection.

First Floor

Prehistoric rooms

(Temporarily closed)
This section includes material from Montlaurès.

Rooms dealing with house decoration

Wall paintings: currently exhibited here, these will be moved eventually to a museum on the Clos de la Lombarde site. The rooms referred to are those of the House of Porticoes.

Outside Pompeii and Herculaneum, the number of wall-paintings recovered in anything resembling a complete state is minimal. That these are so impressive is the result of the work of the Sabrié, who have painstakingly restored whole panels from fragments. The paintings are sensitively lit and framed by wooden balconies that recall the painted Roman versions. A model of the villa gives some sense of their context. The quality suggests that these Narbonne painters had been influenced by artists familiar with contemporary trends in Italy.

Room D: probably a dining-room. The guests could look out over the peristyle through widely set pillars. The wall is 'opened up' by giving the inter-panel 'trompe l'oeil' balconies with vegetation in the background and a very fat pigeon on one balustrade.

Room G: a small room that could have been a bedroom. Candelabra wall-paintings like these are typical early Empire motifs. Richly coloured stylised flowers, hunting scenes, etc. come from the entablature.

Room H: again candelabra are featured. An octagonal ceiling panel has been recovered showing a dancing bacchant carrying her thyrsus or wand. In myth, a wild possessed woman, here turned into a delicate impersonal figure.

Room K: here the grandiose panels are set in an architectural form, using mythological subject-matter. These include a bust of Apollo with his laurel crown and a life-size male figure carrying a cornucopia and *patera* next to a damaged victory, indicated by the wings.

Mosaics: neither of the two exhibited are great examples of the art. One features a mad-looking Dionysos, the other is a coyly named 'two satyrs surprising a nymph'. It is clear what the satyrs have in mind.

Rooms dealing with government, people and religion

Amongst the many stone and bronze records are the following.

The Ahenobarbus milestone: pride of place goes to the earliest known Roman monument in France – 118 BC. Found at the Pont de Treilles, 30 km south of Narbonne, it records a distance of 20 Roman miles from Narbo along the newly surveyed road, the Via Domitia, ordered by and named after the general Cn. Domitius Ahenobarbus who created the Transalpine province.

The Altar to the Augustan Peace: shortly after Octavian had transformed the Republic, described as 'restoring' at the time but which we see as creating the structure of the early Empire, the Senate gratefully thanked him for bringing peace and a new era (27 BC); and a gold disc was made to record this. The provinces were equally grateful, and when the new Augustus arrived in Narbonne the following year the colony set up this altar dedicated to Paci(s) Aug(ustus) – the Augustan Peace – decorated with a crown of oak and olive leaves and at the sides laurel-leaf garlands hanging from bulls' horns.

Other inscriptions: further dedications to Augustus show how he was increasingly identified with god-like characteristics, marking the emergence of an Imperial cult. Note the 'Numen' (divine will) and 'Lares' (family gods) Augusti. Several inscriptions refer to the *seviri*, the freedmen responsible for carrying out the cult. Leading citizens of the city are represented by L. Aemilius Arcanius and S. Fadius Musa. The first managed to become a Senator, the only known one from Narbonne, surprisingly perhaps as Nîmes records over twenty. The long struggle to high status led him to serve in three different legions, his last in Wales with the Legion II.

Fadius Musa was obviously a major figure in the colony. He had made a gift to a workers' guild and they paid for this inscription to him in the forum. His wealth derived from commerce. Many amphorae labelled Fadii have been found in southern France, Rome and Africa. He probably exported wine and olives and even metals as a relative Ti I. Fadianus had the iron-mining rights in the Corbières.

Sculpture: the best of the portrait heads is of a worn, middle-aged man, uncertainly identifed as Mark Antony or Galba (one of the three short-lived Emperors of AD 69), but the outstanding sculpture is undoubtedly the **Silenus**. This marble statue, found near the station in 1856, is a superb example of Hellenistic work, possibly from Pergamon in Asia Minor. The smooth finish of the skin and the beautiful ringlets of his beard contrast with the contorted obscene face and hairy little fat belly, the epitome of an alcoholic ecstatic religion. It must have decorated a rich home. A couple of other versions of the same wily old man-god show how good this one is. The alcoholic theme is continued in the **cupids' sarcophagus**. This early third-century almost baroque work depicts a wine harvest being gathered in by cupids helped by horned fauns. Cupids, or *putti*, passed easily into Christian art as young angels.

Second floor and ground floor

Rooms dealing with daily life

Though a necklace with a tiny bone pendant carving of Hermes and a spoon inscribed 'Utere Felix' – 'Put to good use!' – are interesting, the most important cases contain the pottery, which provides one of the most complete summaries of the developmental sequence of the various pottery styles found in Languedoc from the sixth century BC to the sixth century AD.

Downstairs the most striking cemetery bas-reliefs are those showing the constants of ordinary life in the city: work, bread and entertainment. Dockworkers loading merchant ships, the quizzical dog looking at the donkey trudging round the millstone and the gladiator trainer, whose three names indicate one of the very rare free citizens in this profession – a reward for success or a man attracted by the excitement of the arena?

Early Christian room

The good collection of sarcophagi makes it possible to compare the simple early medieval style of Aquitaine with the late Roman grandeur of Arles, whose biblical scenes are so much closer in spirit to the pagan wine-harvest tomb decoration.

Musée des Beaux Arts

Archbishop's Palace.
Hours: Summer   10.00–11.50 a.m., 2.00–6.00 p.m. daily
       Winter   10.00–11.50 a.m., 2.00–5.00 p.m., closed Monday

Of the twenty or so mosaics found in the city, two of the best are kept in this museum in the 'Chambre à coucher' and the 'Chambre du Roi'.
   Lycurgus killing the nymph Ambrosia: found in the cemetery of La Cité in 1886 close to the La Lombarde houses, this is a fine polychrome work. At the centre is a nymph about to be struck by the mad king's axe (see VIENNE, p. 34–5 for a better and alternative version of the myth).
   Geometric mosaic: this has beautiful colour effects producing a perspective maze image.

Musée Lapidaire

Notre-Dame-de-Lamourgier, Place Lamourgier.
Hours: Summer   10.00–11.50 a.m., 2.00–6.00 p.m. daily
       Winter   10.00–11.50 a.m., 2.00–5.00 p.m., closed Monday

Between 1869 and 1884 a mass of Roman decorative stonework was recovered from the demolished ramparts, most of which ended up in this museum. The sheer bulk of material has made the museum little more than a warehouse that will only really make sense to the visitor after it has been properly sorted. The academic work is now being done and it is hoped the collection will be re-sited soon, sympathetically displayed and appropriately labelled. Until this is done, it is best to wander and examine items haphazardly.
   The vast majority of the blocks are from funerary monuments. A few, particularly the spread eagles in the apse, come from the Capitolium wall.

The others derive from the tombstones, household mausolea and burial enclosures that filled the cemeteries along the main roads out of Narbo. Many of the decorative motifs, such as the cattle heads and rosettes, separated by triglyphs or triple vertical grooves, are thought to have come from tombs put up for Legion X veterans who died here in the years after their settlement in 46 BC. Similar contemporary decoration was found on soldiers' mausolea in central Italy where the troops had been raised. It is probable that the numerous military scenes derive not from a triumphal arch, as many have claimed, but are tomb decoration, possibly also associated with ex-soldiers, and represent a symbolic laying down of arms rather than conquest.

NIMES, Gard

Michelin 83–9
IGN 66–B6
48,70/2,27gr
4°22/43°51

Major urban remains.

Coming to Nîmes from the north, the choking growth associated with nineteenth-century industrialisation is obvious and from the north-east and south-west new commercial zones spread out from the N86/N113 by-pass; yet within, the city itself is dignified and calm with some of the greatest monuments of Roman Gaul. Several dominate their surroundings, whilst others are seemingly hidden until the eye picks them out, often exceptionally well preserved.

Nîmes was named after the local spring deity, Nemausus. The spring line runs along the junction of the coastal plain and the Garrigues, the outlying foothills of the Cévennes. A number of routes from the north and west converged here. The road from the Rhône valley road edged round the Garrigues via Remoulins. The Domitia came due west from Beaucaire. Later, the more southerly route via Arles took pre-eminence. About a kilometre to the east of the Iron Age settlement the roads met at what became the Augustan Gate and may have been the site of an early Roman fort.

Strabo, writing in the Augustan era, described the city of Nemausus as the capital of the Volcae Arecomici, the major tribal federation of eastern Languedoc. The heart of the oppidum was undoubtedly the spring: it poured from the ground with almost the force, if not the splendour, of the Fontaine-de-Vaucluse. Indeed, a powerful god. Its importance to the local population was recognised by the magnificent Roman *nymphaeum* subsequently developed on the site. Rock-cut and rough stone houses dating from the sixth century have been found around the spring at the foot of

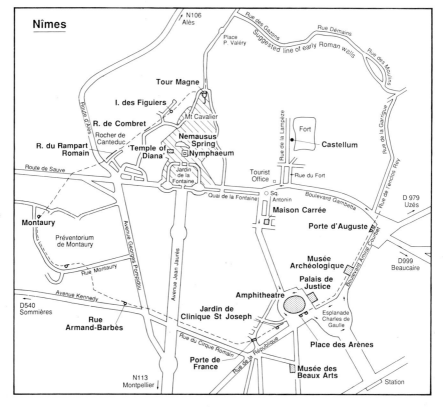

Figure 31

Mont Cavalier, but increasingly habitations are being revealed under other parts of Roman Nîmes.

Nîmes expanded rapidly in the latter half of the first century BC. It obtained colonial status, possibly first from Julius Caesar, and coins were issued here inscribed COL NEM. But it was under Augustus that it emerged as one of the leading Roman centres of southern France. New coins were issued bearing the title COL AUG NEM and on the reverse decorated with palm tree and crocodile, strange choices interpreted as a sign that after Actium, as the Emperor reduced the size of an army bloated by civil war, he decided to settle eastern troops here. At least three major public works were dedicated to Augustus himself: the Maison Carrée temple and probably with it the poorly known forum, the *nymphaeum* and the 6 km ramparts.

During the following century the population perhaps reached 40,000 as the land within the walls was built up. The great amphitheatre and the Pont du Gard aqueduct were constructed. Large public baths have been recognised and there may have been a circus, though the evidence is thin. A large

94

building on the Rue de Sauve with a circular staircased well, floors covered with mosaics and painted walls could have been a public building or possibly a grand *domus*. Rescue digs in the west of the town have shown extensive and fine private dwellings. The enormous collection of inscriptions in the museum testify to the dynamism of the city in the early Empire. Sadly none records Trajan's wife Plotina, who was apparently born here. According to the 'Augustan History', Hadrian was so grateful for her support in winning the succession that he dedicated a temple in Nîmes to her memory; she is certainly the only woman for whom he felt any warm feeling (see VAISON, p. 232–3). The temple has not been identified either.

Little is known of late Roman Nîmes. A section of rampart has been preserved in a basement of the Palais de Justice (normally not open to the public), but the rest of the line is obscure. Although a Christian council was held here at the end of the fourth century, the first known bishop is Sedatus of 506: an appropriate name for an inhabitant of a city whose period of vitality was long past.

Maison Carrée

Place de la Maison Carrée.
Hours: Tourist season   9.30 a.m.–7.30 p.m. daily
            Out of season   9.00 a.m.–noon, 2.00–5.00 p.m. daily

The Maison Carrée is almost perfect. The exterior is one of the finest known examples of a Roman temple. Only the interior has lost its original appearance and that is simply because it has had many uses over the centuries. Henry James first saw the temple by moonlight and described it as 'exquisite', yet it did not overwhelm him. My feelings, too, have always been strangely lukewarm.

Date

Looking above the columns at the front of the temple there are a series of holes on the frieze and architrave that obviously once carried an inscription. These were brilliantly analysed as long ago as 1758 by Séguier, whose deductions have not been seriously challenged despite some doubts about the method. The inscription would read:

C CAESARI AUGUSTI FI COS L CAESARI AUGUSTI F COS DESIGNATO
PRINCIPIBUS JUVENTUTIS

The top line shows that the temple was dedicated to Gaius and Lucius, the two adopted sons of Augustus. Then disaster struck. The 17-year-old Lucius died of fever in Massalia in AD 2, just before taking up his consulship – *cos designato*. Within two years the slightly older brother Gaius also died, from

95

apparently minor wounds received on campaign in Armenia. The unusual use of the architrave was no doubt a rapid decision, made when the magistrates of Nemausus learnt of the deaths and had been told of the chosen funereal phrase designated by Rome: 'princes of the youth'.

Design

The temple embodies the characteristic high podium or platform with a single perspective approach created by placing the *cella* at one end and constructing a single large flight of stairs at the other. This design feature is accentuated by a porch of freestanding columns, whereas the *cella* itself is merely decorated with engaged columns. It would not have been out of place in Rome itself.

The architect must have worked with an up-to-date design book from Rome. He would have selected the decorative elements to be used by the workshops, but stylistic differences in both capitals and frieze work suggest little effort was made to standardise the work of the masonry teams.

The outstanding feature of the design is the refined use of the Corinthian Order. The **columns** used here have the characteristic features that became the norm from the Augustan period onwards. The capital was decorated with two rows of acanthus leaves, taking up two-thirds of the bell-shape (previously this had often only been a half). The **architrave**, too, takes on its Corinthian form here, as a plain area divided into three by a series of mouldings. The **frieze** above is used for decoration on the sides and back of the building. Again the acanthus plant dominates. Waves of foliage culminate in bouquets. The contrasting styles of the different teams are sometimes sharply demonstrated at the junction of stone blocks.

The **cornice** carries the roof. Bands of ornate moulding take the cornice outwards to keep the rain off the walls. After a row of dentils and ovolo come the modillions, another distinctive Corinthian feature. Curved non-functional 'supports', they alternate here with rosette panels, each different. The last four bands include a corona decorated with a Greek key pattern and a Cyma Recta with unusually realistic lion heads, looking like water spouts, but not. The roof itself is modern and lacks both the bronze corner *acroterions* and the earthenware antefixes that concealed the ends of the roof tiles.

The interior

The *cella* once contained the cult statue(s), possibly surrounded by a rectangular alcove. Now it contains a **museum**. This includes 300 restored pieces of a Venus discovered in 1873, a bronze head of Apollo and sections of the frieze around the *nymphaeum* (see p. 101). A finely carved tombstone shows a wife and husband together and the inscription records how he had spent time as an officer in Legion VI. Her hairstyle is typical of

Nîmes

MAISON CARREE (SE corner)

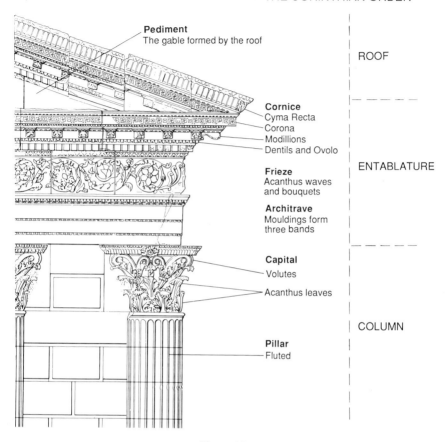

THE CORINTHIAN ORDER

Pediment
The gable formed by the roof

ROOF

Cornice
Cyma Recta
Corona
Modillions
Dentils and Ovolo

Frieze
Acanthus waves
and bouquets

Architrave
Mouldings form
three bands

ENTABLATURE

Capital
Volutes

Acanthus leaves

COLUMN

Pillar
Fluted

Figure 32

Agrippina, the wife of Claudius, a roll of tight curls across her forehead and
a plait on each side, suggesting a date in the AD 50s.

The temple and the forum

The modern enclosure and pavings suggest the original platform and walls
that had been constructed on top of earlier Roman buildings. This temple
area or *peribolus* was created for the altars and their associated ceremonies.
On the northern side were two sets of entrance steps and a portico.

The Maison Carrée stood in the south-east corner of the forum, but the
exact orientation and dimensions of the forum are unknown. Remains of the

marble-decorated town council meeting-rooms, the curia, have been found in the Rue Auguste; the Square Antonin may at least suggest the open area of the forum itself.

The Porte d'Auguste

Corner of Boulevard Amiral Courbet and Rue Nationale, opposite the church of St Baudile.

The façade

There are four entrances with plain semi-circular arches, two for vehicles 4 m wide and two for pedestrians. Grooves along the sides show they could be closed off with portcullis, and sockets in the doorsills show they had leaf doors as well. Above the side doors niches once held statues. The façade is decorated with four pilasters and a central engaged half-column that has lost its supporting half-pilaster. The main keystones are themselves capped with severely battered corbels of kneeling bulls.

Once again holes cut in the entablature identified an inscription, which showed that this gate, along with the rest of the rampart, was built on the instructions of Augustus in 16 BC. Above, there was once an upper storey and remains of this are scattered behind the gate. They suggest, using other Augustan gates as a guide, that there was a gallery above with six windows stretching between the semi-circular towers on each side. The latter are indicated by coloured stone pavings.

The interior

An internal courtyard covered with fine paving links the passageways behind the two main entrances. Underneath run city drains. A moulded foundation stone of one of the towers is used as a base for a modern copy of the Prima Porta statue of Augustus (the original is in the Vatican).

The ramparts

Until twenty years ago isolated discoveries and guesswork had established only a hypothetical path for the ramparts. Now, in the south and west at least, a far more accurate alignment can be drawn.

The rampart is not only one of the longest in Narbonensis, it is also one of the thickest. The curtain wall itself is set on slightly wider foundations. Variations from 2 to 2.95 m suggest different teams working to their own norms, and one very odd junction found in the Rue des Tilleuls suggests they did not always manage to meet correctly. The towers are either semi-circular or tangential circles (see also ORANGE, p. 190). Most surviving sections of rampart are lower than 2 m but study of the exterior of the Tour Magne suggests they were about 7 m high and had crenellated walkways on the top. However, the towers are unevenly spread, some over 70 m apart, and at this distance they could hardly have provided much covering fire. The onlooker's perception was perhaps more important than reality.

Place des Arènes

In the 1970s 90 m of the rampart and two towers were excavated. The western semi-circular tower, by a town or postern gate, was reburied but the rest was consolidated. The tangential tower has worn foundations where carts cut the corner travelling along an external by-pass road.

Jardin de la Clinique St Joseph

Rue Alexandre Ducros.

A circular tower and 40 m of low walling are on view in the garden.

Porte de France

Place Montcalm/Rue Porte de France.

Though only a single semi-circular gate, this was the Via Domitia gate for the south-west. The upper storey is a blind gallery separated by Tuscan pilasters. The curve of the western tower is still visible in the house wall.

Avenue Kennedy/Rue Armand-Barbès

By the corner a short section of rampart and round tower.

The Montaury hill

There is a round tower in the Rue Montaury.

The Rocher de Canteduc

The rampart climbs 150 m across the Canteduc outcrop, used as a major source for the wall's stonework, then rises up the gentle slope of Mont Cavalier. Wedge marks in the quarry indicate Roman workings. Though hard, the stone split easily and it was not used much after the rampart was completed. Sections can be seen by the Route d'Alès (by the 'Parc de l'Empereur' house), the Rue du Rampart Romain, Rue de Cambret and a tower base in the Impasse des Figuiers. After the Tour Magne, little has survived and the route is poorly defined.

Tour Magne

| Hours: | Tourist season | 9.30 a.m.–7.30 p.m. daily |
| | Out of season | 9.00 a.m.–noon, 2.00–5.00 p.m. |

This impressive tower still rises 33 m, despite the seventeenth-century efforts to hack it down in the search for treasure based on one of Nostradamus's gnomic comments. The top has been lost and the north-west side reduced to the vertical vaulting, the rest probably surviving because of the sheer mass of masonry. There are really two towers, one inside the other. First there is a prehistoric tower, a squashed cone shape about 18 m high. Probably built in the third century BC, it was part of the Iron Age settlement defences, though it must have been an exceptionally tall tower. Second, an even more grandiose Roman structure was built, enclosing the prehistoric cone, the alignment of the rampart being adjusted to include it.

Outside

Pierre Varène's excavations in the 1970s revealed that the Gallo-Roman base had a curious design. First the north wall was extended round the tower, then the west wall enclosed that. The line of the junction can be seen on the north-east face. Linked to the base which rises 13 m is an entrance courtyard with vaulted alcoves extending south to join an east–west wall. In the courtyard on the west side of the base survive marks of the external staircase up to the rampart walk and to the octagonal drum shape of the main tower.

The first section is a podium of finely cut *grand appareil* with a horizontal recess in the middle and a cornice marking the division between it and the blind Tuscan pilaster section. On top of this are the remains of a plinth for a crown of engaged columns of which only two bases remain. It is likely that this in turn had a parapet terrace. It must have been over 40 m high.

Inside

The interior has been furbished with a modern column up the centre to help secure the tower and a staircase to the top. The view makes the climb worth it. To the right of the entrance, the rubble masonry of the sharply sloping prehistoric wall is clearly outlined 11 m high in the Gallo-Roman tower walling. On the floor opposite the entrance, crudely shaped prehistoric facing stones lie under the Gallo-Roman blockage.

In both its pre-Roman and Roman forms, it could have been simply a watch-tower taking advantage of the highest point in Nîmes. But more significant could be its proximity to the Nemausus spring at the foot of the hill. A decorative tower like this would serve as a marker for travellers and an assertion of control from above to visitors below: the sanctity of the site had been absorbed and transformed into an epitome of Roman civilisation.

La Fontaine sanctuary

Jardin de la Fontaine.

Hours: Tourist season   7.00 a.m.–11.00 p.m. daily
        Out of season   8.00 a.m.–9.00 p.m.

When Jacques Mareschal laid out the park in 1740 there was still consider-able evidence of the Gallo-Roman sanctuary around the spring. Some buildings he left untouched (the 'Temple of Diana'), others he covered over (the small theatre in the north-east corner) and, in some important cases at least, used them as the base for his own creations. The shape of the spring pool and its semi-circular steps, the channel to the pool with a central platform and its ornate surround, the channel draining away to the main canal into Nîmes (though not the 'U'-shape waterway) all reflect original Roman features.

Its role as a major spring sanctuary has been known for centuries and, like many others, it is also known for its healing properties, as the large number of dedications found here indicates. Here was a Gallic version of Aesculapium at Pergamum: the spring pool for holy washing, a nearby square Celtic temple for the god to visit and a grand portico in which perhaps the sick might sleep and receive healing dreams to be interpreted by sanctuary priests. In 1984 P. Gros argued that this missed a key aspect, the connection with the Imperial cult.

The central element for Gros is the **Nymphaeum** focused on the plat-form. It was not just a decorative mix of architecture and water but the central altar to the spirit of Augustus, tying together Emperor and Gallic god. He showed that the frieze material that Mareschal recovered from around the platform, preserved at the Maison Carrée, was Augustan and that the central lump of masonry could easily have been an altar. He pointed out how very similar open-air sanctuaries were laid out both in the east and in Italy, mixing the worship of local gods with Augustus. A significant number of dedications found here are to Emperors as well as to Nemausus and other gods. One Greek inscription refers to a Dionysic corporation. Gros sees this as a group of eastern artists whose prime role was to hold '*ludi*' in the theatre, as part of the cult. Suetonius mentions how after Augustus re-covered from an illness, grateful cities raised altars and arranged for religious games every five years. The sanctuary would interlock the role of god(s), ceremony, water healing, culture and loyalty.

The 'Temple of Diana'

Partially ruined during the Wars of Religion after its long use as a church, it has survived relatively unharmed since then – except that is for the graffiti and urine; it needs to be guarded, as it was when Henry James visited it in the 1880s. The basis for the popular name is unknown and is

Nîmes

LA FONTAINE SANCTUARY

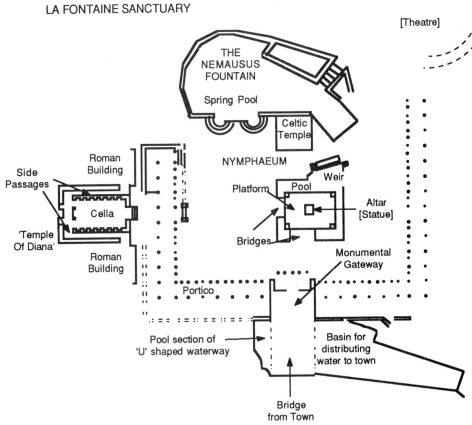

Figure 33

certainly incorrect. Once thought to be a temple ordered by Hadrian for Plotina, it is now believed to have been a library, based on the Celsus library identification at Ephesus. Its date is uncertain. Gros, on stylistic grounds, compromises with an Augustan origin modified in the second century.

The main entrance leads into a large *cella*. It has twelve niches with alternating triangular and round pediments. These seem too shallow for statues, but perfect for scrolls. The roof is constructed like the arches of the Pont du Gard and the galleries of the amphitheatre: the vaulting being a series of separate arches, some set lower and designed to look like ribs. The back of the *cella* has three openings into small linked extension rooms. The central pediment has disappeared and the highly decorated ceiling collapsed, with blocks still standing on the floor. Side passages, covered with stepped vaulting, would help insulate the building from damp and provide access to the upper storeys of the now unrecognisable buildings on either side of the library.

Fragmentary remains of the grand portico are preserved in front of the library.

The *castellum*

Rue de la Lampèze.

Below the massive walls of the seventeenth-century Nîmes Fort is the *castellum* or delivery tank for the aqueduct from Uzès (see PONT DU GARD, pp. 110–20). It has recently been calculated that 20–40,000 m^3 of water per day poured out from the underground channel into the circular basin to supply the fountains, public buildings and houses of the city. The functional section of the tank has survived extremely well, though the roof and much of the surrounding walls have gone. Sadly this includes the interior plaster that was seen during nineteenth-century house demolition, painted with fish and dolphins!

The tank itself is just over a metre deep, with a walkway for the workers who kept the basin clean and controlled the flow. The water enters the tank below the walkway and is distributed through ten pipes on the road side of the tank. Massive blocks had holes cut through them, which secured the absent lead-piping. Three holes in the floor of the tank, which must have had covers, joined the basin with drains running to the sewers under the nearby road.

Operation

The principle is easy. Like a bath tub the water runs from the tap, or aqueduct, to fill the pool, but leaving by the excess pipe rather than the plug hole. In this case the plug holes are used simply to drain it for cleaning. The practical mechanics of determining a constant head of water into the tank are not so obvious.

At the aqueduct channel entrance, grooves in the side stones and holes in the walkway paving indicate that there was some form of gate. G. Hauck has argued convincingly that the Roman engineers would have aimed to achieve the optimum water flow into the pipes, that is a water-level at mid-section of the pipe. He argues that the gate was not used to block off the aqueduct channel which would risk dangerously damaging the aqueduct with back-up, but as a sophisticated control and measuring system. He postulates two short sliding gates, the water normally flowing under them. The job of the man in charge, or *castellarius*, was to check and modify the gates as necessary. There could even have been a measure by the side of the

Nîmes

THE CASTELLUM

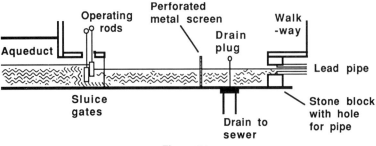

Figure 34

gates to show the *castellarius* the level of flow through the aqueduct; no doubt the flow varied considerably in summer and winter.

Using one gate on the bottom and another above, the flow could be stopped for about 20 minutes. The value of three plug holes was rapid clearing, the residue of water would disappear in 1½ minutes. Plenty of time left for normal cleaning and repairs.

The amphitheatre

Place des Arènes.

Hours: See Maison Carrée

(note special closing for 'manifestations')

The most imposing building in Nîmes is the Roman amphitheatre, no longer vibrant but still dominating. It represents an enormous investment capable of holding audiences of 20,000 plus. The emotional response to a building such as this can only be mixed: admiration for the engineering of such a structure, a difficult but chilling awareness of how civilisation and barbarity do mix and an uncomfortable fascination with what might actually have taken place.

Recent work has shown that Nîmes amphitheatre is Flavian – roughly contemporary with the Colosseum in Rome. It adopts the same radiating walls and vaulting principles of an ordinary theatre to provide quick and efficient access to the mass of people; a safe and well-drained auditorium; and an all-seater stadium with excellent sight lines. It was probably built slightly later than the very similar Arles amphitheatre, whose dimensions are almost identical, as a number of design weaknesses there are not apparent here.

The outside

The façade is made up of two storeys and an attic, the latter surviving rather better than at Arles. There are sixty arcades on the ground floor, duplicated on the floor above but separated by an entablature. This follows the profile of the engaged columns and pilasters, forming a jagged edge and helping to stress the vertical as well as horizontal lines.

There is an entrance at each axis, through rather larger arcades than the norm, though this is difficult to pick out visually. The main entrance was in the north, then as now, facing into the town; it provided immediate access to the loggia of honour. It is most easily picked out by the second-storey pediment. At first-floor level the parapet of the entablature went straight across, not following the profile here, but much of it has been broken. Both storeys have pairs of battered '*protomes*': corbels shaped as the fronts of bulls.

The amphitheatre could be shaded from the sun by a vast awning or *velarium*. Many of the hollowed-out corbels that held the masts for securing the awning are still in place on top of the attic. The masts rested on the second-storey entablature; at the main entrance this meant cutting holes through the pediment. Experienced sailors were employed to put up the *velarium*.

A number of carvings were cut on exterior facing-stones in the Roman period. Two gladiators on the first-floor parapet are badly damaged, but a Romulus and Remus suckled by the wolf are reasonably clear on a first arcade above the keystone, opposite the entrance to the Palais de Justice. A phallus can be found on an arcade near the southern entrance.

The interior

The modern entry is three arcades west of the Roman main entrance. This brings you into the wide, well-lit, ground-floor gallery round the amphitheatre. The roof is vaulted and reinforced with arches, a much more effective solution to the problem of providing strong support for the upper storey than that used at Arles, where many of the flat lintels and pavings have collapsed.

Numerous entrances or vomitoria lead into the amphitheatre itself. To reach a particular row, there is a system of alternating corridors and staircases branching off from the ground-floor gallery. Spectators could circulate easily round the amphitheatre at any level except in the attic passage where staircases went up and down, but then this only gave access to the top tier (*maenianum*) where women and slaves came to sit.

The privileged sat in the front four rows. These were divided up into loggia, temporary structures defining particular sections and separating out groups of the elite, like the executive boxes of modern stadia. Surprisingly,

Nîmes

THE AMPHITHEATRE
Section

(Only major passages are shown)

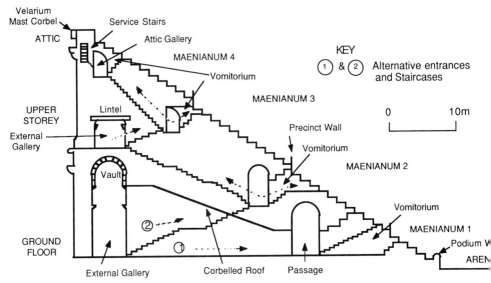

Figure 35

the corporation of *nautae* or boatmen of both the Rhône–Saône navigation and those of the Ardèche and Ouvèze had reserved sections here. Their names were cut on the podium wall above the arena (the inscriptions are now in the museum). Perhaps they helped fund the enormous costs of construction, or were they simply prepared to pay top prices?

The arena

The 3 m high podium wall kept the spectators safe from the action in the typical elliptically-shaped arena. Very similar to Arles, though fractionally smaller, a quite different solution to the problem of raising scenery and 'surprise' entries by animals or beasts was adopted: unfortunately this is now hidden because of the need for a continuous floor for the summer bullfights. Nineteenth-century excavations revealed a cruciform cellar with passages to the axis entrances. Lead-weights demonstrated that lifting gear was installed. A cellar wall inscription 'T. Crispus Reburrus Fecit' could mean that Crispus designed the cellar or that perhaps he was the architect of the amphitheatre as a whole.

The museums

Nîmes has a proud record in the concern it has felt for preserving its archaeological finds. In the eighteenth century the Temple of Diana was already being used as a depot and ever since buildings have been converted to hold the constantly expanding collections. A new purpose-built archaeological museum is projected for completion in the 1990s.

Musée Archéologique

13 Boulevard Amiral Courbet.
Hours: Tourist season   9.30 a.m.–6.30 p.m.
        Out of season   9.00 a.m.–noon, 1.30–6.00 p.m.

Pre-Roman rooms

Most interesting is the statuary. The **Ste Anastasie warrior**, found by a hilltop oppidum 15 km north of Nîmes, is dramatic. A flat rather skull-like face, elongated with large round eyes, is enclosed in a massive helmet, probably made of leather. It has a large crest and rams' horns decoration. Round his neck is a fragmentary torc. Roughly dated to the third century BC, it is a crude reminder of the far finer warriors from Entremont (AIX-EN-PROVENCE) and Roquepertuse (MARSEILLE). The **Grézan warrior** is more sophisticated – and even closer in style – but more battered. Found in Nîmes itself, he probably once had the same large helmet and neck torc, but the emphasis here is on the chest. Thick and powerful, it has a breastplate with a rectangular sun pendant. Perhaps they were dead heroes.

The **Nages frieze** comes from near the spring at the foot of the oppidum (see p. 109). The monolith, engraved with severed heads and vaguely classical horses, was probably a lintel from either a sanctuary or over a gate into the town.

Roman rooms

Few of the many **mosaics** found in Nîmes have survived to be displayed. The best are a complex black and white geometric design and the Endymion mosaic. In the latter, the beautiful young man stretched out by a tree could be Endymion or Ganymede. Appropriately, an Eros looks on. If Endymion, he has been put to sleep by Selene the moon goddess who, on seeing him, fell in love and put him into everlasting sleep in order that she could visit him in his permanent night whenever she wished. If Ganymede, it was Zeus who fell in love, whisking him away to become cup-bearer to the gods.

Naturally there is a vast **lapidary collection**. On the whole the statues are uninspired, though a recent find of a young man posed in the style of

Alexander (long curly hair and a sideways upward look) and a weathered Silenus are reasonable. A marble *oscillum* almost repeats this pairing with a bald, bearded old man and a similar youth, but these probably recall theatre masks.

Amongst the many altars, some are decorated with wheels. These are linked with Jupiter. As a sky-god, where in Roman classical iconography the eagle, sceptre and lightning would be used, in southern Gaul these were replaced by a sun symbol, with an imagery of rotation, hub and rays. One has an inscription recording the Coriossedenses, probably a clan dedication; another links the wheel with the Gallic mallet god Sucellus. As a woodland spirit this could be an appeal to the primal gods of nature, sun and earth.

There are over 2,000 **inscriptions**, many of them funerary. The most interesting are not those proclaiming high status, but those recalling harder and shorter lives, though not lacking in pride. The name L. Spinus is capped by a wedge, hammer, pick and set square: he was a stonemason. Ploughmen and butchers are also depicted by their tools of work. Most moving are the tombstones of gladiators. Fourteen have been found by the Rue St Gilles, implying a special burial site for them near the amphitheatre. Tr. Aptus from Alexandria did well: he either lived to the age of 37 or he had thirty-seven victories, an unusual longevity whichever way the inscription is interpreted!

The amphitheatre provides one of the best pottery artefacts, a terracotta medallion of a myrmillon defeating a retiarius (see AMPHITHEATRES, p. 125). The glassware is good and the coins are outstanding. There is also a collection of Greek, Punic and Etruscan pottery, none of it local.

Musée des Beaux-Arts

Rue de la Cité Foulc.
Hours: see Musée Archéologique.

When the art museum was built, all 'fine' art objects were lumped together with little thought of cultural context. Only one example of Roman art was brought here, the **Admetus mosaic**. Fifteen panels cover 50 sq. m, all decorative except the central panel with a scene from the Greek myth of Admetus and Alcestis. The young King Admetus loved and won Princess Alcestis, shown here standing behind her father, her breasts exposed. This was possible in myth, in reality it would be obscenely shocking. Admetus leads a lion and wild boar yoked to a chariot, a task set by Alcestis' father, King Pelias. His task is merely the earthly result of the struggle between his supporter Apollo and the Fates, who have decreed an early death for Admetus.

Barutel quarry

9 km from the centre of Nîmes by the N106 to Alès. There is quarrying on both sides of the road, but the clearest evidence of ancient workings is on the northern side at the western end.

Stone from this quarry made excellent *grand appareil*. Abandoned blocks lie scattered below a rock-face scarred with vertical lines, divided into layers about 0.6 m wide. Starting at the top, the Roman quarryman swung his pick to create a vertical groove. The horizontal cut was made using wedges to split the stone away from the quarry wall. Nearby a much lower face indicates another technique using a chisel to make vertical holes, then to split the block away with vertical as well as horizontal wedges. It was cruder and needed more finishing work.

Nages oppidum

16 km west of Nîmes by D40 for Calvisson, take D14 south into Langlade and D737 to Nages.

Languedoc has a large number of hilltop oppida, but this is one of the best. The excavations by Michel Py and his team, begun in 1958, have revealed that the hill was settled from the eighth century BC, first on the north-western outcrop of the Roque de Viou and from the fourth century BC until *c.* AD 10 on the main Castels hill above the Nages spring (see Nîmes museum, p. 107). The site is worth visiting for its magnificent ramparts, the evidence of town planning and a temple.

Some parts of the **ramparts** still reach 4.5 m high. They have flat though irregular drystone facings enclosing a thick rubble core. They are often excessively wide as well (up to 7 m!), caused by adding new interior walls on to the older ones. Nages I and II, the third- and second-century occupations, have great bastions on the ramparts. At the highest point a tower with a diameter of 11 m, double the normal, recalls the Tour Magne of pre-Roman Nemausus. The first-century town, Nages III, was four times as big, but its wall had no towers. Py suggests this was Roman influence: a native town could have a wall as long as it was of minimal effectiveness!

Nages I had Greek-influenced **regular blocks** or *insulae* of single houses with 5 m wide streets between. Later the blocks expanded and the streets narrowed. The houses of Nages II and III were bigger and divided into two, three or four rooms. Walling was of the same irregular stonework.

Near the centre of the site and the great tower, what appears to be a small square 'Fanum' **temple** was built in 70 BC, one of the earliest known in Gaul. The excavators interpret its destruction in AD 10 as deliberate, a symbol of the final parting from the site.

Museum: Nages Town Hall houses a collection of site finds.

PONT DU GARD, Gard

Michelin 80–19
IGN 66–A7
2,45/48,84gr
4°33/43°72

Aqueduct.

North-east of Nîmes, 1 km south of D981 Remoulins to Uzès road.

Frontinus, curator of Rome's aqueducts in the AD 90s, claimed that the maintenance of aqueducts was 'the best testimony to the greatness of the Roman Empire'. The Pont du Gard is still one the most glorious testaments, gracefully dominating its Gardon River gorge. The soft, pale yellow limestone blends aqueduct and landscape. No modern buildings disturb its outline or setting, and the visitors, who flood over it in the summer, are totally dwarfed by its scale. It is difficult to be disappointed.

Here it is possible to realise what '*urbanitas*' really meant. Roman remains in the cities of Provence give a sense of the component elements that made up urban life, but aqueducts, more deeply than any other feature, embody the determination of the Romans to support that life; if an adequate source of water was 20 km away and that meant constructing a channel 50 km long, then it would be done.

Exactly when the decision to build the aqueduct was taken is unknown, though the Augustan or Trajanic periods are most favoured. Nîmes expanded rapidly in its early years, perhaps quickly enough to have outgrown its own water resources by the time of Augustus. Espérandieu (1926) linked the aqueduct with Agrippa's visit to Narbonensis in 19 BC, pointing out his known interest in the aqueducts of Rome. However, the scale of the enterprise and its cost, at a time when many other public works were being undertaken (see NIMES, p. 94), seem to support the AD 90s. The recent renewal of research on the aqueduct promises to produce more conclusive evidence.

An appropriate spring was found at Uzès, in the valley of the Ayran, 76 m above sea level, and only 17 m above the Nîmes *castellum* or distribution point. The apparently excessive length of the aqueduct seems surprising at first, but the straight route would have entailed far too many construction problems. The 'Garrigues' are the final outcrops of the Massif Central; they are worn and pitted, winter rains having bitten into the rock leaving thin soil cover and narrow and often deep valleys (some called '*combes*' recalling the coombs of the limestone Cotswold valleys). An additional problem would have been the vegetation; lack of surface soil and water have produced an environment of almost impenetrable dwarf oak, thick brushwood and dense prickly undergrowth. The lack of natural easy routes across the Garrigues becomes obvious if you travel on the direct Nîmes–Uzès road.

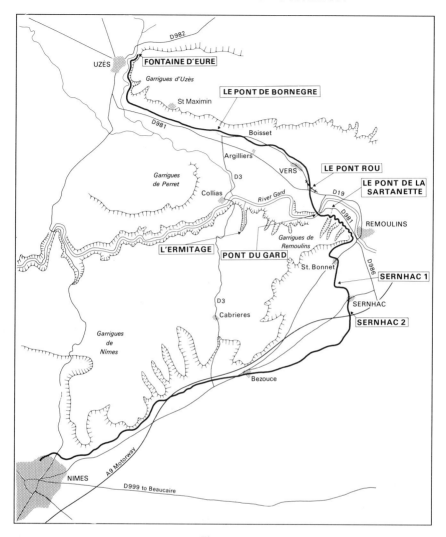

Figure 36

Like most Roman aqueducts, it was built underground where possible. A trench was dug, the stone channel built, enclosed by an arched stone roof and covered with earth. Sometimes it was necessary to tunnel the channel through solid rock. 35 km was constructed below ground level. Inevitably to maintain a steady fall in the gradient, the aqueduct had above-ground sections as well, the channel carried either on a wall or on the classic arches. There is visible evidence of each method.

Sites on the route of the aqueduct

All sites are free. At the Pont du Gard, there are no restrictions on access (and no rails along the edges), but roadside parking is impossible anywhere near and the expensive car parks are well worth while. Even then, it is probably best to try and visit early in the morning or late in the evening when the crowds are at a minimum. But the Nîmes aqueduct is not just the Pont du Gard. Little of the rest of the course is generally known and as yet meeting other visitors is a rare experience.

The source at Uzès

The spring is marked today by a small water-pumping station at the side of the sharply cut valley through which the lethargic Ayran flows. No Roman remains survive, though in 1922 excavators found 4 m diameter circular walls. An inscription found in Nîmes honours the spring divinity (Lyon museum).

Calcium deposits

The Fontaine d'Eure is a high-output, perennial spring. It is a pure water, but for one significant element, the high calcium carbonate content ($CaCO_3$). This is leached out of the limestone as the rain drains through the Uzès Garrigue down to the water-table and out to the spring. In turn the carbonates are precipitated on the surfaces over which they pass. Helped by the hot summers and the low gradient, new 'rocks' were formed along the aqueduct. These are of two types: 'curtain rock' where the walls of the channel are lined with deposits, increasingly reducing the flow of water; and 'calcretes', seepage spray when there has been a break in the channel. Here rapid deposition often created massive lumps of material.

Le Pont Rou (for plan see Figure 40, p. 115)

This name has been given to the raised section that curves round Vers. There are well-preserved wall and arcade sections stretching hundreds of metres, the highest reaching 7.5 m.

Bornègre bridge

The first visible remains come after St Maximin when the channel emerges from its shallow tunnel in the Combe de la Vergue. Here the transitory stream is crossed by a 17 m, triple-arched bridge constructed of *grand appareil*. 5 m to the west of the bridge, the aqueduct provides a fine example of underground channel construction. The tunnel section to the east is lost under impenetrable vegetation.

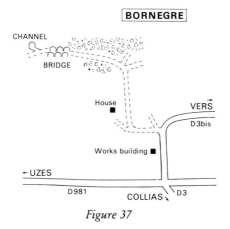

Figure 37

Towards Uzès

This can be followed *c.* 400 m from above the railway. No doubt due to its proximity to the road, the first 60–70 m have been plundered but the foundations of massive double stones 3.7 m wide were unearthed during the early 1980s and there are extensive remains beyond. The piers are at first plain, though the central section has projecting pilaster buttresses, constructed of *petit appareil* with the arch vaults of small *grand appareil*. However, the most striking feature here is that many of the arches are filled in with either single or double walls; the building technique suggests that this was done soon after the original aqueduct was constructed. Further problems in this area are indicated by great masses of calcretes (one estimated at 250 cubic metres) and a section of parallel channel. Close examination of calcretes has shown the marks of wooden pipes cut into the channel to syphon water away.

Towards Nîmes

Again, near the road, the aqueduct has been reduced to the foundations, to be followed by another fine well-preserved section. After some collapsed arches, the aqueduct reduces to a wall and eventually it disappears as the ground level rises. Despite appearances, there is currently no way to walk through to the Pont du Gard; visitors should take the route via the main road D981.

Le Pont du Gard

Technically superior aqueducts were built by the Romans elsewhere, yet despite the apparent awkwardness of the three-tier structure and the lack of

113

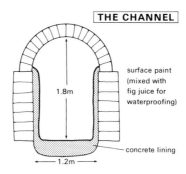

Figure 38

conformity in arch size, the Pont du Gard achieves a breathtaking splendour. When the great historian of Gaul, C. Jullian, called it 'La chose divine', the justification would not simply be the feeling of awe created by its massive strength but also that sense of harmony found in a medieval cloister.

The aqueduct had to carry the channel nearly 50 m above the river. The number of arches standing in the river bed was minimised by making them as wide as possible. The summer flow was probably deliberately concentrated under one extra large arch by deepening the river bed there. It would also have enabled the builders to construct the pier foundations in bedrock without using coffers. The piers were strengthened with sharply pointed breakwaters; they reach above normal winter water levels. The whole structure also has a slight curve facing upstream, generally believed to be a strengthening measure against the pressure of the current.

The second arch tier stands immediately above the first to concentrate the thrust of the arches down to the bottom piers. The top tier carrying the channel spreads the weight with a large number of small arches. Whilst their span remains constant, the pier thickness is varied to allow four arches over the river vault and three over the rest.

Stonework

Most of the bridge is made of *grand appareil*, only the channel walls use *petit appareil* finished with mortar; some stones weigh as much as 6 tonnes, their size being most obvious when looking at the enormous capping stones on top of the channel.

Possibly the use of *grand appareil* reduced the amount of masonry needed; dressing was minimised as well. Many stones are only chiselled at the joints – necessary for hanging plumb-lines – creating bosses of rough quarry pickaxe grooves. As few contemporaries could have looked at the stonework closely it may simply have been time-saving, but the limited

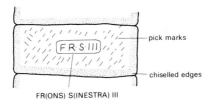

FR(ONS) S(INESTRA) III

Figure 39

and awkward site working area may also have affected the decision. That
the masons worked largely in the quarries is also suggested by the numbering of stones. Vaults on the second tier have voussoirs (archstones) with I,
II, etc., as well as the even more specific FR(ons) D(extra) I or M(edius) I, to
tell the site workers to place the stone on the right-hand side or in the
middle.

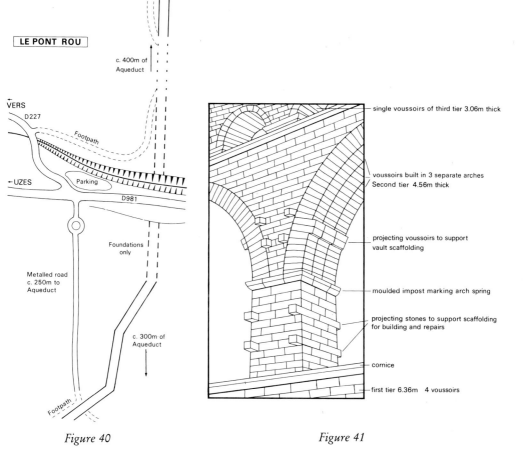

Figure 40   *Figure 41*

115

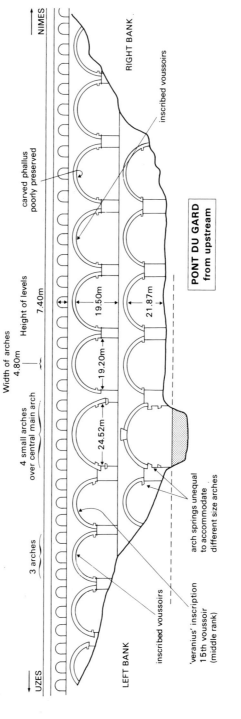

UZES

3 arches

LEFT BANK

Width of arches
4.80m

4 small arches
over central main arch

inscribed voussoirs

'veranius' inscription
15th voussoir
(middle rank)

Height of levels

7.40m

24.52m

19.20m

19.50m

21.87m

arch springs unequal
to accommodate
different size arches

carved phallus
poorly preserved

RIGHT BANK

inscribed voussoirs

NIMES

PONT DU GARD
from upstream

Figure 42

Another sign of minimising construction complexities is building the first and second tier arches in four or three separate 'arches'. This enabled one set of voussoirs to be set in place over its scaffolding, which was then used to construct the next line. It is a system also found at SOMMIERES bridge, ARLES amphitheatre (pp. 143–4) and much later in local Romanesque churches.

Amongst the many inscriptions carved on the bridge during the last 2,000 years, two Gallo-Roman examples have survived. The damaged phallus carving – often placed by Roman masons on buildings as a good luck symbol – has been reinterpreted in the past as a hare and local stories woven round 'Le Lièvre du Pont du Gard'! The 'Veranius' is more enigmatic, a construction worker aiming at immortality? or the architect himself (as Espérandieu suggested)?

Restoration

Frontinus warned 'the parts [of aqueducts] that cross rivers suffer most from the effects of age or violent storms'. In 1958, a flood covered the whole of the lower tier. The aqueduct survived whilst downstream at Remoulins the modern bridge was wrecked. The inherent strength of the structure has enabled it to survive for so long with remarkably little reconstruction. Whilst rain damage, root growth and even earthquakes undermined other sections, the Pont du Gard simply became a medieval toll-bridge. Even the second tier piers did not collapse when they were thinned down to widen the 'footpath' along the cornice.

In 1743 the piers were refilled and the present bridge constructed beside the aqueduct. Though this removed local traffic from the structure itself it also helped bring the first tourists. By 1835, when Prosper Mérimée saw it, the risks of collapse were real. Spandrels had lost solidity, voussoirs had fallen out, many stones were severely eroded. After a patching job in the 1840s, Laisné carried out a thorough renovation between 1855 and 1858. As well as replacing all the badly worn stone and using hidden concrete inside some piers, he separated the bridge from the aqueduct to help drainage. By installing stairs at one end and rebuilding the walls at the other, visitors could walk along the channel itself. The tunnelling in the hillside at the Nîmes end took place in 1863–4, part of an ill-conceived plan to build a new aqueduct 'le canal de Pouzin'. Fortunately this was abandoned in 1866.

Le Pont de la Sartanette

The aqueduct, after leaving the Gardon valley, follows the contour round six small valleys on the edge of the Garrigues de Remoulins. Where economic, bridges shortened the route. The best example is in the Combe de Baune-Sartanette, attractively isolated. It is 32 m long and at its highest point 8.5 m, cut by a single arch. Like le Pont Rou, it was strengthened with parallel walls

Figure 43

on each side and the arch size reduced. The gradient here is amazingly low –
7 cm in a kilometre; however, the engineering skill only served to help create
the thickest curtain rock lining the channel walls: the width was reduced
from 129 cm to only 40 cm.

St Bonnet church

The fortified parish church has stones cut from aqueduct calcretes and
follows the multi-arch design of the Pont du Gard for its vaulting, including
the projecting voussoirs.

Sernhac

Evidence of the aqueduct can be found on both sides of the village.

Vallon des Escaunes tunnels

Follow the small 'aqueduct' signs out of the village to the end of the poor
metalled road and then ask for help as the heavily quarried area with its
many tracks makes the tunnels difficult to find. Two large rectangular
sectioned tunnels of the aqueduct survive, 66 and 60 m long. The frequent
putei or access holes suggest either that the rock caused constant difficulties
or that the surveying was imprecise as there are many changes of direction.
The grim rigour of tunnelling is embodied in the pick grooves.

Railway cutting channel

The last visible section before Nîmes was revealed by the construction of the
Nîmes–Remoulins railway. It is most interesting for the thick curtain rock,
clearly showing distinct layers. A secondary local aqueduct – Roman –
carried water to neighbouring fields.

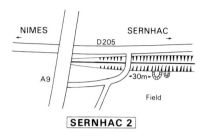

Figure 44

Construction, maintenance and disuse

Finding a suitable spring in an era when springs were both essential for water supply and the embodiment of a divinity would not have presented difficulties. Even the isolated **L'Ermitage spring**, now marked by the chapel of the Notre-Dame de Laval in the wild Combe de L'Ermitage, was worshipped in both the pre-Roman and the Roman period (small collections from the site are held in the chapel and at Nîmes Musée Archéologique). The Fontaine d'Eure would have been well-known.

A *mensor* (surveyor) would have planned the route. To achieve the exceptionally low gradient required, an average 35 cm per kilometre, he would have used a *groma* for sighting, the clumsy *chorobates*, 20 Roman feet long, used for levelling and his 5 or 10 RF measuring poles. Using a wax board, he would have recorded the figures and perhaps drawn a plan with his set square to be written up later on a scroll. Templates could be made for the builders, for example to achieve standard channel widths.

The patron – the city of Nîmes or a rich benefactor, even Agrippa himself? – would hire contractors and their skilled labourers. Construction stone was available near the route in a variety of quarries, most important for the large quantity required for the section between Vers and Remoulins. Equally relevant were the roads, such as the Roman equivalent of the D981, for the ox-carts and sledges carrying the stones and wooden drums in which to roll the largest.

Lifting heavy stones would have involved the use of cranes. Simple twin pole sheerlegs, held in place by guy ropes and operated by windlass, would have been sufficient for much of the work; for the heaviest, power-driven machinery was necessary. Treadmill-driven sheerlegs using pulleys could lift the 6 tonne stones up to at least the top of the first tier and possibly the second. Levers and rollers could also be used to manoeuvre the stones from the valley sides on to the bridge and to place them in position. Wooden treadmill cranes were used in Provence quarries until the beginning of the twentieth century.

How many men were involved and how long it took is unknown, but

119

some estimate of cost is possible by comparison with other recorded examples. With a relatively large amount built above ground, it was probably the most expensive in Gaul. Espérandieu's calculations suggest a figure over 30 million sesterces. An elite legionary soldier was paid 1,200 sesterces a year. It must have taken years to pay off.

As in Rome, where Frontinus had two large slave gangs, there must have been a body of maintenance workers in Nîmes. These would have included skilled men such as clerks, inspectors, architects, masons, plasterers, etc. needed for the upkeep of the system.

Signs of their efforts are conflicting. Reconstruction at Pont Rou and Sartanette indicates major activity. However, the build up of calcium precipitation shows little evidence of having been controlled; perhaps the effort seemed just too great.

No historical or archaeological material has yet been produced to assess how long the aqueduct functioned and so calcium layers have been used for dating. The apparently natural growth of the layers has led recent writers to guess it remained in use for 400–500 years.

Frontinus deserves the final word: 'will anybody compare the idle Pyramids, or those other useless though much renowned works of the Greeks with these aqueducts, with these indispensable structures?' Gazing at the Pont du Gard it is easy to understand his presumption.

* * *

OTHER SITES IN LANGUEDOC-ROUSSILLON

Amélie-les-Bains, Pyrénées-Orientales

Michelin 86–18 or IGN 72–J2
47,18/0,37gr or 2°41/42°28

The Roman spa now forms part of the modern establishment, Thermes Romains, and permission to visit is required. The modern changing cubicles are constructed in a vast Roman room, 24 m × 12 m, covered with a brick barrel vault and lined with semi-circular and rectangular niches; the adjoining room with the swimming pool is built on the Roman original.

Bagnols-sur-Cèze, Gard

Michelin 80–10 or IGN 59–C8
2,55/49,09gr or 44°10/4°37

Musée Léon Alègre contains local finds including those from the oppida sites of Lombren near **Vénéjean**, 5 km north-east, and **Laudun**, Camp de César, 9 km south-south-east. Both were occupied in the Iron Age and

Gallo-Roman periods, and the ramparts and walling are visible. (There is rare late Gallo-Roman evidence of Jewish occupants at Lombren.)

Causses-et-Veyran, Hérault

Michelin 83–14 or IGN 65–C5/6
0,84/48,32gr or 3°05/43°28

28 km north-west of Béziers in the valley of the Orb by the D14/136 are the remains of four circular structures with *petit appareil* exteriors, two over 5 m high. They are of uncertain function, possibly commemorating Cn. Domitius Ahenobarbus' great victory over the Volcae in 120 BC.

Elne, Pyrénées-Orientales

Michelin 86–20 or IGN 72–H/I2
0,72/47,33gr or 2°58/42°36

The modern town covers Iron Age and early Roman Illiberis, and Helenae, the late Roman *castrum* named after Constantine's mother. There is a local archaeological collection in the cathedral museum and Gallo-Roman house remains are preserved in the car park.

Mons-et-Monteil, Gard

Michelin 80–18 or IGN 66–A5
2,05/49,00gr or 4°12/44°07

The dramatic site of **Vié-Cioutat** is 9 km east-south-east of **Alès**. The oppidum was occupied in the early Iron Age and again from the first century BC to the early second century AD when the visible ramparts and houses were built. Finds are displayed in Alès museum.

Montferrand, Aude

Michelin 82–19 or IGN 64–D7
0,62/48,18gr or 1°49/43°23

50 km west-north-west of Carcassonne by the N113 to Toulouse are the remains of a bath system that belonged to a villa or a *mansio*/roadside inn, which was subsequently converted into an early Christian church.

St Thibéry, Hérault

Michelin 83–16 or IGN 65–D8
1,24/48,23gr or 3°26/43°24

An attractive setting *c.* 20 km east-north-east of Béziers for a ruined bridge, claimed to be Roman, carrying the Via Domitia over the Hérault.

Sommières, Gard

Michelin 83–8 or IGN 66–B4
1,95/48,65gr or 4°05/48°46

28 km west of Nîmes, the Roman bridge still carries the main road to Lodève (D40). Eight of the original seventeen arches still stand, though they are considerably restored. **Villevielle** Iron Age oppidum has traces of rampart still visible.

Uzès, Gard

Michelin 80–19 or IGN 66–A6
2,32/48,91gr or 4°26/44°03

Medieval and Renaissance Uzès have limited the excavation of Roman Ucetia. The town museum collection includes an inscription dedicated to a water nymph's temple (see PONT DU GARD, p. 112).

Vendres, Hérault

Michelin 83–15 or IGN 65–D6
0,96/48,06gr or 3°14/43°16

10 km south of Béziers by the D64/37E are ruins on the edge of *étang* marshland which are traditionally considered to be a temple dedicated to Venus. Walls of circular and square structures have also been interpreted as a villa.

THE AMPHITHEATRE: SPECTACLE AND SLAUGHTER

Beginnings

The origins of violent spectacle have been traced back to the sacrificial fights at the funerals of great men in central Italy, long before the development of the Roman Empire. However, it was imperialism that helped turn these low-key events into the orgies of killing characteristic of the 200-odd amphitheatres constructed by the third century AD. Imperialism encourages dehumanisation: losers are outsiders, not 'real' people, by definition beyond the parameters of civilised conduct. Conquest brought the prisoners-of-war to fill the roles of gladiators and victims. Conquest also brought in the loot to finance grand displays by patrons; the scale of the spectacles dramatically increased in the last two centuries of the Republic and established the norms for the Roman audience. Nor was the concept of public sacrifice of either human beings or animals unknown in the Celtic world of Gaul, after all Caesar had moralised about the iniquities of Druid religious practice!

The social role of the amphitheatre

Brutalised spectators continued to be fed by patrons who supplied them with slaves, criminals, religious outsiders (e.g., Christians) and the odd freeman attracted by the heroic warrior image of the gladiator, until inflation, civil war and invasion in the third century undermined urban life, though gladiatorial combat was only banned in AD 404. Contemporary critics are noticeably absent. Amongst pagan writers only Seneca expressed doubts, and whilst Tertullian wrote the most brilliant study of the corrupting horror of the amphitheatre, most Christian writers concentrated their criticism of contemporary entertainment on lewd display rather than violence.

It is easy to see the amphitheatre as embodying the most alien aspect of Roman culture, the least acceptable form of behaviour when compared with today. The certainty of moral superiority is perhaps suspect. Barbarism continues to exist within civilised societies and makes acceptable slaughter on a scale inconceivable to Romans. The deliberate killing of the totally innocent is common – and not just in wartime. Equally the Roman 'peace' is an exaggerated image. Frontier war was endemic, and throughout the Roman Empire there was widespread fear of lawlessness. There was no organised police force and brigandage was rife. For the city magistrates, generally the patrons of amphitheatre shows, public execution before a mass audience was seen as a deterrent, not of course enough to stop criminal behaviour or banditry, but enough to make alternative social and political systems inconceivable. A patron, like Fadius Syntrophus in Narbonne, might celebrate the construction of a new market by paying for a show as well: it equally demonstrated the power of those in authority and the gulf between them and the masses.

Organising a spectacle

Presenting a spectacle was big business. The patron paid an entrepreneur to design and organise a programme that could often last days. The entrepreneur then contacted professional hunters who operated all over the known world collecting animals for the shows: from Africa crocodiles, hippopotami, lions and leopards, monkeys and elephants; from Europe bulls and bears, even polar bears from the Arctic. Next he would get his gladiators from the trainers who ran special schools where the different styles of fighting were learnt. Trainers in southern Gaul are known from inscriptions in Nîmes, Die and Narbonne. Columbus, a gladiator trained at Nîmes, became famous in Rome, but according to Suetonius, he provoked the jealousy of Caligula and was poisoned on the Emperor's orders. Once prepared, the programme would be promoted: the strange animals that would be hunted down in the arena or used to kill criminals and the great fights that would take place. The respective records of the gladiatorial pairs would be listed, no doubt helping the early betting. The night before, the gladiators had a banquet; spectators could come and look and no doubt this affected the betting as well.

Slaughter as entertainment

The day generally began with the animal shows. Some were simply circus acts, such as lions trained to carry hares in their mouths unharmed or men wrestling bulls by grabbing their horns 'Thessaly style'. Most animals appeared as victims. 'Venationes' or animal hunts sometimes featured dangerous beasts, though in European provincial centres harmless creatures such as deer were more common. They would be killed by men or animals, perhaps dogs or predators starved or goaded into action. Equally animals were used to dispatch people. The story of the lion and the runaway slave Androclus (Gellius, second century AD) romantically portrays a lion refusing to attack because earlier Androclus had removed a thorn from the lion's foot: the use of lions on sarcophagi as symbols of death is a much more realistic image of amphitheatre experience. No doubt the best shows had lions, but normally bears would be the most impressive of wild beasts in southern Gaul (see NARBONNE, p. 87).

At midday, according to Seneca's bitter description (*Moral Epistles*, VII, 3–5), the amphitheatre was half-empty, but the entertainment would continue. Unprotected, terrified people, usually criminals, were forced into incompetent, pitiful fights to the death. Sometimes the condemned were dressed up in mythological costumes and scenery constructed to give a perverted story context to the killing: wild beasts tearing apart 'Orpheus' would mock his ability to charm the animals. Sometimes tamer, but still bloody, pleasure was provided by boxers using lead-weighted and spiked gloves.

The amphitheatre filled again for the day's high-point, the gladiatorial show or '*munera*'. Trumpeters led the grand parade, followed by referees in long tunics carrying their batons, men with red hot irons to prod the unwilling and check the dead for pretence – dressed as Mercury, the gods' messenger – men dressed as Pluto – the god of the underworld – to drag the dead away, armed guards and the gladiators themselves. There are at least fifteen different known types of gladiators, broadly divided between the heavily armed and less manoeuvrable and the quick moving but lightly armed. In Gaul there were the *crupellarii*, covered with iron armour, and the *truncii*, who were probably lightly armed as the name has been linked to the human sacrifices of pre-Roman times. The best-known were the **myrmillon** and the **retiarius**. The former was called 'the Gaul'. He wore a large helmet decorated with a fish, carried a long shield and fought with a short sword. The retiarius used a net and trident and carried a sword, but had little armour. When the fighting began he issued his challenge: 'it's not you I'm looking to catch, it's your fish, why are you running away, Gaul?'

Their tombstones show that, like wrestlers today, they gave themselves stage names: Ursius, the bear man; Fulgar, lightning man; Felix, the lucky one. Indeed a few were lucky. They were paid when victorious, received a crown for particularly good wins and some became star performers. But to receive an honourable discharge they had to survive for three years. The crowd roared, the victims bled and the great decided the fate of the defeated. The Emperor or the provincial governor raised or lowered a thumb if they happened to be in the area, but normally it was the local magistrate who had the final say.

Plate 1 Die. Porte St Michel. The late Roman gateway is constructed over an early Roman triumphal arch. The top courses are medieval (see p. 25).

Plate 2 Agde. The Ephèbe. This river-bed bronze has been identified as an Athenian college youth or epheboi. Photograph: Musée d'Archéologie Sous-Marine et Subaquatique, Agde (see pp. 53–4).

Plate 3 Ambrussum. Cobblestone road. The grooves helped guide wheels up the hill into the town (see p. 56).

Plate 4 Carcassonne. Late Roman rampart. At the centre, the Tour de Vieules has been underpinned with medieval foundations (see p. 67).

Plate 5 Ensérune. Houses along the northern slope, above the road and rampart of the town (see p. 73).

Plate 6 Lattes. Roman milestone (see p. 76).*

Plate 7 Nîmes. Maison Carrée (see p. 93).

Plate 8 Nîmes. The *castellum* or water distribution tank for the Pont du Gard aqueduct from Uzès. The water enters by the square hole and leaves via the pipes that once filled the round holes in the stone blocks (see p. 103).

Plate 9 Nîmes. The main north entrance to the amphitheatre, identified by the pediment and the corbels shaped like bulls (see pp. 104–5).

Plate 10 Pont du Gard. The curving arcades of the bridge carrying the aqueduct over the river. The eighteenth-century road bridge runs beside and below (see p. 110).

Plate 11 Pont du Gard. The awesome aqueduct from upstream showing the three tiers necessary to carry the aqueduct 50 m above the river (see p. 113).

Plate 12 Pont du Gard. The massive curtain rock deposits of calcium that narrow the channel and once impeded the flow of water to Nîmes. Sernhac railway cutting site (see p. 118).

Plate 13 The Roman amphitheatre. The interior of the Arles arena, restored for modern spectacles (see p. 123).

Plate 14 Gladiators fighting. The man on the left is a retiarius, on the right is a myrmillon. Medaillon de Cavillargues, Nîmes. Photograph: Musée Archéologique, Nîmes (see p. 125).

Plate 15 Arles. Amphitheatre external galleries showing how the flat stones that once separated the lower and upper passages have disappeared (see p. 144).

Plate 16 The surviving western side of a monumental staircase and entrance that once led up into the forum (see p. 144).

Plate 17 Arles. The exceptional exterior of the Baths of Constantine with the typical late Roman alternating brick and stonework (see p. 146).

Plate 18 Arles. Octavian, later to call himself Augustus, depicted here as a very young man with a thin, wispy beard. Photograph: Michel Lacanaud/Musée d'Arles (see p. 149).

SENATVS
POPVLVSQVE ROMANVS
IMP CAESARI DIVI F AVGVSTO
COS VIII DEDIT CLVPEVM
VIRTVTIS CLEMENTIAE
IVSTITIAE PIETATIS ERGA
DEOS PATRIAMQVE

Plate 19 Arles. A rare marble copy, ordered by the Senate to be distributed round the Empire, of the golden shield given by the Senate to Augustus in gratitude for the peace he brought to the Roman world. Photograph: Michel Lacanaud/Musée d'Arles (see p. 149).

Plate 20 Avignon. Relief of a barge being pulled up a river. Probably from a tombstone dedicated to a boat-owner. Musée Lapidaire. Photograph: Musée Calvet, Avignon (see p. 155).

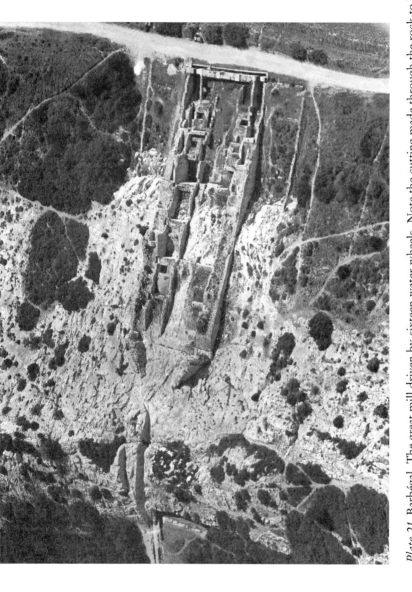

Plate 21 Barbégal. The great mill driven by sixteen water wheels. Note the cutting made through the rock to bring the water from the aqueduct. Photograph: Antoine Chenet, Centre Camille Jullian (see p. 156).

Plate 22 Carpentras. A German prisoner depicted on the triumphal arch (see p. 161).

Plate 23 Marseille. The Lacydon merchant ship being excavated in the horn of the silted Roman harbour. Photograph: Réveillac, Centre Camille Jullian (see p. 175).

Plate 24 Orange. Triumphal arch, looking at the south face (see p. 183).

Plate 25 Orange. The interior of the theatre looking down on to the stage. Note the size of the people and the Imperial statue on the stage building (see p. 186).

Plate 26 St Chamas. The twin memorial arches at each end of Le Pont Flavien Roman Bridge (see p. 200).

Plate 27 St Rémy-de-Provence. Glanum sits at the entrance to the Notre-Dame de Laval valley, one of the easier routes through the rugged Alpilles range. Photograph: Christian Hussy, Direction des Antiquités de Provence-Alpes-Côte d'Azur (see p. 201).

Plate 28 St Rémy-de-Provence. The arch and staircase down to the sacred spring in the sanctuary area of Glanum (see p. 205).

Plate 29 St Rémy-de-Provence. 'Les Antiques', the shrunken triumphal arch, attic removed, and the elegant, well-proportioned mausoleum (see p. 216).

Plate 30 St Rémy-de-Provence. The Mausoleum. This scene on the west relief depicts heroes fighting using a mix of Roman and foreign equipment (see p. 219).

Plate 31 St Rémy-de-Provence. A Gallo-Greek capital from the trapezoidal court in Glanum. The Gallic head of Apollo fills the space between the Corinthian volutes. Photograph: Réveillac, Centre Camille Jullian (see p. 220).

Plate 32 St Rémy-de-Provence. The high cheek-bones and formal bouffant hairstyle show that this portrayed Livia, the wife of Augustus. Photograph: Chéné-Réveillac, Centre Camille Jullian (see p. 221).

Plate 33 Vaison-la-Romaine. The communal lavatories belonging to the Praetorium house with drainage into the sewer in the foreground (see p. 231). (see p. 231)

Plate 34 Vaison-la-Romaine. Statue of the Emperor Domitian wearing the commander-in-chief's uniform with the decorative breastplate. Photograph: Chéné-Réveillac, Centre Camille Jullian (see p. 232).

Plate 35 Vaison-la-Romaine. Statue of the Emperor Hadrian, his nakedness indicating his Greek hero status. Photograph: Chéné-Réveillac, Centre Camille Jullian (see p. 232).

Plate 36 Vernègues. The evocative temple in the sanctuary area, found in the gardens behind the Château Bas (see pp. 237–8).

Plate 37 Fréjus. La Lanterne d'Auguste stood at the mouth of the Roman harbour; its purpose is now obscure (see p. 259).

Plate 38 Fréjus. The beautiful double-headed Hermes, one of the finest examples of classical art found in southern France. Photograph: Réveillac, Centre Camille Jullian (see p. 263).

Plate 39 Fréjus. A section of the aqueduct at the Combe de Rome (see p. 266).

Plate 40 La Turbie. Chained captives kneel below the trophy 'tree' carrying armour and weapons. A symbolic representation of the defeat of the Alpine Gauls (bas-relief from the victory monument) (see p. 271).

Plate 41 Mons. The dark and deep cutting (the Roche Taillée) along the side of the Signole valley to carry the Fréjus aqueduct (see p. 276).

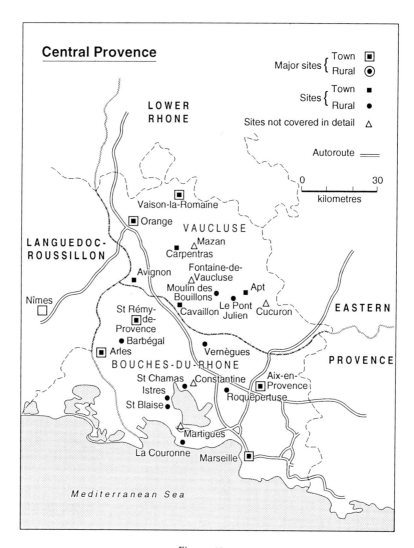

Figure 45

3

THE SITES OF CENTRAL PROVENCE

AIX-EN-PROVENCE, Bouches-du-Rhône

Michelin 84–3
IGN 67–G2
3,44/48,38gr
5° 27/43° 33

Protohistoric town and Roman city.

When C. Sextius Calvinus resolved to establish the first permanent Roman base in Provence, he settled a garrison in the territory of the Salyens or Salluvii, the most powerful Gallic confederation in the region. He chose a site 3 km from Entremont, a major Salluvian oppidum. The location controlled the major east–west route from the coast at Fréjus and a north–south route linking Marseille with the Durance valley. The natural basin protected the site from wind and the local mineral springs (originally hot according to Strabo) led to the settlement being named Aquae Sextiae. By the time Pliny produced his *Natural History* in the mid-70s AD it had become oppidum Salluvii, no longer a *castellum* guarding against an enemy tribe but their city. It had the high status of a colony and when the Empire was reorganised and Narbonensis divided at the end of the third century, it became the metropolis of Narbonensis Secunda.

Extraordinarily little survives from the Roman period; medieval and eighteenth-century Aix have replaced a major Roman urban site more effectively than anywhere else in southern France. No deposits are known from earlier than the end of the first century BC, the *castellum* is simply assumed to have been in the St Saveur district. Excavations under the cathedral suggest that the first-century AD forum and basilica were in this area. The baths, which must have been grander than normal and attracted outside visitors, are believed to have been near the modern Thermes on the Boulevard Jean Jaurès. Odd traces of the wall have been found and gate towers are known from sixteenth-century illustrations. Major areas must have been abandoned in the late Roman period, but evidence of fifth-century

127

ecclesiastical building suggests that its administrative role and the Christianisation of the Empire ensured continuity.

Though an important Roman city, it is most worth visiting for its exceptional picture of the people that were conquered. The Granet museum has one of the finest collections in the south of France while the ruins at Entremont are extensive and interesting.

Musée Granet

Place St-Jean-de-Malte.
Hours: 10.00 a.m.–noon, 2.00–6.00 p.m., closed Tuesday

Entremont rooms (2, 3 and 4)

These basement rooms provide a fine example of painstaking reconstruction of broken statuary and excellent modern thinking about display techniques, especially the use of spot-lighting.

General

There is a good representative display of ceramics and agricultural tools and a small selection of personal jewellery. Fragments of statuary focus the attention on dress: one delicately curved cheek and ear is carved with a wheel-shaped ear-ring and reflected in the metal example found on the site as well and displayed below. As beautifully worked is the pedestal on which only sandalled feet have survived.

The major sculpture

Most of the material comes from the Road VI finds near the portico (see pp. 133–4). They must have constituted the central element of a sanctuary. It has not been possible to restore one complete body, but it is clear that there were a number of slightly less than full-size **cross-legged warriors**. Number 1 head is considered the finest with its fluid lines and tightly curled hair. Others seem to have diadem rolls of hair and one has a metal or leather helmet with cheek-plates and neck-protector. All the chests had mail armour tunics or cuirass, though only the torso, number 6, indicates this clearly with 'pinpricks'. Others were shown in paint, touches of which have survived. The tunic was covered with an additional mail shoulder cuirass, held by a clasp in the middle of the chest; these were a major decorative element, some using great Celtic whirls, another even suggesting Roman Gorgon's head body armour. Some bodies show a Celtic torc at the neck and bracelets round the right upper arm. From a thin belt hangs a sword on the right side. Almost every feature can be found described in the works of Diodorus and Strabo.

128

Diodorus grimly explains:

when their enemies fall they cut off their heads and fasten them about
the necks of their horses . . . and these first fruits of battle they fasten
by nail upon their houses . . . the heads of their most distinguished
enemies they embalm in cedar-oil and carefully preserve in a chest.

The Entremont finds show warrior pride also needed to be recorded in
stone. Eleven of these **severed heads** have been found. 'Deadness' is portrayed by thin straight lips, hollow cheeks and large globular eyes, though
one highly expressive head (number 27) forms a flattened triangle with
jutting cheek-bones and eyes reduced to horizontal slits. Some heads have
the remains of hands holding them, suggesting the seated warriors balanced
them on their knees. One group forms a cluster of five. The join between the
fifth and the others was only recognised in 1974, thirty years after their
discovery. It is probable that a warrior cradled six (one more for symmetry!)
between his legs.

The construction of the sanctuary itself also embodied the same macabre
practice. A monolith stands engraved with twelve schematic skulls; a broken
pillar base has one incised head and two hollows for real examples. **Bas-
reliefs** of warrior horsemen with their typical long Celtic swords seem to
show heads hanging down from their reins. Similar almost full-size examples
must have existed as well: a brilliant outline of a horse has emerged from the
jumble of broken stone and is restored in an iron frame on the wall.

François Salviat, writing in the 1980s, stressed two features: the aristocratic nature of the art and the pervasiveness of severed head cults in Celtic
society. He saw the material here and from Roquepertuse (Musée de la
Vieille Charité, MARSEILLE, p. 176) as essentially dedicatory to the elite
themselves rather than to gods. He rejects both warrior-god interpretations
and ancestor worship, seeing them as 'portraits' of leading families – female
figures were found with the warriors – like contemporary Roman practice,
but modified to a local barbaric Celto-Iberian form. It is perhaps a rather too
anti-mystical view, which the display itself tends to counter.

The Roman rooms

After the Entremont material, these rooms are disappointing. Some well-
made Corinthian capitals and an excellent marble **head of Severus**, Emperor
193–211, with finely smoothed skin and richly drilled beard and curls, imply
the public magnificence of Aquae Sextiae. A reconstruction of the *domus*
found on the Pasteur car park site is unusually restored with a second floor
and hints at its grandeur. Evidence from other rich houses is provided by a
section of decorative marble flooring, *opus sectile*, and some mosiacs.

Amongst the funerary monuments a **veterinary memorial** shows the
shop with the vet on the right blood-letting, whilst the one on the left clips

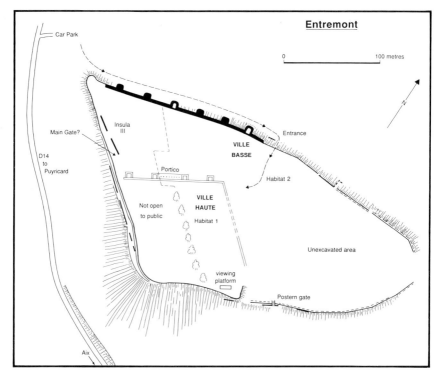

Figure 46

the horse's forelocks; they are separated by a vet's twitch (a similar tool is still used for controlling horses undergoing treatment).

Entremont

Iron Age oppidum.
Hours: 9.00 a.m.–noon, 2.00–6.00 p.m., closed Tuesday

3 km north of Aix, by the D14 to Puyricard. Entremont is 100 m east of the road and is reached by taking the small turning 50 m before the bridge carrying dual carriageway by-pass N296.

Entremont stands on the lip of the southern escarpment of the limestone Chaîne d'Esguilles. It is triangular with sharp slopes to the south, dropping down to the plain 100 m below. To the north the slope is gentler, but here a massive buttressed wall defends the town. The first recorded finds were made in 1817 and the first 'severed heads' were found in 1877, but the major discoveries began in 1943. German troops, sent to build an observation post on the hill, hit on broken statuary. Fortunately, when news of the finds became known in Aix, local representations saved most from disappearing (though one fine head was sold to a Swiss collector and has only been seen in photographic form since). Immediately the war ended, F. Benoit began the series of excavations that revealed most of the site on view today. He died in 1969, and whilst further excavation has taken place, most of the work done has been to clarify the chronology and modify his picture of society in Entremont.

Benoit envisaged the site as two contemporary towns: a Ville Haute as the home of a Celtic aristocratic warrior elite segregated by a rampart from the Ville Basse Ligurian masses with their workshops and agricultural activities. However, clearly stratified ceramic material indicates that the Ville Haute existed for at least forty years before the Ville Basse was built: 190 to 150 BC. Patrice Arcelin, director of excavations in the 1980s, renamed the Ville Haute Habitat 1 and suggested that the dramatic growth in the Ville Basse, Habitat 2, can be explained as an influx of refugees from Marsalliote territory at a time of growing tensions and conflict involving the Salyens Federation, Marseille and Rome. New craft production techniques were introduced by these refugees and were anyway not confined to the Ville Basse (see Insula XXIX, Fig. 47). New building in the expanded town implies the Ville Haute wall lost all meaning.

Benoit noted evidence of two sieges and believed that they took place in 125 and 124 BC, but pottery evidence strongly supports significant occupation until c. 90 BC, followed by some squatting. An alternative explanation has been put forward that there was one siege, in either 125 or 124; that Aix *castellum* was constructed to keep an eye on Entremont and it only became a shell after the Salyens revolt of c. 90 BC.

Numbering for blocks (*insulae*) and roads used on the plan of the site (Figure 47) follows that laid down by Benoit.

The Ville Basse walls

About 160 m of the impressive 380 m northern defensive wall is clearly visible. Around 3 m thick, the rubble core is faced on each side – the exterior is better finished – with uneven rectangular stones quarried locally; gaps in the courses are filled with slivers of the same stone. Along the curtain wall, projecting at 19–20 m intervals, are rectangular towers with curved corners. The wall and towers still reach up to 4.5 m and could have been over 6 m high originally. Small holes on the outside by towers 4, 5 and 6 indicate the drain run-offs. Traditional local drystone walling appears to embody here Greek ideas of rectangular work and regularity in tower design.

Entremont
MAIN EXCAVATION AREA

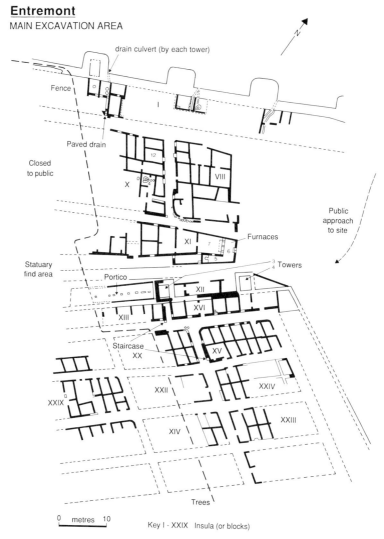

Figure 47

Viewing platform and postern gate

The view is dramatic. Aix, its plain, the Chaîne de L'Etoile and, to the east, the dominating mass of Montagne Ste Victoire stretch out in the haze. The builders of Entremont obviously felt much more secure here and to the west: surviving wall sections are only 1.5 m thick. A narrow postern gate, indicated by a series of steps, lies about 50 m to the east of the platform along the lip of the escarpment.

132

Aix-en-Provence
ENTREMONT
**The Portico: A
Reconstruction**

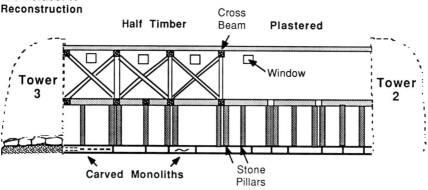

Figure 48

The Ville Haute

The *insulae* form blocks of single rooms, back-to-backs or lean-to houses. Walled with stone that fractures easily in thin slices and floored with beaten earth with a fire or oven in a corner, they could only have been poorly lit, mainly through the open door; few lamps have been found.

Road XVII divides the two sets of excavated blocks open to the public. Throughout the town roads were surfaced with pebble and crushed ceramic, suitable enough for people and pack-horses and perhaps the occasional small cart or chariot, if they could negotiate the tight corners and cluttered streets. Projecting external staircases for the upper storey, large jars to collect rainwater and, inevitably, people living outside their tiny homes, must have made movement difficult.

The Ville Haute walls

Foundation fragments of rampart and two towers are visible; they indicate a wall of 1.5 m thickness of the same design as the subsequent Ville Basse rampart.

The Ville Basse

The portico

A major distinction between a 'protohistoric' oppidum and a Roman town has been the lack of public buildings or areas (e.g. a forum) in the former. At Entremont there is at least the suggestion of shared corporate activity. Room 1 of block XIII looks across the widest open space in Entremont to where block XI has been set back from the road, allowing a crowd to gather. A line of large blocks including lintels and monoliths – they had previously stood as square upright columns – marks the front of the room. Some are slightly hollowed where pillars must have stood, so functioning rather like a Greek *stylobate* or temple base. Along the back runs a parallel bench and down the middle a row of rough pillar bases. Careful re-examination of the site has shown fragments of decorated mortar flooring and plaster walling really belonged to an upper storey. Its sinister connotations are suggested by the snake monolith and the copy of a monolith with head-shaped hollows. Twenty skulls were found scattered in the portico and the road in front, three of them with nail or spike holes. Further down the road the mass of broken statuary was found. This seems to have been a portico reconstructed from an earlier warrior and severed head 'sanctuary' still apparently used to display heads. Perhaps the first and so far unidentified site was destroyed in 124 and this is a poorer version that replaced the original until 90 BC.

Craft production

Block XI: **three furnaces** mark out rooms 5, 6 and 7 as a workshop. Although some slag and a large lump of lead were found here, it is possible this was not its prime function as the lead may have been used for making pellets during the final siege. An **oil press *'lapidum'* or counterweight** stands in room 10.

Block X: in room 4 lies a pear-shaped **oil *'ara'* or *scourtin* base**. The *scourtins* or baskets of olive mush were piled on this to be crushed by the weight of the beam. The oil is steered by grooves to the lip at the end where it would have been collected in bowls. (For details of operation and explanatory diagrams of oil production see MOULIN DES BOUILLONS, pp. 178–80.)

More developed housing

Block VIII is dominated by much larger houses than elsewhere. Not only are some rooms linked to make two- or three-room dwellings (excluding the upper floor), but the rooms themselves are larger than those in the upper town. Block I's lean-to houses, with their drainage culverts and pavings, remind the visitor of the communal needs of a hilltop urban site.

Jardin de Grassi

Avenue Grassi.

An atrium or small peristyle of one of the grand *domus* of this part of Aquae Sextiae has been turned into an attractive sunken garden. A fountain and a large perspective-painted wall help to give some sense of the attractiveness of these city villas. The remains were once much more extensive as the 1940 civil defence work revealed three villas.

Cathédrale St Saveur

Rue J. de Laroque.

The baptistery embodies a fifth-century structure and reuses eight Roman columns. The fourth-century St Mitre sarcophagus is a fine example of early Christian decorative work showing Christ handing the laws of the church to St Peter.

Aqueduct remains

There are five aqueducts known to have supplied Aix; there are visible remains of two.

The *Traconnade aqueduct* was the longest, coming from near Jouques, 30 km to the north-east of Aix.

Meyrargues: on the N96 road to Manosque and Digne. Take turning south into town and left at Avenue de la Pourane, following signs for the château. Outside the town, after the cemetery, take left turning for 50 m. Two tall arches and the remains of other pillars survive. They once carried the no longer existing channel across the narrow valley. Most of the rest of the aqueduct was subterranean.

The Eastern *St Antonin aqueduct* brought water from the Le Bayon spring, 13 km away below the hamlet of St Antonin.

Le Tholonet: signposted on Aix inner ring road by the D17. The 'Mur des Romains' is a section taking the aqueduct across a rocky ravine. The arch itself is gone but the walls that carried the parapet with the channel survive 15 m high on each side. Constructed with the usual rubble core and *petit appareil* facing, it is about 3 m thick and a few large blocks suggest where the arch was buttressed. The place is idyllic in the summer months. There are a waterfall, luxuriant bushes, ash and pine trees, butterflies and lazy bees, whilst on the other side of the wall lies an empty and mysterious valley. Unfortunately, the direct route to it by the side of the la Cause stream is fenced off and the visitor has to hope to get through the premises of the CEMAGREF organisation.

'Trophy of Marius'

100 m to the north-east of the junction of the N7 and D23 to Pourrières, south of the river Arc, is a mound of cemented rubble. There are also remains of walling that could be an enclosure. It is claimed to be a trophy raised to the Roman general Marius who defeated the Teutons near Aix in

102 BC, when an estimated 1–200,000 Germans were slaughtered. The attribution is dubious and could be the product of anti-German feeling in the late nineteenth century, after the French defeat in the 1870–1 war. Even the name Montagne Ste Victoire is a relatively modern renaming of the windy mountain, Mt Ventoux. Perhaps it is best simply to look out over the plain from a quiet spot on the slopes below the mountain. The quiet, the colours and the beauty enable the imagination to work in a way impossible near a noisy modern road; the plaster walls and red roofs of the farmhouses suggest even more vividly the numerous villas that once filled the area.

APT, Vaucluse

Michelin 81–11
IGN 67–C2
3,40/48,75gr
5°23/43°53

Museum and theatre remains.

52 km east of Avignon on N100 to Sisteron and Gap.

The summer trickle of the Coulon/Calavon River winds round the northern side of Apt; like the town itself, it gives little impression of its role in the Roman period. It had, of course, once helped create a valley between the Vaucluse and Luberon that the Romans utilised as one of their major routes from Italy to Spain (see LE PONT JULIEN, pp. 167–8). It had also been powerful enough to create two streams around the site of Apt. This island was turned into the colony of Apta Julia when either Caesar or Augustus saw its potential for securing the road and romanising the local people. The Albici soon abandoned their hillfort at Perréal, 6 km to the north near St Saturnin, to join the new settlers.

During the early Middle Ages the once thriving town was deserted; the southern branch of the river silted up and deposits, washed down from the hillsides, covered Apta Julia. The remains of Roman Apt exist now 3–10 m deep in and below the cellars of the modern town. It has inhibited excavation and the serious study of Apt only began in the twentieth century.

However, there have been many chance discoveries and some have ended up far away, such as two fine statues in Chatsworth; others have simply disappeared. The most famous of the latter is a dedication to Hadrian's horse Borysthenes, which died here on his visit to Gaul in 121. Two literary sources record the death and that Hadrian composed a memorial poem. In the sixteenth century in the archbishop's palace yard the inscription itself was found and fortunately was transcribed by contemporaries. Translated it starts:

Borysthenes the Alan
Caesar's hunter

Over plain and marsh
And the mounds of Tuscany
Went like the wind. . . .

(translated by S. Perowne)

Redolent not only of his passionate love for horses and hunting, but also of his commitment to the cultured man who can compose poetry when needed.

The museum

Rue de l'Amphithéâtre.
Hours: Tourist season   10.00 a.m.–noon, 2.30–5.30 p.m. daily
        Out of season   2.30–4.30 p.m. except Tuesdays
                      Saturdays 10.00 a.m.–noon, 2.30–5.00 p.m.

The museum is housed in a mansion once owned by the Orange family. Despite the provincial display quality, the contents hold some interest.

Ground floor

Amongst the better sculpture is a seated woman. Her stool is decorated with fine drapery and she wears a long gown and cloak. She could be a personification of the Roman earth mother **Tellus**; unfortunately she is headless. A far more Gallic form is represented by the **three-headed capital** with its deep-cut locks of hair and calm stylised faces.

Two **inscriptions** commemorate members of the **Allius** family. They must have been powerful figures. C. Allius Celer was himself a magistrate in Apt and L. Allius Severus was probably a magistrate in Avignon where an inscription was found recording the same name. As with Antista Pia Quintilla (see VAISON, p. 232), it implies that great landowners had widely spread estates in southern Gaul.

Another small room contains **Perréal material** ranging from a reconstructed late Bronze Age tomb, to Iron Age burial and settlement finds (fourth to first century BC).

Second floor

The most interesting material here is a collection of **altars** found at a small Roman temple site at St Saturnin. They are dedicated to Silvanus, the Roman god of the countryside. A mass of **votive lamps**, too tiny for practical use, come from a Romano-Celtic temple at Le Chatelard, near Lardiers.

The theatre

Ask an attendant for access to the museum cellars.

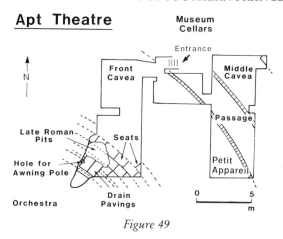

Figure 49

The Nassau mansion was built over the remains of the town theatre, recognised in the 1960s when two local archaeologists decided to investigate the debris in the cellars. On top of the *cavea* remains, traces of late Roman houses show that the theatre was already out of use in the fourth and fifth centuries.

ARLES, Bouches-du-Rhône

Michelin 83–10
IGN 66–8C
2,54/48,53gr
4°38/43°41

Major urban remains.

The atmosphere of Arles is quite different from that of, say, Orange. There the majestic theatre and triumphal arch dominate their surroundings. Standing alone, they proclaim the survival of a past civilisation. Arles has swallowed up its Roman remains. Houses surround the amphitheatre and once covered it. The slope of the hill almost allows you to look in: the amphitheatre cannot overpower, it simply exists. The theatre bears no comparison with Orange, but it is part of the town: the remains merging with the Jardin d'Eté and the nearby buildings. In no other city of Provence do the relics of the ancient world provide such a strong sense of being part of an organic continuum.

Arles is built on a low hill at the apex of the Rhône delta. In Antiquity there were probably three mouths, though this was a matter of contention amongst ancient authors. But then as now, the Grand Rhône was the main route to the sea, probably a few kilometres less than the 40 km of today. Just north of Arles one of the surviving minor branches, the Petit Rhône, took a

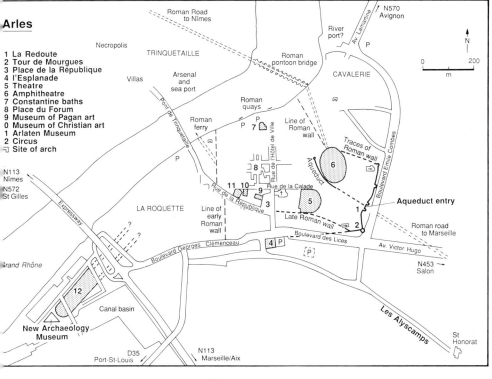

Arles

1 La Redoute
2 Tour de Mourgues
3 Place de la République
4 l'Esplanade
5 Theatre
6 Amphitheatre
7 Constantine baths
8 Place du Forum
9 Museum of Pagan art
0 Museum of Christian art
1 Arlaten Museum
2 Circus
⌐ Site of arch

Figure 50

westerly route. Arles provided a secure resting point for boats making their way up river and, of course, for the inhabitants, a means of controlling the traffic. In addition it was the lowest east–west crossing point, competing with the Beaucaire/Tarascon crossing 16 km further north.

Chance finds have long made it clear that Arles was occupied from early on and Avienius, in the fourth century AD, wrote that Arelate was originally a Greek town, 'Theline'. Until the 1970s excavation of the Jardin d'Hiver site (in the area now east of the tourist office), little more could be said. Now it is certain that the southern slopes of the hill were occupied in the sixth century BC and here, at that time, Greek pottery far exceeded indigenous: probably this was a staging post for the Massaliote Rhône traffic to central and northern Gaul. Even though by the second century BC the Jardin site had become like many others in southern Gaul, with single-room houses filled with local pottery, few doubt that Massalia controlled the delta region in this period. Perhaps, if we knew it, the centre of the settlement would give a very different picture, or maybe another town provided an alternative trading base, such as Espeyran, believed then to have overlooked the Petit Rhône. Certainly there is a suspicion that the Grand Rhône was not an easy

139

shipping route in this period as Marius found it necessary in 102 BC to order the construction of his canal, the Fossae Marianae, cutting out the lowest reaches of the river. Massaliote efforts to improve it further, by constructing towers to help ships find their way in such a low-lying landscape, certainly helped Arles. Caesar was able to use its shipyards for constructing warships to operate against Massalia in 49 BC.

Arelate, 'the town by the marshes', became Colonia Sextanorum when Caesar's general, Ti. Claudius Nero, settled sixth legion veterans here in 46 BC and gave it a large territory taken from both Massalia and the Salyens tribe. The ferry here was still used but soon a new pontoon bridge was built to the north of the town providing a permanent link with Trinquetaille, which developed rapidly as a suburb. The Augustan rampart only included the hilltop and the western slopes, primarily the public centre of Arles, but quayside urbanisation along both river banks must have featured from early on. Triumphal arches marked the town's supposed limits, respectively by the roads to the ferry and bridge (both pulled down, one as recently as 1683), but new quarters soon enveloped them in the north and south. The ceremonial role of the northern wall was ended when the Flavian amphitheatre was constructed on top of it, whilst the circus had to be built beyond the river wharfs of La Roquette. Even the area south of the Boulevard des Lices, once thought to be marsh, became a suburb. Across the river, Trinquetaille not only had its port and arsenal but also its own portico square, whilst mosaic finds indicate a whole series of *domus* houses, perhaps the homes of rich merchants. Unfortunately very little survives *in situ* on this side of the river, but it must have been remarkably like St Romain-en-Gal (see VIENNE, p. 36).

Although described amongst the '*urbes opulentissimae*' by P. Mela in the first century AD, it was only really at the end of the fourth century that Arles achieved a leading role in Gaul. Following the reorganisation that heralded the emergence of the late Empire, Arles gradually rose in status, though within Vienne's new province. Constantine held an important Church Council here in AD 314 and his son, the future Constantine II, was born here whilst it met. The town took on the features of an Imperial base: a mint for coining army pay; an arms factory; a workshop for officers' armour and silversmithing; and a woollen factory (no doubt for uniforms). None have been identified, nor has any Imperial palace, though there is a grandiose fourth-century baths and outside Arles a multiple mill for grinding mountains of corn (see BARBEGAL, pp. 156–7). New city walls, using stonework from the theatre, arches and tombs, enclosed a slightly smaller area than previously, but evidence from the suburbs shows these were still occupied. Possibly the most telling sign of the late Roman wealth of Arles is the largest collection in western Europe of marble sarcophagi outside Rome. For Ausonius in the later fourth century it was 'the little Rome of Gaul'.

Honorius, Emperor from AD 395 to 423, withdrew the Imperial administration from Trier as the north had become too vulnerable to barbarian attacks and made Arles the capital for his praetorian prefect of Gaul. He convoked an assembly of Gauls here (AD 418) claiming that 'all that is best in the opulent east, in perfumed Arabia, delicate Assyria, fecund Africa or fruitful Gaul, is offered here in abundance, as if all the magnificence of the world originated here'. No doubt hyperbole, but the letters of Sidonius Apollinaris highlight the continuation of Roman life here. The Forum, filled with columns and statues, is still the place the 'rabble' gathered and he can be accosted in his sedan chair and accused of writing scurrilous unsigned leaflets. He can be invited to an Imperial banquet held in honour of games in the Circus and take pride in his courtly skills. Yet this was written in AD 461, only fifteen years before the last shadowy western Emperor was deposed and even less before Arles finally fell to the Visigoths!

However, appearances were deceptive. The forum and the circus were anachronisms in late fifth-century Gaul, while the daily concerns of the late Roman world led naturally enough to the early Middle Ages. For years, reality for Sidonius had meant hanging on to his land, negotiating with and working for barbarian kings and ultimately obtaining a bishopric: these were the elements of real power, not senatorial titles. Arles did not stop being a Mediterranean trading centre (the goods were still wanted) and it had been an episcopal see for many years. The world of small churches and the great stone tombs of the Alyscamps had begun long before the Roman era ended and continued without a break when Visigoth and subsequent barbarian rule began.

The streets of Arles are narrow and driving down them is not only difficult but discouraged. Most sites are anyway better seen on foot. The best placed **parking areas** are either on the **Boulevard des Lices**, near the post office or by the Rhône on the **Quai Marx Dormoy**.

The ramparts and aqueduct

Montée Vauban and Boulevard Emile Combes.

The slope down from the Tour Rolland at the theatre to the Tour des Mourgues marks the line taken by the southern **late Roman rampart**. Using a mix of large blocks, small blocks and reused stonework, parts of it can be distinguished from the Jardin d'Eté outside the theatre and running down the Montée Vauban.

The **early Roman rampart** diverts south of the late Roman wall on the Montée Vauban and is represented by a few courses of neat, rough-cut *petit appareil* facing. Elements of the large Tour des Mourgues are also early Roman, but behind later Roman and medieval additions. The surviving eastern rampart provides the only significant evidence of the early Roman walls, which, on the basis of their building technique and design, are Augustan in date. Evidence of small block-work can be periodically distinguished along the base of the rampart line. The eastern gate, **la Redoute**,

141

is of the Fréjus type: a half moon inset in the rampart, marked originally by circular towers (traces on the ground), is filled at the centre by two semi-circular towers on each side of the gate. It uses well-dressed large blocks at the base though it has clearly been rebuilt many times. This kind of gate design is considered to be Augustan. On the left of la Redoute gate the **aqueduct entry point** is clearly marked. It came from the Alpilles (see BARBEGAL, p. 156) and from here went underground in two branches, one to the town centre and the other to the amphitheatre where it curves round to a *castellum* or distribution point whose remains were found under a house. Lead-piping found in the river suggests that fresh water was also carried to Trinquetaille by a syphon.

L'Esplanade

Boulevard des Lices.

The steps down from the Esplanade west of the bandstand divide the two sections of the excavations. The eastern half is below the tourist office but the remains are visible through a window. The western half is fully exposed.

Rebuilding work here revealed a previously unsuspected suburb outside the southern gate, once thought to be marshland. An area of shops and houses, one a fine villa, it had become very delapidated by the late third century. Revitalised *c.* AD 400 by new building it gradually turned into a rubbish dump during the fifth century.

Theatre

Rue de la Calade.

Hours:	June–Sept	8.30 a.m.–7.00 p.m. daily
	October and March	9.00 a.m.–12.30, 2.00–6.00 p.m.
	April (May)	9.00 a.m.–noon, 2.00–6.30 (7.00) p.m.
	November–February	9.00 a.m.–noon, 2.00–4.30 p.m.

The modern entrance recalls the convent created on part of the site; however, 'l'arc de la Miséricorde' is the one surviving northern arcade of the theatre. The clearance of later buildings behind the stage has left an attractive area of grass, trees, large blocks and ancient decorative stonework. It is possible to sit here and wonder at the superstition that saw the twin columns described in the Middle Ages as a place for pagan sacrifices and later compelled the nuns to make them a feature of their garden! The convent and the rest of the houses were cleared and serious excavation and restoration begun in the nineteenth century and completed by J. Formigé in the 1900s.

The hill was too low to consider using the slope to form the base for a *cavea*; Arles theatre is one of the earliest free-standing theatres using radiating walls and galleries. They supported a semi-circle of thirty-three rows, capable of holding an estimated 10,000 people. Its dimensions are very similar to those of Orange, with a diameter of 102 m. Its perfect alignment beside the *decumanus*, the modern Rue de la Calade, various elements of the decoration and the discovery of the statue of Augustus suggest an Augustan date.

The '**Tower of Rolland**' was adapted from the southern projecting wing as part of the defences against the Saracens in the ninth century. It preserved the whole bay, not just the exterior arcade, to the full height of the theatre, making it possible to visualise the structure of the whole theatre with its twenty-seven arcades on three floors. The **orchestra** floor is paved with green and pink imported marble. The hole in the middle marks the site of the altar of Apollo (see p. 150) while the raised area was used for moveable seats for town dignitaries. Five staircases divide the remaining rows of seating behind the groove left by the *balteus* wall.

In the summer months a wooden stage covers much of the *scaenae* remains. The **pulpitum** is represented by two courses only; many of the museum theatre reliefs derive from here. The **ditch** behind held the curtain and its counterweights, indicated by stone grooves once lined with wood. A winding drum for lifting the curtain stood at the southern end. The two columns with their fragment of entablature are the lone survivors of the *frons scaenae* once covered with perhaps a hundred.

The amphitheatre

Rond-Point des Arènes.
Hours: as for theatre.

Entrance: on north axis. This way in had a passage into the arena, wide enough for the carts needed to remove dead animals and people.

The amphitheatre has survived because it has fulfilled new functions since it lost its original role. The three towers, once four, recall its medieval role as a fortress; as this disappeared the poor filled its warren of galleries and tunnels, and houses soon covered the seats and arena. The nineteenth-century interest in the past and sense of civic pride stimulated its clearance, though the compensation paid out was only half that paid to the middle-class dwellers in the much smaller theatre.

The outside

The general design and size is very similar to that of Nîmes and was built AD 70–80. Like Nîmes there are two storeys with sixty arcades each, though these vary more in width, probably to utilise the strongest bedrock. It must have been roughly the same height, though here the attic has been removed entirely. The entrances at each axis are again slightly larger, the western on the short axis being the one for dignitaries – it led straight to the loggia of honour.

The interior

The outer ground-floor gallery is not vaulted, instead flat monolithic stones were used. Most of these have disappeared and it is believed they represented a design weakness – at times they must have given in under the weight of circulating crowds in the upper gallery. It suggests the use of vaulting at Nîmes must have been a subsequent and deliberate choice!

The thirty-four rows of seats, including the assumed attic rows and using the standard *c.* 40 cm width per person, give a capacity of 21,000. A feather-like mark setting off blocks of five seats is visible on some lower rows.

The podium wall still has much of its marble paving veneer and an inscription (second century AD) put up by C. Junius Priscus. It records how he paid for the podium, a gold statue to Neptune and four bronze statues (which probably decorated the loggia of honour), as well as two days of games and a banquet.

Entrances through the podium under the front seats, presumably covered with stone doors, allowed performers to enter the arena. They would not need to jump down into the arena because Arles, unlike Nîmes, had a huge wooden floor *c.* 2 m above the rock surface, shown by the notched stones and slots at the foot of the podium. Trapdoors could provide 'surprise' appearances or allow scenery and props to be pushed up for the different performances.

The stairs up to the attic survive and it is worth going up. The view is evocative and it is not simply the sense of unchanging rivers and mountains; modern Arles with its pink tile roofs, so like their *tegula* and *imbrex* predecessors, also provides a hint of the past Gallo-Roman community.

The forum complex

The forum covered a vast rectangular area and its surrounding portico had to have a flat surface. To achieve this on the slope down to the Rhône, a *cryptoporticus* or 'U'-shaped cellar was built: this has survived almost perfectly, though evidence of the forum itself is limited.

Monumental entrance remains

Place du Forum.

Two columns with fragments of the western section of an entablature and pediment have been embodied in the walls of the Hôtel du Nord. These are the survivors of what was once an open archway entrance, reached by a

Arles

CRYPTOPORTICUS & FORUM

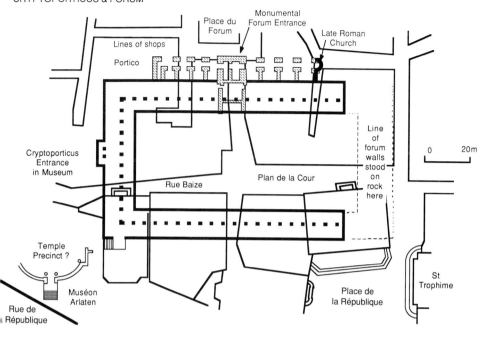

Figure 51

grand staircase. Originally the slope on this side would have exposed the supporting *cryptoporticus*, fronted by shops and a portico on each side of the staircase.

The cryptoporticus

Entered by stairs inside the Musée d'Art Chrétien (from 1993, this will be an extension of the Muséon Arlaten).

Hours: see theatre.

These porticoed crypts or cellars have long been matters of controversy because none of the ancient sources are clear on why they were built. An airless, damp environment, and this *cryptoporticus* has its puddles, suggests only emergency storage for foods. Lit by little more than holes in the vaulted upper walls, could they have been winter promenades? Or were they barracks for public slaves? Archaeologists are only agreed that they provided strong foundations on which the above-ground forum buildings could stand.

The long sides of the 'U' are nearly 89 m long and the short end is *c*. 59 m.

Each branch is divided down the middle by a series of low arches creating two galleries. The decoration is minimal, confined to simple mouldings and cornice. Now lit by suitably gloomy electric lighting, the window openings, once lined with grills, are visible above the vault springs all along the inside galleries and very intermittently on the outside. In the middle of the northern branch the massive foundations of later entrance buildings, of which the Place du Forum remains form the end, nearly block the way. In the final part of the branch was found the sculpture of Octavian and Tiberius; no doubt somewhere in the forum was a temple of the Imperial cult.

Muséon Arlaten

Hôtel du Laval, Rue de la République.
Hours: as for the theatre but closed on Mondays.

The courtyard of the museum was excavated in the early 1900s and revealed a large **curved wall with niches** on the inside and small columns standing on top, enclosing a paved area. Formigé thought it might be the apse of a basilica, but this is very unlikely. The apex of the curve has a monumental entrance, the 'apse' was c. 25 m wide and there is no evidence of internal columns to support a roof. The most likely explanation seems to be a temple precinct attached to the forum, copied from Augustan, Trajanic or Hadrianic examples in Rome. The presence of a **late Roman rampart** to the south of the courtyard (nearer the door), with its reused stonework and large blocks, shows how this rampart took a new path defending a narrower area of public Arles.

Baths of Constantine

Rue D. Maisto (a continuation of the Rue de l'Hôtel de Ville).
Hours: as for theatre.

The great apse seemed so remarkable that it was commonly assumed to be part of a 'Palais de Constantine'. M. J. Formigé was able to show that it belonged in fact to what must have been the largest bath system in Provence and one of the last to be built in southern Gaul. The **exterior** of the apse shows the widespread use of brick together with large stone blocks for window sills, both Late Roman features. Corbels with holes indicate that there were wooden shutters to keep out the worst of the mistral.

Inside, another late Roman feature is the extensive use of concrete, most apparent in the 40 cm thick flooring that separated the tile hypocaust pillars from the marble paving, now almost entirely disappeared. Inevitably the apse is the dominant feature: even the cupola survives supported by its brick,

Arles

BATHS OF CONSTANTINE

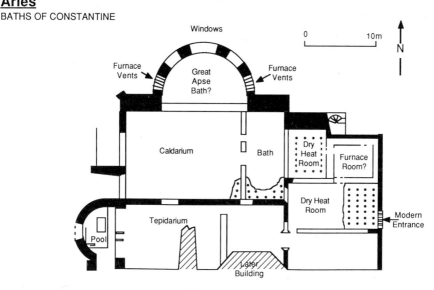

Figure 52

not stone, arch. It probably covered a large pool heated by external furnaces. The windows would have been glass filled, held by a framework of bronze.

The main rooms are extremely big, the *caldarium* alone was more than 10 m × 20 m, excluding the apse. Extending much further up the hill, there must have been an equally large *frigidarium*, a swimming pool and an exercise yard. However, excavation here has not been possible.

Because baths of this scale were extremely expensive to build and to maintain, they were nearly always the donations of wealthy men. By the late Empire such gifts had become increasingly confined to members of the Imperial elite. It is quite possible therefore that Constantine did order their construction, perhaps for the bishops in AD 314 or maybe to celebrate the birth of his son.

Les Alyscamps

Avenue des Alyscamps.

Les Alyscamps was a place of legend – a place of great Christian victories over Saracens: it deserved wonder and prayer, so provoking medieval pilgrimages. In reality the awe had been stimulated by the great marble sarcophagi that filled this late Roman necropolis south of the Roman road to Aix. The best sarcophagi have all been removed to the churches – for example, St Trophime – and museums of Arles, yet the pleasure in walking down the avenue is not less. Surprisingly, Van Gogh's vision of cedars and tombs is little changed. The cemetery was used from the mid-fourth century until the sixth century AD. The avenue culminates with the early church of **St Honorat** into which a number of good quality tombs have been taken (reopening by 1993).

The circus

Avenue de la 1ère Division Française Libre, Faubourg du Cirque.

(The new Musée d'Arles, displaying all the ancient material previously kept in other museums, is expected to open next to the site by 1993.)

Circuses were the largest public buildings of the ancient world, up to four times the length of an amphitheatre, but, unlike the latter, when the culture that supported the costly professional sport of chariot-racing died, there was little alternative use for the structures, except as ready-made quarries. Arles is no exception. Fortunately though, the flat but low-lying land surface beyond the Roman suburb in La Roquette, chosen at the end of the first century AD as the site for the circus, has sunk over 1.5 m since Antiquity, leaving the foundations of the circus waterlogged but almost intact. In the 1900s, Formigé identified the outlines of the structure. The new canal basin and the N113 expressway in the 1970s brought renewed excavation and led to the decision to build an archaeological museum by the site.

Sections of the circus seating foundations are visible: first, a part of the southern arm by the **north-west bank of the canal basin** from the parapet of the Avenue de la 1ère Division bridge; second, a section belonging to the arc of seating at the end of the circus in the area to the **south-west of the avenue**, designated as the 'Jardin Archéologique'.

The foundations follow a standard design, using *petit appareil* and rubble stonework. A podium wall 4 RF wide separates the *cavea* from the arena. Behind it, rectangles, 20 × 10 RF, are created by a rear wall of 5 RF and cross-walls between. In the wettest areas, oak logs were laid below the stonework, which was itself at least fifteen courses down. Alternate bays had drains as well. These massive foundations suggest stone not wooden seating, but nothing has survived. As the circus fell into ruin the bays and what was above were used by squatters.

Nearby, archaeologists found housing, remains of a necropolis (first to third century AD) and a large mausoleum, possibly that of the Imperial pretender Constantine III who held court in Arles and was executed here. It was bulldozered away.

The arena, though narrower than Vienne, would probably have had twelve chariots racing at a time, but this can only be confirmed if the starting gates can be found at the other end, at present under the houses of La Roquette. The audience at this end would have been able to see the crashes as the chariots rounded the barrier or *euripus* down the middle of the circus. Traces of this barrier have been found and it was from here that the obelisk was taken. It once marked the finish line in front of the judges and the Imperial box, near which Sidonius Apollonaris would have sat in AD 461.

The obelisk

Place de la République.

In 1675 the obelisk was hauled, with difficulty, to the centre of Arles and set on a new base to celebrate the rule of King Louis XIV, the sun-king. It would not have surprised Augustus who had brought the first obelisk from Heliopolis to Rome to identify himself with the sun god worshipped in Egypt. In the circus it was seen as a sunbeam and used as a sundial casting its shadow over the arena. Genuine Egyptian granite obelisks like this are extremely rare in the west (see VIENNE, pp. 33–4), it was probably part of the fourth-century Imperial upgrading process.

Musée Lapidaire/d'Art Païen

Place de la République.

The museum is in an old and badly-lit deconsecrated church: the collection will be getting the modern museum it deserves, when the new Musée d'Arles opens by the Circus.

The apse at the far end brings together four pieces of monumental stonework illustrating the emergence of the Augustan family as emperors. The head of Octavian, the inscribed marble shield and the head of Tiberius were all found in the **crytoporticus** and probably once belonged in a forum temple of the Imperial cult; the statue of Augustus decorated the *frons scaenae* in the theatre.

The **head of Octavian** is an unusually early one and represents him with a thin wispy beard which he only wore whilst he was in mourning for his step-father Julius Caesar. When he married Julia in 38 BC he cut it off. In the six years since Caesar's murder, Octavian had already established himself as joint ruler of the Empire with Mark Antony. As one of the triumvirs, he had control of Gaul and visited it for the first time in 39 BC. This head was probably set up in Arles to commemorate that visit. He was 24 years old then, but shown here with a mature creased brow. His hair is depicted with a feature retained all his life, the lobster-claw lock on the forehead.

The **inscribed marble shield** is a copy of a golden shield ordered by the Senate to be distributed round the Empire in 26 BC. It is one of the few surviving. It is not simply an attractive example of Roman lettering, but an important historical document, specifically mentioned in Augustus' will, the *Res Gestae*. It simply records 'The Senate and the Roman people to the

Emperor Caesar Augustus, son of the divine [Julius], eight times consul, has given this shield for his courage, his clemency, his justice, his piety towards the Gods and the Homeland.' It seems purely ceremonial, but it is the culmination of the events following 31 BC when Octavius defeated Mark Antony in the battle of Actium and established himself as the single ruler of Rome. The inscription embodied the Senate's acceptance of the end of the Republic. Octavius received a new name, Augustus, embodying priestly status rather than majestic power. His political hold was recognised by his title of Emperor, holder of permanent 'imperium' – the right to rule.

The **Augustus statue** is the physical embodiment of that settlement. Gone is the creased brow: instead we have a mature, serene, noble figure. Although Suetonius comments on his calm appearance, this is not realism. Augustus is a demi-god, given a body based on a Greek ideal of virility, suitable for a divine being. The hard dry patches on his body, caused by using the strigil too much in the baths, do not appear and his hair retains the same curls. This idealism marked the decline of Republican realist portraiture.

The **head of Tiberius** is less god-like; he was the inheritor (Emperor AD 14–37) not the founder of a dynasty. But continuity there is. The overall picture is the same, most apparent in the curly hair which had become an established feature of the Julio-Claudian family. His head is more triangular and he has a fatter nose.

Confident and delicate stoneworking is represented by the material from the theatre, sadly rarely undamaged. The small **swan's wings altar to Apollo** stood in the orchestra, attractively decorated with garlands of laurels and palm trees on the rear corners. The larger **figure-decorated altar to Apollo** stood at the centre of the *pulpitum*. A seated Apollo rests his elbow on a lyre, the sacrificial tripod, seen as the god's throne, placed by him. On the right Marsyas hangs from a tree, about to be skinned by the Phrygian on the left sharpening his knife. He had made the fatal mistake of challenging Apollo to a flute contest and had lost. A reminder for modesty amongst theatre performers!

Other *pulpitum* fragments include two opposed fat-bellied Silenus statues lying on sofas and a lovely dancer – or victory – whose dress swirls, but who has lost her head and shoulders.

Two of the most striking and well-preserved sarcophagi are probably third-century. The white marble **sarcophagus of Hippolytus and Phaedra** was found in Trinquetaille. The source of the relief is tragic myth. Phaedra sits on the left. The second wife of Theseus, she fell in love with his son Hippolytus, committing suicide when he failed to respond. His chastity made him a devotee of the goddess Diana the huntress. He is therefore shown here surrounded by hunting companions, and the relief is filled with dogs. An older woman, perhaps Phaedra's nurse, points him out, carrying a lance and nude except for his floating cloak; she was the one who persuaded

Phaedra to send a letter to Theseus accusing Hippolytus of seducing her. The scenes on the right end side and on the back develop the hunting theme; they are clearly by another inferior artist. The lid, again less ably carved than the front relief, portrays the dead man, now headless, book open before him.

I like the **hunting sarcophagus**, simply because of its lively naive realism. Three dogs attack a wild boar, a man grabs the muzzle of a stag, others on horseback have wrappings round their legs to protect them from bites. Amongst the rest of the collection are inscriptions stressing the economic role of Arles: '*navales*', the shipbuilders, an '*architectus navalis*', a ship designer, '*navicularii marini*', ships' captains, '*utricularii*', rivermen. The **dockers relief** has two men tying a sack with ropes: it is a vivid glimpse of the daily work of the port.

The mosaics come from rich suburban houses in Trinquetaille. The pleasant **mosaic of Europa** was restored in Antiquity. The **Orpheus mosaic** is a richly decorated example of the same type as that displayed in Aix, where Orpheus is encircled with charmed animals, rather than placed in individual surrounds as at Vienne.

Musée d'Art Chrétien

Chapelle du Collège, Rue Balze.
Hours: as for theatre.

This is also the entrance to the *cryptoporticus*. The collection will be housed in the new Musée d'Arles by the Circus.

The museum brings together a large number of sarcophagi of the third to sixth centuries AD. As samples of the Arles school, I will simply describe the three that I found the most interesting.

The **shell imago** coffin was found in 1974 in Trinqueville with two others. The figures in the large shell, clearly the deceased, are the most compelling feature. A middle-aged man wears high-status clothes and carries a book. His young and attractive wife rests her arm round his shoulders, her hair dressed in turban style, an early fourth-century fashion set by Helena, Constantine's mother. The top register of reliefs show on the left the creation of Eve and a triple image of God. Adam and Eve also appear here as small figures. On the right of the shell Christ carries out miracles. On the bottom register the Magi appear before Mary, seated in a Roman basket chair, followed by further miracles including Christ and the loaves. The lid reverts to the Old Testament with Abraham about to sacrifice his sons. The discs here are uninscribed; however, male and female skeletons were inside. Both died in their 50s but the coffin was reopened in Antiquity; was this to allow the burial of a younger wife?

The **olive harvest** is also early fourth-century and this time reflects the reality, not of individual experience, but of work. Cherubs pick the olives standing on the top of pole and crossbar ladders; they transfer them from their paniers to baskets which are then taken to the olive press. It was mutilated in the Napoleonic era.

Hidden in a side chapel is the grandest narrative sarcophagus, **passage through the Red Sea**, made of imported Carrara marble late in the fourth century. On the right Mary the Prophetess leads the way beating her dulcimer. The Israelites follow, Moses walks with a stick and a child is carried on a man's shoulder. The sea closes behind them on the Pharaoh and his army. He is shown with rich curls standing in his chariot carrying a lance and shield. At the bottom of the scene three symbolic figures lie down: Egypt, the Earth and the Red Sea.

AVIGNON, Vaucluse

Michelin 81–12
IGN 66–9A
2,72/48,83gr
4°48/43°56

Major museum.

The dominating image of Avignon is improved medieval. The fourteenth-century walls benefited considerably from the work of Viollet-le-Duc, the famous 'bridge' is a carefully preserved stump of four arches going nowhere and the papal palace, despite extensive work to restore its palatial aspects, still looks more like a fortress. My sour response is I suppose a result of the pervasive atmosphere of mass tourism, intense summer heat and the almost total absence of any Roman remains. The compensation is that what there is can be seen easily and the museum collection has some outstanding pieces.

Avenio was an important Roman city, listed by Mela in the first century as the third richest city of Narbonensis. The rocky prominence by the Rhône had attracted intensive settlement in the Bronze Age and emerged as the major Iron Age centre of the Cavares tribe. Massaliote coinage and pottery confirm the expected Greek presence. The St Agricol excavations (see p. 153) revealed Greek large block walling; a hint that during the later second century BC Avignon may have formed part of Massalia's inland territory, securing the Durance valley. The wealth of the Roman city, awarded the prestigious title of 'colonia' early on, is hinted at by the forum remains, traces of a theatre, the fragments of battle scenes preserved in the museum that might represent a triumphal arch and the large number of mosaics found here and subsequently destroyed.

The Forum remains

Only isolated features are known and do little more than confirm what was suspected in the eighteenth century, that the Place de l'Horloge and the area nearby was the site of the public centre of Avenio.

Built into the wall at the junction of Rue St Etienne and Rue Petite Fusterie is a double arcade of *grand appareil*. They once formed the foundations on the sloping land surface for a level forum, much as a *cryptoporticus* (see ARLES, p. 145). A few metres away, at the end of the Rue St Etienne, are pavings, capitals and entablature blocks from forum buildings on the northern side. They may have come from the large building whose *grand appareil* foundations are at the corner of the Rue Racine and Rue Molière. By the **church of St Agricol** are three parallel sections of walling that marked the southern limit of the Forum. The inner wall of *petit appareil*, with a semi-circular buttress apse, is the best preserved. They have been interpreted as supporting inner and outer porticoes – or as part of a basilica. At a deeper level, this site produced Greek masonry.

On the other side of the Place de l'Horloge, via the Rue Vilar and Rue Peyrollerie, in the public garden at the Place de la Mirande are the ruins of a double row of arcades presumed to be those of a theatre.

Musée Calvet

65 Rue Joseph-Vernet.
Hours: 10.00 a.m.–noon, 2.00–6.00 p.m., closed Tuesday.

The Calvet museum was one of the earliest museums in the region, created in 1823 from church confiscations during the revolution and the personal collection of Esprit Calvet. Its curators sought out material not only in Avignon but all over the Vaucluse and beyond; throughout the nineteenth century, towns like Vaison lost their major finds to the Calvet. In the 1900s the museum split its collection, moving its sculpture and many of the mosaics to the Musée Lapidaire. It is an artificial and unsatisfactory division.

Hercules and Hesione mosaic: this is the centre piece from a much larger mosaic found in St Paul-Trois-Châteaux: the rest somehow disappeared. It recalls one of the many stories about Hercules, obviously copied from the Perseus and Andromeda myth, in which he rescues a princess from a sea-monster. It was much restored in Antiquity, turning the rock and monster into a confused mass between the figures. It has been called '*très mediocre*'.

Musée Lapidaire

27 Rue de la République.
Hours: 9.00 a.m.–noon, 2.00–6.00 p.m., closed Tuesday.

153

Despite the poor lighting and unsympathetic setting in yet another deconsecrated church, there are things here that should not be missed.

The 'Tarasque' of Noves: this fearsome sculpture is of a man-eater or *'androphage'*, named after a monster of medieval myth that haunted the Rhône by Tarascon. It was in fact found by the Durance at the foot of Noves oppidum, 10 km south of Avignon. The monster's body is broadly that of a lion, though its back could be scaled. It sits on its rear legs with human heads placed under each paw, while also dismembering a human body. Most writers have considered this a prime example of early Celtic art symbolising the triumph of death over life, some even postulating a very early fourth century BC date. Doubt has been cast by F. Salviat (1979) who suggested the Tarasque was really medieval, analogous to a gargoyle, whilst the men's beards reminded him of biblical prophets. For me, the existence of other Celto-Ligurian lion *androphages*, the dead eyes of the men, so reminiscent of others at Entremont, even the severed head cult itself (see AIX, p. 129) are persuasive. It is interesting that at St Rémy a conventional seated warrior is also shown with an erect penis: these figures usually held heads in a pose like the Tarasque.

There are a number of **reliefs** showing the integration of Gallic gods in the romanised life of the region. Two from Séguret near Vaison show contrasting affects. Unusual care has been taken to give a strong classical veneer to **Sucellus**, yet he can be clearly identified as the Celtic god of nature and the underworld by his hammer. His woodland aspect is stressed here by the pan-pipes he carries. On the other hand **Jupiter** is turned into a Celtic god. He appears as a Roman general, appropriate dress in a land conquered by the Romans but not normal in the Roman world! He has his attributes, an eagle and an oak tree, but the latter is turned into Celtic tree-worship by the addition of a snake and his shield has become a wheel – the symbol of the Celtic sky-god.

A more straightforward kind of integration is depicted by the finest statue in the museum, the **Gallic soldier from Vachères**. The pose is naturalistic, the face self-assured, the hands relaxed, the man confident. His Gallic heritage, and wealth, is affirmed by his torc necklace. The shield too is Gallic (see ORANGE triumphal arch, pp. 183–6). Chain mail was possibly an independent Gallic invention of the third century BC; it certainly took skilled metal craftsmen to make it. Yet the representation is in the Roman realist tradition, quite different from the Gallic seated warriors of the second century BC. His tousled waves of hair suggest an Augustan influence and most likely he was a Gallic aristocrat recruited into the Roman auxilliaries. Next to him the headless **warrior of Mondragon** perhaps embodies the same spirit, by carefully draping the cloak over his shield to stress the Gallic fringes.

Roman rule is epitomised in the **Imperial statue heads**. The workshops of Rome had evolved a demi-god image for Augustus, suitable for the development of an Imperial cult. However, all the male members of his family are identified with the same overall image. Distinguishing them is a matter of nuances when the overall facial features and haircuts are so similar. Here the most interesting are **Tiberius**, Augustus' immediate successor (AD 14–37) and his son **Drusus**, the former with a wide forehead, small mouth and large eyes, the latter marked by thin lips and a long hooked nose, unfortunately broken here. Well-made in Italian marble, they were found at different times in the forum area – perhaps they stood together in a cult room constructed before the early death of Drusus in AD 23. Later Emperors in the collection include a **Trajan** (AD 97–117) brought from Carpentras. The hair and smooth face hint at the Augustan tradition, but the low forehead, long face and puffed cheeks are quite different. A totally new approach is embodied in the late **Antonine** heads of Marcus Aurelius or Commodus and perhaps Lucius Verus (160s–90s). The Imperial image now has thick hair in wild locks, a beard and shiny skin surfaces. The source is Greek: a mix of the philosopher and Alexander heroic. The masons went mad with their drills, typically adding pupils where paint alone was once enough.

Two Imperial women have been recognised. **Julia Drusilla** (died AD 38) was the sister of the mad Gaius. This proper and dull portrait may imply her status as his favourite sister, but not the rumours of incest. **Julia Domna** (Empress, AD 193–211), the cultured wife of Severus, is perhaps worse served by the sculptor: her dramatic hairstyle is turned into a heavy helmet.

A very different world is recalled by the **river barge relief**. Probably a tombstone relief, dedicated to a boat-owner, it was found at Cabrières-d'Aigues in the foothills of the Luberon above the Durance. A man sits with his steering oar on a boat with two large barrels. From a forward mast three ropes stretch out to the towing men, two of whom survive. Above them are a row of locally made amphorae, some basket-covered. Probably the owner specialised in wine, but barrels were used for beer, mead and foodstuffs like salted fish. He would have been a member of the rivermen's craft guild or college, one of which existed in Cavaillon. But my eye is always drawn to the men on the ropes as they hobble along with their sticks, a rare glimpse of the mass of ordinary people whose labour maintained the privileged life that fills so much of the archaeological record.

The mosaics are disappointing. Only the **Orange mosaic** is interesting, largely due to the border: a stylised city wall of black on white. As the mosaic is dated to the first half of the first century AD, it might embody local pride in Orange's new ramparts. After all the town's leading citizens would have contributed to their construction and seen them as enhancing their prestige.

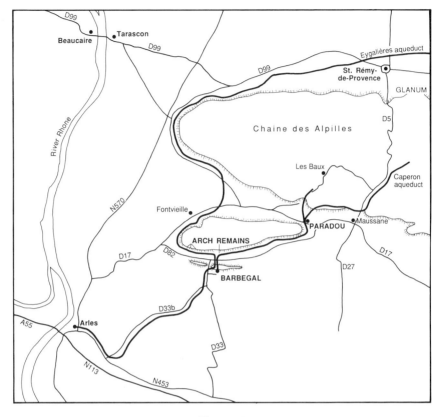

Figure 53

BARBEGAL, Bouches-du-Rhône

Michelin 83–10
IGN 66–C9
48,56/2,67gr
4°44/43°46

Mill and aqueducts.

Arles 13 km and Tarascon 14 km; 3.5 km south-south-east of Fontvieille. Coming from Arles, take the N570 Avignon road for 3 km, turn right on the D17 for Fontvieille and after *c.* 5 km, the D82 for Paradou to junction with the D33. Then either: (1) continue on the D82 *c.* 500 m (note arches of Eygalières aqueduct parallel to the road *c.* 150–200 m to the north; parking on eastern side of aqueduct arches crossing the D82); (2) turn right and after *c.* 1 km take left turning, signposted for Meunerie Romain (about 750 m, parking at foot of mill foundations).

The Roman mill that once covered the hillside at Barbégal is the largest surviving powered industrial unit in the classical Mediterranean world. There were mines that employed more people and whose production over the centuries was staggering, but they were driven by muscle power, largely human. At Rio Tinto in southern Spain, twelve bucket wheels, set in a sequence down a shaft, were trodden by men enabling water to be lifted painstakingly up to the surface. At Barbégal the principle was reversed. Here, water gushing downhill was used to turn sixteen wheels, each one driving a millstone. It is the scale of the enterprise that is so striking. Small single wheel undershot water-mills were an innovation of the period, but such a concentrated exploitation of natural power was only achieved again in the eighteenth century.

The aqueducts

The mill is driven by water from the **Caperon** aqueduct, fed by springs north of Maussane some 9 km away and joined by a feeder channel from l'Arcoule. Arriving from the north-east, it meets the **Eygalières** aqueduct, coming c. 35 km from the north-west. They run due south side by side for c. 320 m across the appropriately named *vallon des arcs*.

To the north of the D82

The two aqueducts are together for a short distance. The Caperon can be followed c. 120 m through the gorse and over the drainage ditch until the low wall that supported the channel disappears.

To the south of the D82

There are noticeable differences between the two aqueducts. The Eygalières retains the classic arch structure when the Caperon aqueduct reverts to a solid wall. The latter uses *petit appareil* facing and is rather better made. The Eygalières has large block foundations and mixes courses of stone and brick facing on the rubble core. On reaching the hill, the Eygalières turns abruptly westwards; shrubbery makes it difficult to follow the channel very far. The Caperon channel goes straight on through the rock in a steeply cut trench.

The mill

It was F. Benoit's excavation of 1936–8, probably his greatest work, which established all the major features of the structure (see Figure 54). Subsequent studies have vindicated nearly all his cautious conclusions.

At the foot of the mill the water-wheel 'chambers' have survived much better than higher up the hill because they were cut into bedrock; they were

Barbégal Mill

PLAN

Cutting and aqueduct

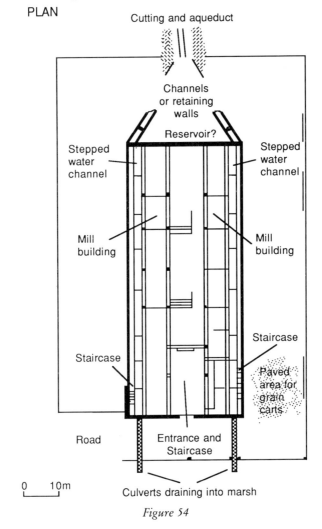

Channels
or retaining
walls

Reservoir?

Stepped
water
channel

Stepped
water
channel

Mill
building

Mill
building

Staircase

Staircase

Paved
area for
grain
carts

Road

Entrance and
Staircase

0   10m

Culverts draining into marsh

Figure 54

the key to Benoit's analysis and reconstruction. The fall of 20 m in 61 m gave space for eight wheels of about 2.1 m diameter, though it meant the bottom one was half buried. None could have worked with direct drive: the bottom three wheels must have driven millstones above the axles, whilst all the levels above must have been geared to mills below. The overall efficiency of the mill would have depended in part on the precision of this machinery, but more on the force of the water flow from the aqueduct.

Benoit retained the idea of a reservoir at the top and in this he was probably wrong. The two diagonal walls were seen by him as sides with a

158

Barbégal Mill

RECONSTRUCTED SECTION

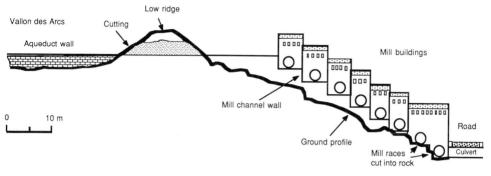

Figure 55

retaining wall across the width of the mill; its supporting bench is visible. However, Sellin (1983) has argued that this would only permit a thin wall vulnerable to being undercut by water and causing disaster. He argued that the walls in fact supported channels from the aqueduct.

Flour production and the late Imperial world

Wonder at the size of this factory has led many uncritically to accept an estimate that it could produce 28 tonnes in a day – enough to feed 80,000 people (Sagui 1948). However, this was based on the assumption that each wheel drove two millstones, the mill worked continuously for 24 hours a day and grain was always available for grinding. Sellin convincingly shows that water discharge could never have been strong enough to drive two banks of millstones and that 9 tonnes would be a more reasonable total for 24 hours. He then talks of a 'load factor' of 50 per cent, meaning breakdowns, reduced water-flows, undelivered grain, absent foremen, etc. Finally, if we consider a day governed by daylight we are reduced to a more probable 2–3 tonnes. Benoit had looked at nineteenth-century water-mill production and arrived at 2.4–3.2 tonnes a day! However, even this could have fed 10,000 people a day.

It is a method of production that demands centralised decision-making. In Gaul, most corn was ground by handmill in people's homes. Mass production like this was no benefit for them, adding transport costs, that must have been considerable, simply to keep a mill this size working. The only other example of a similar mill, far more fragmentary than here, is on the Janiculum ridge in Rome. Grain had to be brought from North Africa and Egypt to feed Rome under the Imperial corn supply or *annona*. Large-scale milling may have been a refinement linked to the free distribution of bread to 150,000 privileged citizens. Both Barbégal and Janiculum have been dated to the end of the third century AD. There was no hand-out in Narbonensis, but the period was one of fundamental change, especially for Arles. The third century had ended with contraction, but the city re-emerged as an Imperial base (see ARLES, p. 140), populated with new kinds of people, courtiers, soldiers, Imperial slaves, factory workers, all with a privileged status that necessitated their needs were met: the flour produced at Barbégal was their hand-out; Barbégal was built to supply them.

The contrasting building methods of the two aqueducts can be explained by the changing historical environment. Excavations in 1987–90 support an Augustan date for the Caperon aqueduct. It would make sense if it originally supplied water to Arles, using the section from here to Arles of what became the Eygalières aqueduct. The latter would then have simply been a new tributary, constructed when demand rose in Arles during the later second century: Barbégal was then a junction point. By Constantine's time, water needs would be lower in Arles and the Caperon could be diverted through its man-made ravine to supply the mill with power and the water carried away by a culvert into the marshland. Who built the mill? Perhaps the master carpenter Q. Candidus Benignus, a specialist in 'organa aquarum' or hydraulic devices, recorded on an inscription in Arles, had something to do with it.

Paradou

On La Burlande camping-site and 'Le Domaine des Alpilles de Paradou' housing estate. By the north of the D17 to west of Paradou village.

Building work, followed by archaeological excavation, has revealed a subterranean section of the Caperon aqueduct. A low bridge that once carried the Via Aurelia is marked by massive foundation blocks on each side of the channel.

CARPENTRAS, Vaucluse

Michelin 81–12
IGN 66–11A
3,02/48,95gr
5°03/44°03

Arch and museum.

Only one Roman monument has survived in Carpentras, but an interesting one: a triumphal arch. The best time of the year to visit this market town is spring. Not only is Carpentras well known for its early strawberries, but the open-air theatre will not have been put up. An advantage, perhaps, of a summer visit is that although the lower half of the arch is hidden, the stage platform can allow a really close look at the reliefs. You might need to persuade the attendants to let you in.

The Memini, one of the tribes in the Cavares confederation, lived on the eastern side of the Ouvèze plain, their main oppidum probably on the hill of La Lègue 2 km east of the centre of modern Carpentras. Both huts and imported pottery show the site was occupied from at least the sixth century BC. A Roman foundation here, about 25 km from Orange, Avignon and Cavaillon, ensured domination of this key route from the north into Provence and Italy. Called 'Forum Neronis' by Ptolemy, this might hint at Carpentras as a settlement for some of Caesar's legionaries arranged by Tiberius Claudius Nero (the Emperor Tiberius' father) in 46 BC, after the fall of Marseille. Pliny provides us with its usual name Carpentoracte Meminorum, which could derive, as so many other southern French sites do, from the divinity of a local spring, Carpentus.

The historical development of Carpentras during the Roman period is obscure; inscriptions shed little light on ordinary life, with one exception (see p. 162) and virtually nothing is known from literature.

The triumphal arch

Place d'Inguimbert, in the courtyard of the Palais de Justice, behind the Cathédrale St Siffrein.

During the Middle Ages the arch was moved from elsewhere, probably the main *cardo* leading out of town. It became the porch of the bishop's palace, converted at the revolution into the Palais de Justice. The single-span arch has suffered. The four corner Corinthian pillars are without upper shafts and capitals. The superstructure, from the start of the vaulting up, has been lost and is replaced by a simple sloping roof. Fluted pilasters support acanthus roll decorated arches, but the real focus of attention is the larger than life-size relief figures. The arch commemorates victories in the early first century AD.

The west side

The west side reliefs are best preserved and most compelling. The Romans copied the Greek practice of making a monumental pile displaying defeated enemy equipment and then elaborated on it in two ways: first by ensuring a permanent memory of the victory by carving 'trophies' in stone, second by showing the defeated secured to trophy pillars bearing the trappings of war (see also ORANGE, p. 185, ST REMY, p. 216, and LA TURBIE, p. 273). Here, chained to the pillar, are German and eastern enemies. The German is shown wearing only a thick woollen cloak, his hair in wild curls and blowing out behind him. His wide chest and firm look emphasise the need to control such a powerful, barbaric force. The easterner, head bowed in defeat, wears the Phrygian hat of Asia Minor, an Iranian tunic, baggy trousers and fringed cloak. The pillar between them has part of a breastplate on the top, balanced by two quivers. The Parthian people, ruling Iran at the time, were famous as bowmen. Below is a helmet with two large horns, associated with Germans. The double axe and the curved knife with a bird handle are eastern weapons.

The east side

The eastern reliefs are much more worn. The prisoners, one tall and long-haired, the other squatter, almost dumpy, both wear Greek costume and are from the east, perhaps Syria.

Comtat Venaisson (Comtadin) and Lapidary museums

Boulevard Albin-Durand.
Hours: Tourist season   10.00 a.m.–noon, 2.00–6.00 p.m., closed Tuesday
        Out of season   10.00 a.m.-noon, 2.00–4.00 p.m., closed Tuesday

Comtadin museum

The small finds are kept on the second floor. The display mixes not only artefacts from local excavations and sites in other countries, but also Renaissance bronze figurines with genuine Greek and Roman material. The labelling is minimalist.

Lapidary museum

On request an attendant at Comtadin will take you to the stonework collection in the nearby Rue de Collège. It is simply a storehouse combining quite a large ancient collection with medieval material. In the Middle Ages and later, Carpentras provided a haven for Jews and there is a fine eighteenth-century synagogue in the town. More surprisingly an inscription records the existence of a **Jewish community** in the Roman period as well. It honours Decimus Valerius Dionysus who assisted the Jewish community here by constructing an amphitheatre and decorating it with murals – presumably really funding a communal auditorium for meetings and entertainment.

CAVAILLON, Vaucluse

Michelin 81–13
IGN 66–11B
3,01/48,72gr
5°03/43°52

Arch and local museum.

Modern excavations have shown that Cabellio – or rather the hill of St Jacques, overlooking modern Cavaillon – was occupied from Neolithic times. This was a junction site and remains so, the traffic slowly grinding its way round the modern town, fortunately outside the old centre. Augustan milestones confirm that during Strabo's time the main Italy–Narbonne road came through Cabellio, but crossed the Durance by ferry; there is no evidence for a bridge before medieval times.

The local tribe, the Cavares, seem to have been absorbed first into the orbit of Greek Marseille and then after 49 BC into Roman Narbonensis. By then the focus of the town had moved down from the oppidum on St Jacques into the plain. Ptolemy talks of Cabellio as a 'colony' but there are hardly any other literary references and finds of inscriptions have been few. It was supplied with water by an aqueduct from FONTAINE DE VAUCLUSE, though few traces of its course have been found in the town itself. No public buildings or house plans have been discovered. Of the street plan only the main *cardo* has been identified, traces of Roman road having been found under the Avenue Clemenceau. It met the *decumanus* to the east of the forum, placed roughly by the Cours Sadi Carnot near the church of St Veran. This was the original site of the Cavaillon arch.

The triumphal arch

In the Place François Tourel next to the Place du Clos.

The 'arch' was once a four-sided structure, now reduced by the collapse of the linking vaults to two separate and rather battered arches. Its form probably embodied both Cavaillon's role as a crossroads whilst at the same time proclaiming Roman power, one surviving victory stretches out her palm and crown in a spandrel. The exterior pilasters and their bases, especially that on the north-east corner, show the high quality of the craftsmanship here. The scrolling acanthus design with its birds and butterflies is very like the frieze on the Maison Carrée, but without the mistakes. This stylistic link to Nîmes and Augustan monuments in Rome has led most scholars to accept a date of AD 0–10, as proposed by Gros (1979). It would have been covered with an attic and a statue of some kind.

Cavaillon museum

Porte d'Avignon, in the eighteenth-century hospital (Hôtel-Dieu).
Hours: 1 April–30 September   10.00 a.m.–noon, 2.00–6.00 p.m.
        1 October–31 March   10.00 a.m.-noon, 2.00–5.00 p.m.
        Closed Tuesday.

This collection came into being thanks largely to the devoted efforts of André Demoulin, the museum curator appointed in the 1940s and responsible for most of the limited excavation work in the town itself and on St Jacques hill. Much of the material is from burials and some of the pre-Roman grave goods have been kept together. The presentation is quaint, the wooden cases resonant of provincial traditions and minimal expenditure.

Two broken monolithic stones with skull-shaped cavities show that here too, before the Roman conquest, there was a Celtic head cult (see AIX-EN-PROVENCE, p. 129). There is a fine Roman **Arretine vase**, a product of Cneius Ateius, beautifully decorated with fighting Greeks and Amazons and a **dedication to Diadumenian**. He was the 9-year-old son of the short-lived Emperor Macrinus, who lasted only 14 months (AD 217–18). An elegant lawyer commanding the praetorian guard, he had organised the assassination of the vicious Caracalla, but failed to win the commitment of the army before leading them on an unsuccessful war with the Parthians. He was murdered and along with him his unfortunate child 'Augustus' or joint Emperor. It is a sad insight into the efforts made by Gallic towns to curry Imperial favour by putting up dedications to the new Emperor's family – and the harsh realities of Roman political society.

ISTRES, Bouches-du-Rhône

Michelin 84–1
IGN 66–11D
2,95/48,33gr
5°00/43°31

Museum and oppidum.

Although the town is dominated by the nearby airbase, the attractive new museum (1989) is worth visiting.

Musée d'Istres

Place du Puits Neuf.
Hours: Tourist season   2.00–7.00 p.m. and Saturday also 10.00 am–noon*
        Out of season   2.00–6.00 p.m.
        Closed Tuesdays
        (* groups by appointment other mornings)

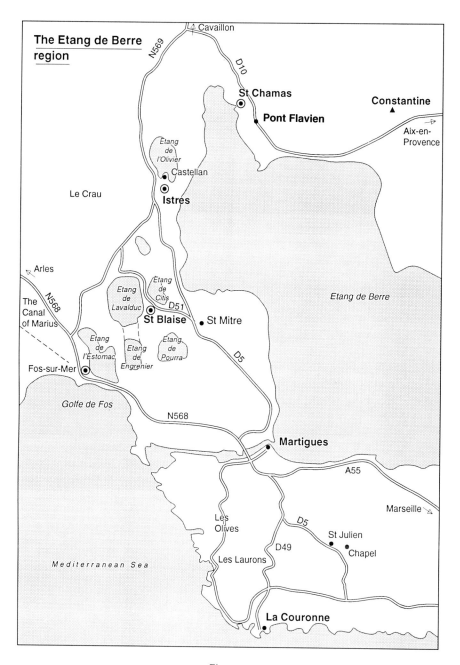

Figure 56

The most important archaeological material in this collection is from underwater excavations in the Golfe de Fos, especially those associated with the Roman port of **Fossae Marianae**.

In 102 BC, during campaigns against the Teutons and Ambrones, the Roman general Marius had ordered the construction of a canal to by-pass the awkward lower waters of the Grand Rhône, enabling ships to sail more easily from the coast to Arles. At the mouth of the canal or fossa a major port and road junction town developed. Changes in the sea level in late Antiquity resulted in most of the town, its harbour installations and its necropoli ending up under at least 4 m of murky water. The large-scale industrial development of the modern Port de Fos has destroyed whatever survived on land. The museum displays selected evidence of the ancient port and shipwrecks recovered from very difficult underwater research work.

An early find in 1960 was the only known **bronze figurehead**, a superb, hairy wild boar still secured to the bronze cap that held it on to the ship's timbers.

Subsequent wrecks have produced one of the finest sequences of amphorae in any museum. A large number come from Lusitania (Portugal) and Baetica (southern Spain) containing various fish sauces. Some have hand-painted labels, showing that they should have ended up with troops guarding the Rhine frontier.

Castellan oppidum

On the hill overlooking the Etang de l'Olivier to the north of Istres. There are directions from the museum and the site has identification labels.

Exposed are a few walls and the stairs cut directly into the rock linking the terracing on which the houses stood. An enigmatic inscription cut in the rock recorded 'a matron', a wife or mother, but using a Greek script.

LA COURONNE, Bouches-du-Rhône

Michelin 84–12
IGN 66–11D
3,02/48,14gr
5°03/43°21

Ancient quarry workings and bas-relief.

The Cap Couronne was well-known in Antiquity as the promontory marking the point where the coastline turns away from Marseille and into the Golfe de Fos, familiar to the coast-hugging seamen of the period. Strabo notes that it was near some stone quarries. Their remnants are now on the shoreline due to the rise in sea levels by 2–4 m in the region.

Quarry workings

10 km from Martigues by D5 and D49 turning right for La Couronne.

La Couronne is a small seaside resort on an outcrop of the bare l'Estaque massif. Take the Chemin de Sémaphore from the town centre down to the parking area in front of the lighthouse. The workings are on the east of the promontory.

Ancient quarrying in this context, beside the vast and timeless sea amongst water-smooth rock, allows the imagination to focus on people undistracted by new or old buildings. It is the quarrymen with their hammers and chisels and the hard labour necessary to break out the stone that spring to mind. One wonders how many were men bound by tradition, and how many were slaves who knew nothing else or criminals condemned to this life.

More workings are visible on the Point de l'Arquet between the Tamaris and Boumaderie bays. The Iron Age village excavated here suggests that exploitation began in the sixth century. The stone was used in Hellenistic Massalia for both the ramparts and the quays.

St Julien-les-Martigues

7 km from La Couronne. By the D9 to Marseille turning left at the next junction, the D5 for Martigues. Access is on the northern side of the road by the signpost marking the beginning of the sprawling village of St Julien.

A badly weathered bas-relief, presumably from a tomb linked to a nearby villa, now decorates the outside wall of a small chapel on a low hill, almost hidden by a pine wood. The style is similar to the mausoleum at Glanum, particularly the tassels (see ST REMY, p. 217); it might have been made by the same team of masons in the late first century BC.

Le PONT JULIEN, Vaucluse

Michelin 81–13 or 84–2
IGN 67–C2
3,30/48,73gr
5°18/43°52

Roman bridge.

8 km west of Apt on the N100, 1 km south on the D149 towards Bonnieux.

The main route from Cisalpine (northern Italy) to Transalpine Gaul (Provence), used throughout the Roman period, crossed the Alps far to the north via Turin, Susa and Briançon, then followed the Durance valley for much of the way. Winding its way down, the road crossed many rivers: this is the only surviving bridge. It is amazing how well the structure has been preserved.

Roman milestone finds from the Mt Genèvre pass to Beaucaire on the Rhône are rare, and none are earlier than the time of Augustus. However, written sources indicate that this was the normal way Roman armies entered Gaul. Perhaps this traditional route, without a serious competitor until the coastal Via Julia was secured and marked out by Augustus (see LA TURBIE, pp. 271, 274), did not need formal establishment, unlike the Via Domitiana, created by Ahenobarbus when he sent out the first colonists to Narbonne in the 120s BC, which extended the road to Spain (see BEAUCAIRE, p. 59).

The bridge itself is a three-arched structure. As with virtually all Roman bridges the arches are semi-circular to minimise the tension on the abutments. They are also different sizes; this ensures that the piers stand on the best foundations possible, here solid bedrock. The Romans constructed their bridges in the summer when the flow was light and the river-bed exposed in many places. The Calavon could, however, be much more dangerous in the winter and to prevent the torrent smashing the bridge the piers were strengthened on the up-river side with buttresses (remains only) and the spandrels have storm-water apertures.

The technique suggests a Republican date: massive masonry is used both for the voussoirs, the wedge-like arch stones, and the rest of the structure. The approach section on the northern side has been rebuilt later as the change in stonework clearly shows. But the Roman parapet support remains, its straight lines clearly showing the pointed hump caused by the wider and therefore higher central arch. Evidence of the building method survives in the corbels under the arches that would have supported the wooden scaffolding while the voussoirs were put in place. The holes in the lower stonework are the result of later damming.

Its attractiveness as a quiet picnic site is largely spoilt by the sewer exit 20 m from the bridge.

MARSEILLE, Bouches-du-Rhône

Michelin 84–13
IGN 67–I2
3,35 /48,11gr
5°22/43°17

Greek and Roman port.

About 600 BC, colonists from Phocea in Greek Asia Minor chose to settle on the low hills of the northern shore of a deep-water creek, a *calanque*, now known as the 'Vieux Port'. It offered considerable benefits: the security of a promontory site, a natural harbour with a narrow defensible entry, only a

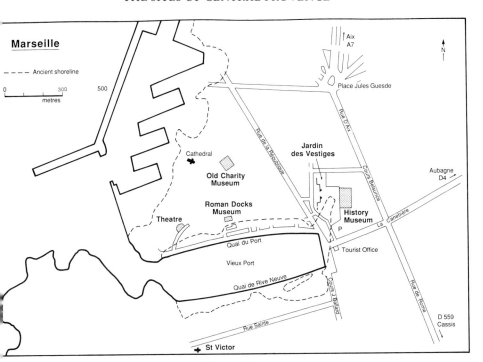

Figure 57

day's sailing from the Rhône River with its markets in the Gallic interior and the potential to develop the long-distance Spanish and Atlantic trade. The antagonism of the local Segobrigii Gauls, according to Justin, was disarmed by the chieftain's daughter Gyptis, who chose the Phocean leader Protis as her husband (a story faintly echoed much later by Pocahontas and Captain Smith in the early English settlement of America). It embodies the normal Greek priorities in colonial settlement, where possible winning acceptance rather than conquest.

Massalia became rich, cultured and famous in the ancient world. Even when it chose the 'wrong' side in the civil war between Caesar and Pompey and the city was captured by Caesar after a long siege and two sea-battles in 49 BC, he did not sack Massalia. The city kept an independent status; though reduced, it retained some inland territory and subsidiary colonies (see NICE, p. 277). Tacitus was not untypical when he wrote on his father-in-law Agricola's education in Massalia: 'a place where Greek refinement and provincial puritanism meet in a happy blend'.

Massalia rapidly established itself as the major Greek power in the west. Her own colonies stretched from Nice to Ampurias (in Catalonia, northern Spain), her goods and those she carried for the Greek cities of Italy and the eastern Mediterranean have been found throughout southern and central

France. We know her ships competed with Carthage for the Spanish metals trade via the Straits of Gibraltar, until Carthaginian Gades (Cadiz) strangled this. Even then some captains managed to push out into the Atlantic: Pytheas reached as far as Norway and Euthymedes returned to describe the crocodiles of the Senegal River.

The position of Massalia was undermined from at least the third century BC as Rome and Carthage emerged as great states locked in struggle: she backed the winning side, but as an increasingly dependent power. A comparison of the origins of amphorae found on Gallic sites shows that Massaliote types are overtaken by Roman ones and that the former virtually disappear in the later second century BC. Certainly some of the great expansion of Roman wine exports must have gone via Massalia, but as passing trade carried by Italian shippers.

It has been suggested that the Massaliotes compensated for their loss of trade by selling Greek technological expertise: city layout, military equipment or economic development, such as olive-oil cultivation and lever-press design. More certainly, territorial expansion took place, and while it could increase opportunities for exploitation, the costs were greater conflict with the Gauls and further dependence on Roman help.

Apparently decisive evidence of Massalia's decline is provided by shipwreck statistics. These suggest that Mediterranean trade peaked in the late Republican period. Massalia could not therefore have compensated for the reduction in territory after 49 BC by returning to international trade, especially in competition with the ports of Arles and Narbonne. Traditionally then, during the Roman era Massalia has been seen as something of a backwater.

The city's own archaeology is not easy to interpret. One problem is a lack of remains. Much of Marseille's development seems to have happened with eyes closed: Massalia was simply not noticed. When it was, a cursory look was followed by rapid destruction or, as in the case of the discovery of an ancient shipwreck in the 1890s, public silence was maintained by the property developers in case the archaeologists came along. Serious study has not been helped by a late nineteenth-century museum curator's habit of claiming finds as new discoveries from excavations in Marseille, when they were in fact bought from an antique dealer who had acquired them from all over the Mediterranean.

Greek pottery and habitation evidence from the sixth century onwards on all three hills immediately north of the *calanque* suggest significant and rapid early success, a city of 50 ha quickly being created. Later, the mid-second-century BC 'Hellenistic' evidence of a water-supply system and the impressive ramparts confirm wealth, even if in a possibly threatened form.

The Roman material is the real surprise. Archaeology reveals large-scale construction of port facilities at the beginning of the era that remained in extensive use into the third century. Excavation in the port area and early church remains confirm written evidence that during the late Roman period Massalia was an active centre. As one of the new generation of Marseille archaeologists has argued, if Massalia experienced decline during the Roman period, it was short-lived.

Theatre

Rue de Martégales.

The small surviving remains of the Roman theatre built at the bottom of the slopes of the St Laurent hill are now surrounded on three sides by school buildings. The remains are not impressive. A few ranks of *cavea* seats can be made out through the railings when the gates of the school are shut.

Although first century AD, it was Greek in design with a circular marbled orchestra and no vomitoria. The most interesting detail is that the seats have been carved with a lip to prevent feet slipping into the backs of people in front: a feature found in Greek theatres in Sicily and the eastern Mediterranean.

Musée des Docks Romains

Place Vivaux.
Hours: 10.00 a.m.–5.00 p.m. daily

The museum covers the eastern half of a warehouse that stood beside the Roman quay. No doubt this was one of many, as the quay, then as now, stretched the full length of the *calanque*, some 400–500 m. These docks were constructed either on the shore itself or on wooden piles. The interior of the museum is dominated by thirty-three massive storage *dolia* – giant pots 1.75 m wide and over 2 m high. They were buried in the floor for coolness and easy access, the foodstuffs inside the jars protected by circular earthenware lids. The east wall has upright roof tiling to allow the air to circulate and keep the temperature down, whilst a north–south channel drains water from the hillside. The south wall opened on to the quay to allow dockworkers access. During excavation, F. Benoit found remains of a second floor which would have given access straight on to the main east–west road. Polychrome marbling and mosaics suggest that this was the business area for merchants and dockmasters. It was built in AD 40–50s and remained in use until the fourth century when a fire destroyed it.

The rest of the museum is almost entirely devoted to shipwreck material. The exceptions are a case of pottery and small pieces found in Benoit's 1947–8 excavations and the **'baigneuse' mosaic**. More than fifty ancient wrecks have been discovered in the *rade* or bay of Marseille. In one corner are stacked various anchor types, lead plumb-weights and metal rings for securing sail ropes. Video programmes (in French) range from the techniques of underwater archaeology and the importance of amphorae, to ancient ship design.

Specific **shipwrecks**, named after the site of sinking, have their own cases. **Planier I** (the first found of at least seven ships that sank around this small island) with its two rare wooden statuettes, one wearing a toga and the other a *priapus* figure whose giant penis has disappeared; perhaps they are the rough-cut workings of a superstitious sailor. From **Planier III** came a set of smooth serpentine weights with their poundage cut on them (X, V, II and an S for semis or half). Lost also was the mixed cargo of oil, dyes and tableware from Puteoli in central Italy sent in the mid-first century BC. The amphorae were stamped and this has made it possible to trace the producers, name the combine formed to ship the cargo and even to suggest that they fell out over the losses sustained and went to court!

The **Grand Congloué** was the first wreck to be excavated using aqualungs and combined the talents of Benoit and the underwater explorer Jacques Cousteau. It did not go well. The specialised techniques necessary for underwater archaeology were only developed gradually in the 1960s and 1970s. Treasure-hunting excited the divers and no archaeologist knew how to dive. The result was that two ships were confused with one another and vast amounts of material were removed by divers tempted by the publicity. It is now clear that the earlier ship sank at the beginning of the second century BC, whilst the second was a first-century BC ship carrying wine amphorae stamped SES, a product of the Sestii family, major aristocratic estate-owners and one of the largest exporters to Gaul in this period.

Jardin des Vestiges

Rue Henri Barbusse.

Marseille is lucky to have one of the best compromises between the need to preserve important ancient remains and to invest in commercial development. The park/museum combination has been imaginatively integrated. Locals and tourists can relax in the gardens and get a taste of the ancient dock area. The museum's large windows and the upper-floor entrance from the shopping precinct all add to a feeling of accessibility to the city's past and its links with the present day.

When the Phoceans arrived at the beginning of the sixth century BC, the eastern side of their settlement was marked by marshy ground merging with the *calanque*. The Greeks rapidly discovered the freshwater springs here, the largest named the Lacydon or Sacred Stream. Gradually the marsh was brought under control, a simple causeway became the major eastern entry to the city and the creek was deepened into the 'horn' that eventually became a harbour.

Marseille
JARDIN DES VESTIGES

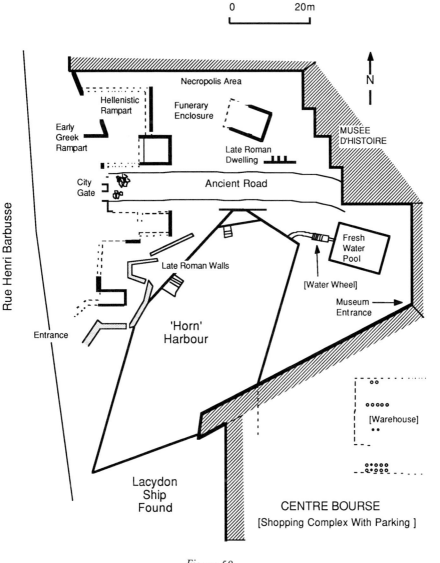

Figure 58

The gate and walls

The 3 m thick Hellenistic rampart is built of large blocks from the LA COURONNE quarries 25 km west of Marseille. The walls are known for at least 200 m further north and remained the city walls throughout the Roman period. The defences were modified in the fifth century AD when a lower curtain wall was added.

The road

A well-constructed road replaced the causeway when the ramparts were built, but the surface of limestone slabs from Cassis, marked with transverse grooves to stop horses slipping, is late Roman work. A milestone dedicated to Constantine II, AD 337–40 was found 30 m east of the gate.

Funerary monuments

A necropolis stretched out beyond the marshes from the fourth century BC. Some early cremation burials are enclosed by stone walls decorated with temple-like triglyphs and metopes. Many more burials are now covered by the commercial centre.

The horn

The Roman dockyard was Flavian. Nine courses of stone blocks made the quays 4.40 m high. A large warehouse, now hidden by the commercial centre, stood on the eastern side. Silt became an increasingly serious problem and modifications had to be made: the freshwater basin was constructed, steps down into the harbour pool added and a low platform built at the tip of the horn. The difficulty was not solved and by the early third century the dock was abandoned. The horn quickly became a disease-ridden, rubbish-filled swamp. In the late fifth century it seems to have been partially cleared for use by boats, but soon reverted to marsh. Surprisingly, late Roman artisans' dwellings were built beside this area! The 'Lacydon' ship, preserved in the museum, sank at the mouth of the dock.

The freshwater basin

This must have seemed a neat solution to a problem. The spring water causing the silting would be used to fill a basin 650 m^3 that could then supply ships with drinking water. Pine pitch was used to seal the masonry. A further refinement was an overshot water-wheel drawing water from the pool.

174

Musée d'Histoire de Marseille

Centre Bourse.
Hours: 10.00 a.m.–7.00 p.m.
    Closed Sunday and Monday

The discovery of the 'Lacydon' ship in 1974 led to the decision to create a museum not only to display the ship but also to portray the development of ancient Massalia.

The Lacydon ship

The ship, minus its prow, which was severed by a mechanical digger, is preserved in a concrete and glass chamber using a freeze-dry technique allowing a controlled, airtight environment. Only the bottom of the Roman merchant ship has survived. A keel 19.2 m long (with prow, estimated 23 m) has timbers attached to it by lead pegs, some internal planking, joined with wooden pegs and caulked with resin. Study of the timbers suggests that from the wood used it could have been built in Massalia and that it had a working life of about forty years. According to the pottery in the deposits that settled on the wreck, the ship sprang a leak in the already heavily silted harbour in the late second or early third century. Perhaps this sinking marked the decision to abandon active use of the horn as a port area.

Greek Massalia

The material surviving from the Greek period is rather thin and broadly religious in focus.

Roman Massalia

A collection of catapult balls marks the siege of 49 BC and introduces the Roman section. There are reconstructions of a pottery furnace and the water-wheel found by the freshwater pool, but the outstanding display of the museum is the **full-scale copy of the Lacydon ship**, a crane poised over it. More than anything else, it shows that the purpose of archaeology and history is to understand the past. A mass of (genuine) amphorae and ingots lie on a quayside waiting for loading; a nearby case has Campanian A pottery stacked with straw. They illustrate vividly that these artefacts – ships and metal, jars and plates – were part of work and commerce as well as art, typology and 'daily life'.

Musée de la Vieille Charité

2 Rue de la Charité.

Hours: noon–7.00 p.m. daily except Saturday and Sunday 10.00 a.m.–7.00 p.m.

This newly renovated museum is housed in the seventeenth-century charity hospital.

The Roquepertuse gallery

In the modern fashion, the sinister aspects of the site, linked as it was with the severed head cult, are stressed with darkness and spotlit highlights. The material seems to be earlier and more stylised than that at Entremont (for a description of the cult see AIX, p. 129). The sanctuary is hinted at with the pillar and lintel portico, decorated with engraved heads and hollows for skulls, framing a cross-legged, headless warrior.

The man wears armour, the square and diamond decoration suggesting plates, with a rigid square projection protecting his shoulders and breast (the Entremont types are chain-mail and clearly more comfortable). His now shattered right arm possibly once held a severed head by his knee.

The strange bird might have stood on the top of the sanctuary roof. At first glance a harmless duck, but note the clawed feet. A less intimidating aspect of the structure is suggested by the fragments of plaster decorated with fish.

Two 'Hermes' heads linked by a mortise and tenon joint with a large lump in the centre implying that they too fitted in the structure, have slightly upturned lips, giving the impression that they are almost smiling. Perhaps the first Gallic stone sculpture derived from Hellenistic examples, but they are absolutely distinctive. The technique is like woodworking, the features sweeping in rather geometric shapes, each individualised and very impressive.

The Gallo-Roman gallery

At time of writing, this was being organised.

St Victor

Place St Victor, Rue Sainte.

The crypt cuts into a necropolis used from the fourth century BC, but is itself late Roman, probably fifth century AD. The two chapels, St André and Notre-Dame de Confession, might be part of the St Victor basilica to which the Marseille bishop fled in the plague of 591. Despite modern excavations, the origins and function are obscure; nothing specific has been found to link them with the abbey of John Cassian (*c.* 360–*c.* 433), who came from Palestine to become an early architect of western monasticism.

MOULIN DES BOUILLONS, Vaucluse

Michelin 84–2 or 81–13
IGN 67–C2
3,17/48,75gr
5°12/43°53

Olive press of Roman design.

On the D148 south of Gordes. 20 km west of Apt, 17 km on the N100 and 3 km north of Beaumettes. Also signposted to Musée du Vitrail.

The Moulin des Bouillons is an old farmhouse in the Calveron valley. The largely sixteenth-century building with its eighteenth-century frontage, the herb garden and geraniums, the whitewashed interior walls and the low vaulted rooms all create a pervading sense of peace and antiquity. A perfect place to find the ingredients of Cato's hors-d'œuvre '*epityrum*', made of stoned and chopped green, black and mottled olives mixed with oil, vinegar, coriander, cumin, fennel, rue and mint.

The mill

Hours: Tourist season   10.00 a.m.–noon, 2.00–7.00 p.m. daily

The inside has been carefully restored to show traditional olive processing. The most important piece of equipment is a massive lever olive press, still in working order and claimed to be of Gallo-Roman origin. This is rejected by J. P. Brun. Unfortunately, no professional excavation has taken place at Bouillons, though there have been Roman finds at the mill and the well-cut 40 m water tunnel from a local spring might have Roman origins. Despite the doubts, nowhere else is it possible to see even an approximation of Gallo-Roman olive processing differing in only minor ways from the technology described by Pliny. Brun has described a second- and third-century AD oil mill with not one but six lever presses – see his study: 'La Villa Gallo-Roman de St Michel à la Garde (Var). Un domaine oléicole au Haute Empire', *Gallia*, 46 (1989). It includes drawings of rather simpler reconstructed presses. There are no excavated oil mill sites open to the public.

Olive exploitation in Provence

Olives have been fundamental to the Mediterranean peasant diet since early classical times. Cato describes how his estate workers lived on bread and olives washed down by wine. They also made a cake from olive paste and were allowed an additional pint of oil each month. But olive cultivation was for more than just local consumption. As well as a food, it was used, then as now, extensively in cooking. It was used in the ritual of cleansing in the baths and as the fuel for lighting. It provided a base for various cosmetic and medical preparations. By Cato's time in the second century BC it had long been a major commercial crop, not just in Italy, but throughout the ancient world where conditions allowed.

Possibly the olive tree was first deliberately cultivated in Provence by the Phocaeans through their colony at Marseille in the sixth century BC. Finds from Gallic sites suggest increasing oil production from the third century BC onwards. Excavations at Entremont and elsewhere have even revealed signs that lever presses were being used prior to the Roman conquest. The growing size of *dolia*, food storage jars, has been interpreted as a sign of the commercial expansion of the olive industry, climaxing in the Gallo-Roman period.

'*Huileries*' have been found at various sites; the best-dated suggest the industry reached a peak in the second century AD. Some seem to have been independent specialist workshops or *officina*, but most have been found as part of villa complexes, forming a major element of the 'rustica' or farming section (as opposed to the 'urbana' or owner's living area).

Olive processing at Bouillons

Harvested at the beginning of winter, the olives were laid out on rush mats and washed, then they were soaked in hot water to soften them and thus make extracting the kernel easier. The stones were extracted by milling, leaving a thick pulp or '*sampsa*'. The stones and residue were not wasted: they were used as fuel to heat the water. The riveted iron pot displayed on the old fireplace is no doubt similar to those used in the Gallo-Roman period.

There were two main types of mills used: the **trapetum** and the **mola olearia**. Remains of the *trapetum* type, particularly the upright curved millstones, the orbs, have been found at sites in Provence, but the mill here is not of this type, despite the label. It is a refined example of a *mola olearia*. The base is a raised, circular, flat surface on which millstones could be wheeled round on their thin edge. The position and base may be ancient, even the use of animal power to turn the '*cupa*', but the Bouillons' example is a highly refined *mola* type – and therefore of largely recent construction – indicated by the complexity of the machinery to control the height of the millstone, the use of iron and the single millstone (the Roman *mola* used two).

Moulin des Bouillons
ROMAN OIL MILL TYPES

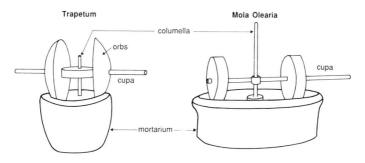

Trapetum
Mola Olearia

columella

orbs

cupa

cupa

mortarium

Figure 59

The lever press

The *sampsa* was put in rush baskets, called in French '*scourtins*', which were then stacked under the press. The first pressing is always the best because it is the purest, but the pulp is squeezed a second and third time after adding water to help separation. The workers still had the job of carefully separating the water waste from the oil; this semi-poisonous mix was, as Pliny pointed out, still useful because it could be used as a weed killer.

Working the press

The press is massive, the beam made of an oak tree-trunk weighing about 7 tonnes and 0.80 m in section. The '*ara*' or plinth for the *scourtins* is placed as near as possible to the thick end of the press. The aim is to release the weight of the tree-trunk and, by attaching it to the floor at the thick end and pulling down the other end, to use the beam as a lever, pressing out the oil into a basin below the plinth.

1 The press rests in equilibrium. The screw shaft holds the beam balance on the wedges at the centre posts. The beam is also held in position by further wedges at the end posts beyond the *scourtin* stack and the screw is secured by the stone weights at its base.
2 The beam is released to begin pressing. The screw is turned to lift the beam off the end wedges, which are then removed from the posts. The weight of the thick end of the beam falls on to the *scourtin* stack.
3 The beam is used as a lever. The thick end of the lever is attached to the ground with a hook and chain. The screw is wound up to lift it from the centre post wedges and these are removed. The screw is then wound up, lifting the stone counterweights from the ground; the beam, held at the

179

Moulin des Bouillons
THE SCREW AND LEVER PRESS

Figure 1 Plan and section   Press set to start operations

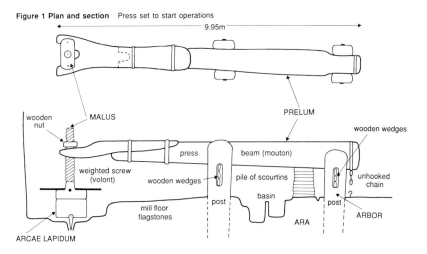

Figure 2 Section   Press at completion of operations

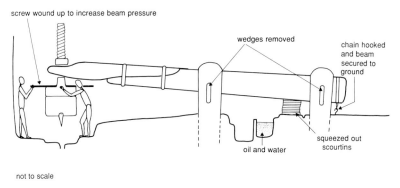

Figure 60

other end, squeezes the last drops of oil and watery scum from the
scourtins.

Musée du Vitrail

In a separate museum of glass-making, there is a small display of Roman
glasswork.

180

ORANGE, Vaucluse

Michelin 81–12
IGN 59–D10
2,75/49,04gr
4°48/44°08

Major urban remains.

The very name Orange is quintessential Provence: redolent of lush fruit, intense impressionistic colour and the threshold of the Mediterranean. This final fancy is not far from the truth. The great north–south route of the Rhône widens at this point and St Eutrope's hill, overlooking modern Orange, dominates the wide and rich agricultural plain. By the second and first centuries BC it was a major settlement site of the Cavares confederation.

According to Strabo, the Cavares dominated the region from Cavaillon to the Isère (Valence). Their key position led Marseille and then Rome to cultivate their friendship, but it was the migration of the Cimbri and Teutons from Jutland that made the vital strategic role of Orange apparent. It was here that two Roman armies concentrated in 105 BC, probably with at least one camped on St Eutrope, but still managing to suffer the worst Roman defeat since Hannibal's victory at Cannae. Subsequently, Marius was able to organise and train a new army which won the decisive victory below Ste Victoire (see AIX, pp. 135–6).

The Roman colony of Orange was the creation of Augustus. In 36–35 BC, whilst he was still called Octavian and still struggling for domination in the Roman Empire, weary and disgruntled veterans of Legion II Gallica were given land here. The full name of the town – Colonia Julia Firma Secundanorum Arausio – encapsulates this military role in the use of '*firma*' or enduring. Arausio was derived from the local spring-god. The intermittent finds of the Augustan city wall suggest they stretched about 3.5 kms and enclosed *c.* 70 ha, a sizeable town. The Avenue de l'Arc and the Rue Victor Hugo follow the alignment of the main *cardo* and the Rue de la République the *decumanus*.

Orange's fame rests on the great triumphal arch and the magnificent theatre, whose serious study and restoration was begun in the mid-nineteenth century by Caristie. During the 1920s–30s the Formigés, father and son, did much to complete the work on the theatre, open up the complex next to it and reveal the Roman foundations on the hill above. Recent excavations have found evidence of public baths and houses on the western and eastern sides of town, but the forum has not been certainly identified yet. Modern work suggests that, like most other cities in the area, the third century saw decline and destruction, but occupation continued and it became a bishopric in the fourth century. Possibly for us the most interesting inhabitant was Ulpius Silvanus. Sometime, probably early in the

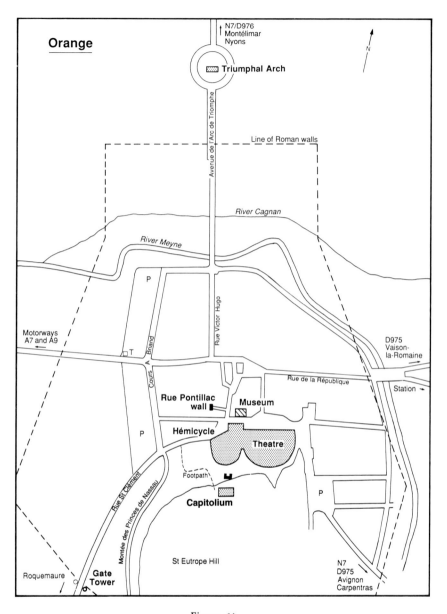

Figure 61

third century, he joined Legion II Augusta, then based in Britain. When a veteran in London, he set up a dedication in the temple of Mithras; perhaps he had worshipped as a boy across the Rhône at BOURG-ST ANDEOL, only 35 km from here.

The triumphal arch

Avenue de l'Arc de Triomphe.

600 m north by the N7 from Orange town centre. Binoculars useful for upper reliefs.

The arch has survived because in the Middle Ages it was converted into a castle guarding the northern approaches to Orange. Caristie carried out a careful study and major restoration work in the 1850s. A hundred years later R. Amy, with the support of J. Formigé, completed what has become the standard study of the arch and more accurate restoration work replaced Caristie's efforts.

Structure and original appearance

The Orange arch was designed to be both massive and flamboyant. Four levels of construction have survived: the three arches; the architrave; a first attic including the pediment, and a second attic, separated from the first by a cornice, modelled into a series of pedestals. Originally it was topped by statues, though what they were is unknown. Probably in the centre there was an emperor standing in a chariot or riding a horse, whilst on the other pedestals might have stood statues of prisoners. The structure from the ground up to the top attic was highly decorated: projecting columns added depth to each side of the arch; rich floral relief was carved on pilasters and arch stones; as many flat surfaces as possible were used for scenes demonstrating Roman might in battle. The whole would have shone with bright paint and the various golden bronze figures and inscriptions, now lost but indicated by the clamp holes. It epitomised the Roman approach to glory and proclaimed victory on land and sea.

The north front

Above the lower side arches are the '**spoils of war**' reliefs. Bundles of lances, curved swords, trumpets, battle standards (animals perched on top of poles), drapery and shields. On the left-hand relief, the central shield has the name Catus engraved in a cartouche. Over the main arch, there is nothing. Normally the corners would be filled with female 'victories': the clamp holes suggest that they were probably in bronze but have been removed. Unusually the frieze is blank. Instead, the architrave below is pitted with the

183

Orange

TRIUMPHAL ARCH
North Front

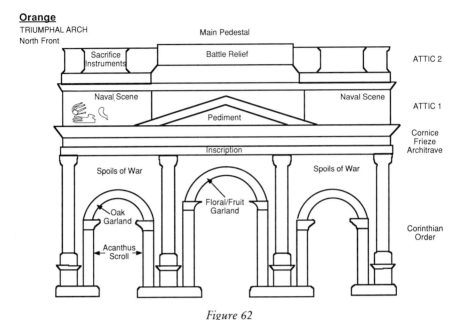

Figure 62

tell-tale **clamp holes of the inscription.** Above the central section a pediment rises from the cornice; once it too was decorated with bronze sculpture.

The first attic carries the **naval scenes** – for me the most striking feature of the arch. There are no complete ships, only elements, giving a rather mysterious underwater effect. Resting on an anchor, a sloping mast dominates the **right relief**, with rigging and a double pulley hanging from it. There is the prow of a ship decorated with a dragon's head and the evil-warding eye; the stern of a ship with its fan-shaped timbers; up-turned three-pronged rams and trident standards. The **left relief** includes more complete rams, these having the bronze sheets that must have encased a ship's prow. Dislocated prow decorations, curving up and ending in a disk, float disembodied amongst more standards and flags.

The second attic has three pedestals, the central one much larger than the others and covered with a **battle relief.** This follows a Greek model depicting a mêlée in which a group of Roman horsemen dominate the group. The most interesting figure is a Roman foot soldier, left of centre, carrying a shield decorated with a capricorn, the symbol of Legion II Augusta. The equipment shown is very accurate and the barbarians are also carefully differentiated between the Gauls, with breeches and bare chests, and Germans, with long breeches and leather caps. On the left pedestal are instruments associated with sacrifice, possibly linked to the setting up of the arch or the foundation of the colony.

Orange

TRIUMPHAL ARCH
East Side

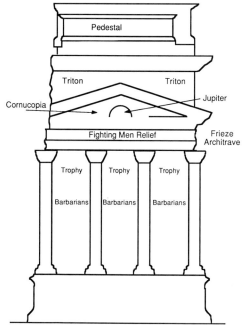

Figure 63

The east side

The four three-quarter-length Corinthian columns create three zones used for **trophy reliefs**. In the middle register – the bottom is blank restoration – and in a poor state of preservation, are barbarian prisoners, hands tied behind their backs, each pair secured to a wooden pillar. Much larger and better versions can be seen on the arch at CARPENTRAS (p. 161). Over them are the actual trophies, cross-shaped clothes horses with tunics hanging from them, helmets covering the upright posts, shields, swords and lances around them and above, the wild boar standards of Gaul.

The frieze carries a register of fighting men. In the centre of the pediment is Jupiter, identified by his sun-god rays, but the attic has the most lively sculpture; two tritons, half-men, half-sea-monsters, fish tails swirling.

The south front

This face is much less well-preserved and has been more heavily restored. The overall design is exactly the same as the north face, but there are differences in the individual reliefs. The right-hand **spoils of war** has more shields with clearly distinguishable names, such as MARIO and AVOT, but the most significant is SACROVIR on a badly broken shield in the bottom left corner.

The **naval scene** on the right includes a gangplank or boarding ladder. The central battle scene on the second attic again depicts Romans fighting both Gauls and Germans.

When and why was it built?

There will always remain some uncertainty about when and why it was built because the clamp holes, unlike those on the temples at Nîmes and Vienne, have not provided an indisputable reading of the inscription. A recent study claims that it is Severan, but most scholars consider that it names Tiberius and that he restored the arch – or perhaps the colony as a whole – in AD 26–7.

The context for the arch was found in the name SACROVIR. Tacitus describes him as the leading figure in a revolt in AD 21 focused on Autun at the other end of the Rhône–Saône valley. The veterans of Orange would be keen to commemorate this victory, if a major role was played by their descendants in the II Augusta. The Legion was based nearby on the Rhine frontier and its capricorn symbol appears on the arch.

This may be too literal an explanation. The name of Sacrovir is not uncommon in Gaul nor is there any written evidence that this particular legion took part in crushing the revolt. Gros (1979) has pointed out that the presence of Germans as well as Gauls and the naval scenes are difficult to explain. He prefers to see it as initially dedicated to the victories of Germanicus on the Rhine, but turned into a more general statement about Roman power by an emperor who had become increasingly resentful about the popularity of his nephew.

The theatre

Place des Frères-Mounet.
Hours: Easter to 30 September 8.00 a.m.–6.45 p.m. daily
        Out of season   9.00 a.m.–noon, 2.00–5.00 p.m. daily

Tickets include the 'hémicycle' complex and a visit to the museum.

The **stage building** totally dominates the square and its surrounding cafés. Its condition is astonishing. An arcade decorates the lower level, and above it are a groove and cornice, which indicate a portico roof that was once supported by a gallery of granite columns running in front of the wall. The western arch end of the portico still stands. Small corbels above show where the exterior sloping roof rested. In the centre three rectangular entrances cut through the wall and took the actors out on to the stage. Other arches gave access to rooms behind the stage. Above the plain moulding and blind arcade are the corbel bases for the curtain masts and, running along the top, the hollow corbels that held the masts upright.

Entrance

The visitor comes into the theatre through one of the barrel vaulted corridors, reserved for the more privileged in Roman times. They were entitled to sit in the two to three rows of wooden seats that once stood on the raised section of the orchestra. They were separated from the rest of the audience by a wall; traces of this *balteus* were found when M. J. Formigé fully excavated and then reconstructed the *cavea* in the 1920s. The excesses of VAISON theatre (p. 229) have been avoided and the seats enable people to enjoy live performances in an ancient context.

The cavea

The seats sit on the natural rock divided into three tiers, enclosed by a semi-circular wall that climbs up the hillside. There were no vomitoria. The audience in the lowest tier came in via the side entrances at the bottom. Those in the top two tiers climbed up steps outside the *cavea* wall and entered at the appropriate level via galleries, one backed by caves, or from the top through a portico (two column stumps have been re-erected on modern bases). A recent estimate suggests 9,000 could have filled the theatre.

The stage and stage building

It is difficult not to be overpowered by the scale of the stage building, to know that the statue of the Emperor in the central niche is double life-size, to see the projecting wings where the actors, musicians and dancers had their rooms, still standing to roof-top level. Yet, as well as the admiration, there is also the regret that there are only hints at the grandiose excess of the *frons scaenae*; the front of the stage building, unlike the sober exterior, gloried in rich embellishment.

Caristie estimated that 122 **columns** filled three levels. Even Formigé's more likely seventy-six can hardly have reduced the impact. He was also responsible for re-erecting a half dozen columns found in the rubble below, adding to the single example that survived *in situ* (second level on the left of the central scene). Scraps of **facing marble** and the clamp holes that held others in place hint at the original bright glare of the surface. Scatters of tesserae show that mosaics must have added colour to the effect. The overall richness would have been further intensified by the **statuary in the niches**.

The broken remains of a Venus were found under the right-hand centre niche.

Perhaps the Imperial statue would not have stood out in the way that it does today, as it would have formed part of a larger composition. The base survived in the central niche and Formigé carefully replaced the legs and torso found in the rubble below. The head and arms he added, choosing to give them an Augustan appearance. The base had a figure in breeches kneeling at the left leg of the emperor, probably a defeated enemy, whilst the space on the right suggests that there must have been a balancing figure there – perhaps a prisoner.

The brown stones are pitted with larger **holes** as well as those for nails and clamps. Many of these are medieval, but some might represent cubby holes for surprise entrances by actors playing gods, just as we know from written sources that some performers were lowered from the roof. The row of nineteen rectangular holes in the top quarter of the back wall show how this **roof** was held in place. Beams sloped upwards until they were level with the front of the *vesurae*. Vitruvius asserted that roofs such as this helped the actors to project their voices, though as contemporary productions here show, the acoustics are splendid anyway.

During the summer season the foundations of the Roman stage structure are hidden by a modern platform. It is not then possible to see the parallel ditches for the curtain, lifted up from the floor by counterweights, with its guide-holes for curtain masts and weights. The fragments of the highly decorated wall, fronting the wide Roman stage area or pulpitum, can be seen in the museum.

No dating evidence has been found for the theatre. Formigé considered that it must be Augustan as the dimensions are similar to those of the theatre at Arles. His conviction accounts for the closeness of the re-creation head of the Imperial statue to Augustus. However, it is quite possible that the theatre is somewhat later, and doubts have been increased by the uncertainties concerning the adjacent site.

The 'hémicycle' complex

The visitor can follow a Roman staircase and landing that lead out from the theatre down to a Roman alley between the theatre and what had become, by the second century AD, a temple enclosure. The rock-face was cut to form a steep semi-circle. J. Formigé, excavating in the 1930s, noted evidence of stairs curving up the face of this rock. These, he discovered, gave access to a small temple 30 m above the precinct, perfectly aligned to the main *cardo*. The scant remains he found are hidden by a water distribution tower.

Portico and temple

The feature that is immediately striking is the massive capital, 1.36 m high, suggesting columns of around 15 m. It is the only complete survivor of the twenty-six that once capped the colonnade surrounding an imposing temple; it is in keeping with a mid-second-century date when large and rather florid styles were in fashion. What survives are the battered remains of the **podium** or temple base.

Around the curve of the rock-face there are sectioned foundations, badly damaged by the medieval housing that stood here. Smashed surviving columns show that these supported a porticoed gallery, awkwardly close to the temple building. This clumsiness of design helped reinforce the belief that the temple precinct represented a change of function on the site. No consensus has been arrived at on its original role.

Circus? Gymnasium? Theatre? Imperial cult precinct?

Caristie thought the hémicycle represented the curved end of a circus. The wall standing in Rue Pontillac (see below) he took to be on the long side of the track. The excavations carried out by both Formigé in the 1920s and Amy in the 1950s mean that this must be rejected: the podium remains and the road across made it an impossible idea. Formigé proposed instead a gymnasium complex: the podium as a wrestling site and the rectangular area, of which the Rue Pontillac wall formed one side, an athletics track. This too seems extremely unlikely: the podium hardly warrants any explanation other than a temple base. The most convincing current interpretations suggest that at first the hemisphere held a theatre, but following the construction of the great theatre next door, the site was used for a temple. The Rue Pontillac wall is explained as the forum enclosure (traditionally the forum has been placed due north of the theatre). Most recently it has been argued that the temple was simply a replacement of an earlier altar: this was the precinct of the Imperial cult, aligned with the *capitolium* on the hill and the forum. The debate continues!

Rue Pontillac walling

The wall is still 16 m high and crosses the narrow street at right angles. A tall arched entrance cuts through here, one of four known as traces of the wall have been found up to Rue Victor Hugo. On each side of the simple entrance are blind arcades. The lower courses are large stonework, the upper *petit appareil*. Formigé noted evidence of a portico running along the inside of the wall. See above for possible interpretations.

Gate tower

Route de Roquemaure, opposite garden centre and the cemetery.

The tower confirms that Orange's defences were built to the same design as Nîmes and are Augustan. Up to a dozen courses of *petit appareil* survive of the 2.5 m thick wall and the circular tower set at an exterior tangent. For what is believed to be a mosaic depicting Orange city walls see the Musée Lapidaire in AVIGNON (p. 155).

St Eutrope hill

Montée des Princes d'Orange Nassau or footpath.

The shaded park is pleasant and the municipal swimming pool might be useful to entertain children – or to cool off after sightseeing. None the less the best reason for coming up here is the superb view. Below Orange and its major sites are laid out before you. Most pleasing of all, the silent wonder of looking down into the theatre and hémicycle.

The Capitolium

On the north-western slope above the hémicycle are the remains of the sixteenth-century Dutch Orange family fortress. Below it, in the north-western corner, are the huge vaulted remains of the foundations of what was probably a *capitolium* platform 60 m wide by 30 m deep facing over the town. Traces of two possible temples were found by J. Formigé and he argued that there must have been a third to provide the triple dedications to Jupiter, Juno and Minerva. Like the inaccessible temple below by the water tower, this too is aligned facing the Cardo Maximus.

Orange Municipal Museum

Place des Frères-Mounet.

Hours: Tourist season	9.00 am–7.00 p.m. weekdays
	Sundays 9.00 a.m.–noon, 2.00–7.00 p.m.
Out of season	9.00 a.m.–noon, 1.30–5.30 p.m.

Tickets include visit to theatre and hémicycle complex.

The museum should be visited because it has a unique find: a Roman land survey inscribed in stone for display in a record office or *tabularium*. Nowhere else has a record of this type survived. These fragments obviously cannot appeal in the way great public buildings or art can immediately win our attention. Nevertheless this aspect of local government takes us to the heart of Gallo–Roman life: land, wealth and ownership.

The tabularium *excavation and display*

In 1949, whilst building a bank strongroom, workers discovered Roman remains. An **emperor's torso** in a military cuirass, an **inscription** recording Vespasian's decision in AD 77 to carry out a land survey and the shattered, incomplete pieces of **three different area surveys**. The walls of a museum room have been used to recreate the record office display, except here there are large empty areas and disconnected jigsaw pieces which at first seem just a jumble of compressed and meaningless script squashed into rectangles. It was the brilliant work of the epigraphist A. Piganiol that managed to make sense of the material.

Cadastration

Cadastre is a French term for the Roman method of land surveying that could be used, as in this case, to cover hundreds of square kilometres. Its basis was the division of land into squares or more rarely rectangles, generally of about 50 ha. The process is called today 'centuriation' after '*centuria*', the Latin name for a block of this type of land, originally meaning 100 holdings, though in reality by the first century AD holdings were much bigger. The Romans called it '*limitatio*' or making balks.

The surveyor and his assistants used a sundial, a *groma* (a cross-staff sighting pole) and measuring rods. A point would be chosen giving a reasonably clear view and a sighting made on an agreed point. Using the *groma* an alignment was made (often a few degrees off the cardinal) and then workers would begin the task of creating four tracks at right angles: the surveyor had created a crossroads. These two principal ways, 40 RF wide, were named the Decumanus Maximus (DM) and Kardo Maximus (KM). Points 2,400 RF along each way would be marked and then narrower right-angle tracks constructed (12 RF wide with every fifth track 20 RF). These would automatically cross, creating standard squares of land in which holdings could be allocated to both new settlers (colonists) and the original inhabitants. Each *centuria* was divided into 200 *iugera* (1 *iugerum* = 0.25 ha) which would be allocated by lot into holdings. Then the surveyor would take the owners to their land and show them the limits which had to be marked with stones. The surveyor would draft a map on papyrus recording the relevant details from which two bronze master maps would be made, one sent to the Rome *tabularium*. The large marble copy was made for tax purposes.

Cadastre '*B*'

Of the three surveys, *cadastre* 'B' was best preserved – 14 per cent survived! Piganiol placed it in an area north of Orange with a sighting point near

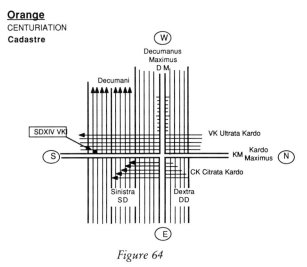

Figure 64

Bollène. The northern most point is the edge of Montélimar and the 1,500–1,700 *centuries* reach near to Orange. Aerial photography has confirmed his identification. It is possible that the survey might have included Arausio itself as the photography shows similarly aligned paths around the colony.

Reading cadastre 'B'

West is the orientation point at the top, and therefore north is on the right. There is little attempt literally to represent the centuriated area. The blocks are shown as rectangles, though the measurements are the standard 2,400 RF square; the tracks are shown as extra wide double lines in the case of the DM and KM tracks, and by a single line for all the others. Most rivers, but only a few major roads are shown. The Rhône and a road figure in fragments at the top (the west!). No attempt is made to portray mountains or settlements, forests or farms.

Centuriae are identified by the concept of facing the orientation point and a numbering system based on the main crossroad. All the tracks running parallel with the DM – the *decumani* – would either be to the left – '*Sinistra*' – or to the right – '*Dextra*'. The Kardo tracks – the *cardines* – were seen as being on the far side – '*Ultrata*' meaning in *cadastre* B west of the KM – or on the near side – '*Citrata*' meaning on the east. These *cardines* paralleling the Kardo Maximus would be identified with either VK or CK. The letters and numbers are used as co-ordinates and are written at the top of each *centuria* block on the survey.

Figure 65 reproduces fragment IIIc 171, a *centuria* in an upper central left position. It was on what is now the north-east of the Ile de St Georges on the

192

Orange

CENTURIATION: CADASTRE B

Fragment IIIc 171	Expanded text	Translation

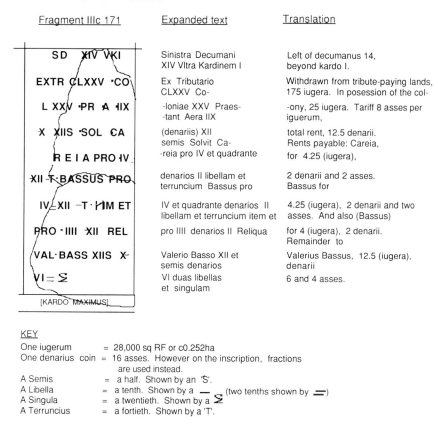

	Expanded text	Translation
SD XIV VKI	Sinistra Decumani XIV Vltra Kardinem I	Left of decumanus 14, beyond kardo I.
EXTR CLXXV ·CO	Ex Tributario CLXXV Co-	Withdrawn from tribute-paying lands, 175 iugera. In posession of the col-
L XXV ·PR A IIX	-loniae XXV Praes--tant Aera IIX	-ony, 25 iugera. Tariff 8 asses per iguerum,
X XIIS ·SOL CA	(denariis) XII semis Solvit Ca-	total rent, 12.5 denarii. Rents payable: Careia,
R E I A PRO IV	-reia pro IV et quadrante	for 4.25 (iugera),
XII ·T·BASSUS PRO	denarios II libellam et terruncium Bassus pro	2 denarii and 2 asses. Bassus for
IV·XII ·T · ΗM ET	IV et quadrante denarios II libellam et terruncium item et	4.25 (iugera), 2 denarii and two asses. And also (Bassus)
PRO ·IIII XII REL	pro IIII denarios II Reliqua	for 4 (iugera), 2 denarii. Remainder to
VAL·BASS XIIS X-	Valerio Basso XII et semis denarios	Valerius Bassus, 12.5 (iugera), denarii
VI = Ɀ	VI duas libellas et singulam	6 and 4 asses.

[KARDO MAXIMUS]

KEY

One iugerum	=	28,000 sq RF or c0.252ha
One denarius coin	=	16 asses. However on the inscription, fractions are used instead.
A Semis	=	a half. Shown by an 'S'.
A Libella	=	a tenth. Shown by a — (two tenths shown by ⹀)
A Singula	=	a twentieth. Shown by a Ɀ
A Terruncius	=	a fortieth. Shown by a 'T'.

Figure 65

west bank of the Rhône (2,62/49,12gr or 4°43/44°13); low-lying land, it is not very fertile, but since Roman times the course of the Rhône has changed significantly and it could have been much richer then. It specifies, like all the other *centuries*, the types of landowner represented here and the taxes due. The Valerius Bassus specified as an owner here may be the proconsul (governor) of Narbonensis asked by Vespasian to carry out the surveys, or at least a relative.

Other fragments use abbreviations not found in Figure 65. IUG is spelt out sometimes for *iugera*. TRIC RED occurs meaning '*Tricastinis reddita*' or restored to the Tricastini tribe, one of the Cavares federation. It may have marked a reconciliation of colonial and tribal interests, but most of the land restored seems to have been in the least cultivable areas! REL COL stood for *Reliqua Coloniae* or left to the colony: this was generally rented out for pasture. Some land was never allocated, it was *subseciva* – 'leftover'. Usually this was in marshland or mountains.

Cadastres 'A' and 'C'

Aerial photography has shown up a number of other Roman centuriations in the lower Rhône, but there is less agreement on which ones 'A' and 'C' portrayed. Though there are only forty-seven fragments of *cadastre* A there is now agreement that they show the Avignon area by the junction of the Durance and Rhône. However, the area covered by *cadastre* C is still disputed: it has been argued that it really covered the Arles area, rather than Carpentras as Piganiol thought. The emerging consensus is that the *tabularium* in Orange was responsible for much more than the colony, perhaps acting as a regional record office.

Finds from the theatre

Pulpitum wall and *frons scaenae* frieze figures feature Amazons, centaurs and nymphs. In addition there is a copy of a fine *oscillum* (the original is in Geneva) showing Pan.

Mosaic

From the seventeenth to the early nineteenth century, Orange had the most celebrated mosaic in the south of France: somehow it disappeared. A similar fate nearly befell the one mosaic now in the museum. It was found in 1936 in a vaulted room (possibly part of a *nymphaeum*) on the south-east side of the theatre *cavea*. Unfortunately, though almost perfectly preserved, it was left exposed *in situ* and half of this carpet mosaic was destroyed, including the central Medusa's head. The dolphin and fruit decorations remain attractive.

ROQUEPERTUSE, Bouches-du-Rhône

Michelin 84–2
IGN 67–G3
3,25/48,37gr
5°16/43°32

Sanctuary site.

Hidden on a rocky spur 1.5 km north-north-east of Velaux. The Chemin Roquepertuse runs along the southern side of the railway, near the roundabout linking the turning to Velaux and the main D20 Berre L'Etang–Aix road (see Figure 66).

Roquepertuse

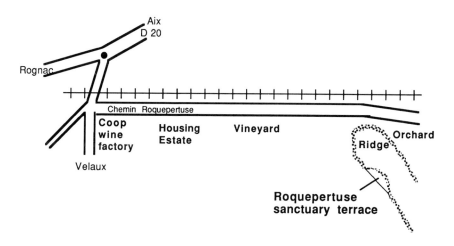

Figure 66

The sinister bird, striking seated warrior and remains of the sanctuary itself are on display in the Musée de la Vieille Charité, MARSEILLE (p. 176), but the site of Roquepertuse provides the context that a museum cannot give. The low hill projects north towards the River Arc, concealed in the valley beyond the railway. The sanctuary itself is hidden on a terrace in a natural hollow behind the spur. Pine trees cover the slopes and the site is approached through these woods. This enclosed approach, shaded and seemingly cut off from the modern world, insinuates a feeling of mystery and enigma.

Roquepertuse was first excavated in 1919–27 by Gérin-Ricard, who found the sanctuary remains and a half dozen dwellings. He suggested a third-century BC date. In the early 1960s Ambard re-excavated the site, trying with little success to get a better picture of its stratigraphy, though he confirmed the lack of significant habitation in the immediate area. However, recent survey work has shown the sanctuary was at the centre of a large number of oppida in the neighbourhood: Rognac, Roquefavour and St Propice are just some of those known on nearby hills. Perhaps it was a spot dedicated to the fighting spirit of the Salyens, or the aristocratic warriors who did the fighting. Lucan, in his epic, the *Pharsalia*, perhaps meant this place when he described the shocked and frightened soldiers ordered by Caesar to destroy a sanctuary during the siege of Marseille in 49 BC:

A grove there was, untouched by men's hands from ancient times,
whose interlacing boughs enclosed a space of darkness and cold shade

195

... gods were worshipped there with savage rights, the altars were heaped with hideous offerings and every tree was sprinkled with human gore.

Remains of the 22 m long walls forming a platform and the steps made with large blocks can still be made out at the back of the terrace just below the top of the hill. In front were buried nine storage *dolia*: the guardians' food supplies? water collection? or offerings? Gérin-Ricard had no suggestions. The sanctuary remains and the statues were found scattered on the terrace, and amongst these finds were catapult arrowheads, ballista bolts and stone shot: apparently the final destruction was Roman work, but there was no clear dating evidence. Was it 49 BC, or the 125–123 BC campaign?

ST BLAISE, Bouches-du-Rhône

Michelin 84–11
IGN 66–11D or 67–G1
2,94/48,29gr
4°59/43°27

Gallo-Greek ramparts and town.

Amongst the *Etangs* of the eastern Rhône delta, the easiest approach to St Blaise is from St Mitre-les-Remparts on the Martigues–Istres D5 road, 5 km west on the D51. St Blaise is about 40 km west-north-west from Marseille and 43 km south-east from Arles.

Obvious Roman involvement at St Blaise is minimal: little more than responsibility for its destruction. Interpreting 'Gallo-Roman' in a broader sense, then fifth- and sixth-century late Antiquity is certainly represented, but the real justification for visiting St Blaise must be to see the finest stretches of Hellenistic fortification in southern France. Henri Rolland divided his life's work between St Blaise and Glanum (see ST REMY, p. 202) and he cleared most of the visible remains. Since his death and burial in St Blaise church (1970), new work, inspired by Bernard Bouloumié, has led to significant revisions.

The 5.5 ha plateau of St Blaise rises sharply above the *Etangs* of Lavalduc and Citis; sloping up from the north, it reaches 63 m near the southern end. The view is astonishing. To the east, looking out across the Etang de Berre, the Equilles hills around Aix shimmer in the heat haze; to the west the bleak desert of the Crau stretches away; to the south the petrochemical plants of Fos glow malignantly. Once this was open sand bars with narrow channels allowing low draft boats access from the sea, at least some of the way into the *Etangs*. St Blaise had natural strength, nearness to the sea and relative ease in reaching it, close proximity via Fos to the Rhône and the internal markets of Gaul and the resources of the *Etangs* all around, primarily salt and salted products like fish and oysters. It did not have water – the spring line is 25–30 m below the plateau – and an inland hilltop site cannot have been convenient: it was a site used when such compromises were necessary.

Settlement before the seventh century BC was minimal, but the sudden appearance c. 625 BC of a large walled town suggest conditions were now appropriate. **St Blaise III** with its irregular stone-built houses, streets and a 400 m rampart securing the weakest side of the hill is a typical local oppidum. However, recovered from the remains was the largest collection of Etruscan pottery and amphorae found anywhere in southern France. The Etruscan cities of central Italy perhaps used St Blaise as a trading entrepôt, mixing its long distance opportunities with the development of local resources, the site and its rampart providing essential security against Greek competitors and local jealousies.

However, during the second half of the sixth century competition with the Greeks in the western Mediterranean and the rise of Massalia (see MARSEILLE, pp. 168–70) severely limited Etruscan involvement in Provence. St Blaise III, although probably never abandoned, certainly experienced serious decline and new building is extremely rare in the next three centuries.

Dramatic change occurred at the end of the third century when the town was totally reconstructed. **St Blaise V** was created by levelling the old site, covering it with a layer of sand and building new stone and mortar-lined houses on a grid pattern design based on a main north–south road: features characteristic of the trends in local oppidum design. The mix of Massaliote, Campanian and indigenous pottery can be found in many other Provençal sites. There are even hints that the notorious severed head cult (see AIX, p. 129) was practised here as pillars, one with the hint of a skull hollow, linked to severed head sanctuary design, have been identified recently. But unlike most other sites, except Glanum (see ST REMY, p. 204), there is the striking evidence of direct Greek involvement: the ramparts.

The sophisticated design, distinctive stonework and high-quality workmanship are typically Hellenistic Greek. Current dating suggests that they were built c. 170–140 BC, when Massalia too put up major new defences. Unlike Massalia, here there is evidence that the ramparts were quickly breached. Stone shot and metal bolts scattered in the houses round the gates and the deliberate dismantling of the walls show that the town was captured by a well-equipped army. Once again a period of minimal occupation followed.

As the pottery sequence ends in the later second century BC, the most obvious date for the siege would be during the 125–124 BC Roman campaigns. Who then were the defenders? The Massaliotes had asked the Romans for help, it therefore seems unlikely that they controlled St Blaise. Perhaps this was a native oppidum governed by the local Avatici tribe (part of the Salyens confederation) who had paid for Greek fortification expertise but had not conceded any political control. As a major stronghold, the

Romans would have felt the need to crush its occupants. No doubt the survivors moved down to Fos or to the villa estates that emerged in the area.

The final phase of occupation on the hill began with the onset of unsettled conditions in the third century AD. **St Blaise VI** grew in the fifth–sixth centuries to cover most of the hill again. Another new rampart was constructed, using many of the stones taken from the Hellenistic wall and following a very similar line. This time the defences were strengthened with ten towers. A major sacking by the Saracens in the ninth century began a steady decline, represented by the new wall across the centre of the hill in 1231, creating the shrunken settlement of Castelveyre. By the fourteenth century, its church, St Blaise, had become a hermit's home and the rest of the hill was given over to olive trees, pines, sheep and shepherds.

Site

At the beginning of the 1990s, there was no proper site museum, and the bulk of Rolland's finds were still hidden from the public in St Rémy. There are a few signs to help visitors, but they are old and now inaccurate, particularly the dates. By the car park, the first is enigmatic, simply stating 'St Blaise', but giving no indication of direction. Avoid downhill paths! See Figure 67.

Eastern postern and rampart

The eastern end of the wall has been lost, but there must have been a gate to the nearby spring. The path takes you outside the defences.

Rolland's excavations exposed some 30 m of Hellenistic curtain walling rising five courses. Above and behind it, half hidden by vegetation, there is the cruder fifth–sixth century AD tumble of walling with a semi-circular tower in the centre. A line of merlons that once formed the walkway crenellation about 6 m up now stand facing the rampart; and behind them, a rough outer defence that might have been emergency building in the 120s BC.

The Hellenistic stonework is the exterior facing of a 3–4 m thick rampart. The elegant blocks are *c.* 50 cm thick and of varied length. Placed on deep foundations often cut into bedrock, they have been laid with headers to strengthen the rubble core, but no mortar was used. The chevron chisel marks are typical of Greek workmanship. Some blocks have Greek letters on them, put as masons' team marks or to define different rampart sections. Occasionally headers are left embossed, though why is unclear.

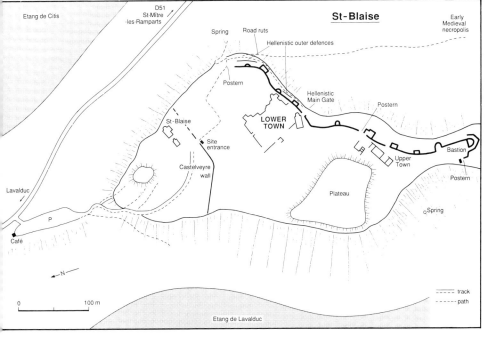

Figure 67

Main gateway and lower town

The main gate of both St Blaise III and V was set at the point where the plateau begins to rise towards its highest point. In late Antiquity this was closed off by the new rampart. There is evidence of all three periods of rampart construction.

The large **square tower** projecting from the northern medieval wall looks Hellenistic as it is entirely built of Greek stonework, but uses mortar. The square Greek tower guarding the gateway was separate from the rampart itself creating a false postern; it has been reduced to two courses. Inside the gate, there are buildings of all periods. **St Vincent church**, built across the main north–south second-century BC road, was the town's oldest (fifth–sixth century AD).

Upper town and southern bastion

Amongst the upper town houses, some with small mills and olive presses, there is a **pit** enclosed by a metal fence. It goes down 25 m, but stops short of the spring-level. Was it a failed attempt to reach a secure source of water during the siege?

The **best preserved Hellenistic walls** are at the southern tip of the plateau, the most vulnerable point for the town. Behind this facing was a particularly thick rubble filling including archaic tombstone-like pillars. A postern on the western side gave access to the spring, 30 m down the slope.

Behind and above the Greek bulwark is ruined medieval walling and a wall of uneven large stones, part of St Blaise III's defences.

The plateau

Largely unexcavated except for some massive foundation stones that might have been a watch tower (see Tour Magne, NIMES, p. 100), naturally the views are best from this vantage point.

ST CHAMAS, Bouches-du-Rhône

Michelin 84–1/2
IGN 66–11C or 67–F1
3,01/48,37gr
5°04/43°33

Roman bridge.

Le Pont Flavien stands near the northern shore of the Etang de Berre, by the D10 road, 37 km west of Aix-en-Provence and 7 km short of Miramas.

The setting is a little bleak: glaring, exposed rock with the summer trickle of the Touloubre River on the outskirts of semi–industrial St Chamas. But the small humpbacked bridge, with its two ceremonial arches at each end, is one of the most delicate and beautiful Roman bridges outside Italy. The modern bridge skirts it 50 m to the south.

Its attractiveness and use have contributed to its durability. By the end of Antiquity the wheels of carts were digging deep ruts into the arch stones, having worn right through the road. Resurfacing, particularly in the seventeenth century, helped prevent the collapse of the bridge. None of the rutted pavings exposed on the bridge today are Roman and the parapets too are modern. Only one of the four lions, that on the right-hand side of the eastern bank, is original; the other three are eighteenth-century copies, made when the western arch collapsed and was rebuilt, fortunately using ancient stone. The blocks added at the foot of the arches, to prevent wheels catching the pilasters, did nothing to stop the western arch yet again suffering. During the Second World War first a German tank ran into it, then an American truck completed the collapse! The arch was once more painstakingly reassembled. The decision was at last taken to by-pass the bridge.

Le Pont Flavien probably replaced an earlier wooden bridge, since even in the pre-Roman period the *Etang* was surrounded with settlements and actively involved with trade. The arch stones must have been lowered into place by crane; their grip holes are offset so that they would hang at an angle and could therefore be lowered into place with minimum adjustment. It represents a striking example of Roman engineering refinement.

The bridge and the arches appear to be contemporary: though the arches themselves use a white limestone, their bases are made of the same yellow limestone as the bridge. The inscription seems to embrace both and points to their funding from a private source:

> L(ucius) Donnius, son of C(aius), Flavos, flamen [cult priest] of Rome and Augustus, has ordained in his will that [this monument] be built under the direction of C(aius) Donnius Vena and C(aius) Attius Rufius.

Flavos probably owned land here and is likely to have been both a major figure in the local tribe, the Avatici, and a leading citizen of Arles, to which this area belonged. His mausoleum may have stood nearby, though no remains have been found. A recent study of the stylistic elements stresses the memorial features: the wave pattern on the frieze was frequently used as a funerary symbol, implying the constant rebirth of life; eagles, above the capitals, and the free-standing lions are commonplace on tombs; arches and bridges in themselves can reflect the passage of life. Though the inscription is undated, the most likely period is 20–10 BC. The wave pattern and the acanthus leaves on the capitals seem a little earlier than the Maison Carrée, whilst lions were particularly popular in Provence in the latter first century BC. The death of Flavos could therefore have occurred when Agrippa was carrying out his road-building programme for Augustus in the 20s BC. Like the Julii family of Glanum (ST REMY, p. 218), with their grandiose mausoleum, the bridge and its arches would state to everyone who travelled the road that this Gallic aristocrat had become truly Roman.

ST REMY-DE-PROVENCE, Bouches-du-Rhône

Michelin 81–12
IGN 66–9/10B
2,78/48,65gr
4°50/43°47

Major ruins of Glanum, arch and mausoleum.

30 km south of Avignon by the D571.

Provençal towns like Orange, Arles and Vaison, with a continuous history from Antiquity, grew amongst and over their Roman ruins. St Rémy though, developed round a road-stop 2 km to the north of Glanum. Strangely, the atmosphere of the two places is similar: both seem almost to wish to hide themselves away from outsiders. However, appearances and feelings can deceive because the existence of both Glanum and St Rémy has been based on their position at a road junction. The Vallon de Notre-Dame de Laval provides the one relatively easy valley route south through the jagged peaks of the Alpilles. In Antiquity, the main east–west route from Italy skirted the range, creating a crossroads at Glanum. Communications stimulated both the original urbanisation of a spring sanctuary and the subsequent emergence of St Rémy on a realigned east–west road, now the D99.

Recognition and excavation

The site of Glanum has never been lost. 'Les Antiques', the local name for the triumphal arch and mausoleum, were already well known in the Middle Ages. Glanum had been plundered in Antiquity for its cut stone and was covered with a layer of alluvial wash brought down by the winter torrents, but in the seventeenth and eighteenth centuries there were still walls and columns poking above the surface. Treasure-hunting was both popular and successful.

It is surprising then that organised excavation only began in 1921 when Jean Formigé joined with the local scholar Pierre le Brun to carry out work on the eastern side of the D5 until the Second World War brought this to an end. They exposed many of the houses in the northern sector. In 1928, the great **Henri Rolland** began work on the western side of the road where the valley narrows to a bottleneck. He discovered the sanctuary and then left for work elsewhere (see ST BLAISE, p. 196). Already a veteran of Verdun during the First World War, he fought again at Dunkirk, was captured and interned. His release in 1942 coincided with the death of Le Brun, one of the many civilians to 'disappear' in the war. Rolland now became responsible for the entire site. His achievement here was immense, revealing most of the remains visible today. A new team, including Anne Roth-Congés and Pierre Gros, began work at Glanum in the 1980s and have been able to refine, clarify and extend Rolland's work.

Evolution of Glanum

The Vallon de Notre-Dame de Laval attracted intermittent settlement from the beginning of the first millennium BC. By the sixth century BC, a small permanent site had been created by a perennial spring in the gorge and a deep natural crevice on the hillside above. Finds of strange monolithic pillars, reused for Gallo-Roman building, suggest that it was a sanctuary site from the beginning and that the associated beliefs go back to similar and equally mysterious Neolithic megaliths.

Glanum I is the term Rolland used for the town that had emerged by the second century BC. The gorge itself had little space and the town emerged to

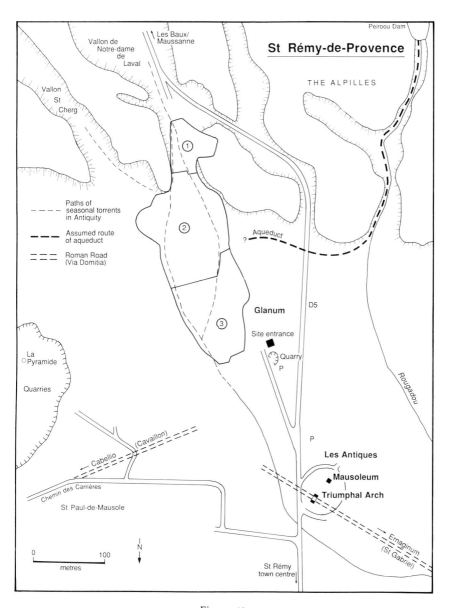

Figure 68

the north. A rampart was built sealing off the 'sacred' area; the striking feature of this short wall and gateway is its distinctive Hellenistic construction, something that also typified much of the public and private buildings elsewhere. It seems likely that Greek engineers acted as advisers here. So strong is the Greek influence, that Glanum seems to have developed as a Gallo-Greek town rather than a Gallic oppidum.

Two destruction levels mark the end of this phase. The first is dated to the 120s BC, the second to the 90s BC. They have been identified with the Romans' initial defeat of the Salyens confederation, to which Glanum would have belonged, and their subsequent abortive rising. This last thirty years saw Hellenistic Glanum reach its peak with a number of buildings of apparently pure Greek type, yet without Gallic elements totally disappearing. It could be that in this period, Glanum was made part of Marseille's territory.

Glanum II: at first, following the ransack and ruin of the 90s BC, there was barely more than a squatters' occupation, suggesting only a gradual return to urban life. Subsequently, homes of irregular stonework were built over the public buildings in the monumental area. From the mid-first century BC, they were replaced by well-constructed houses, rich in mosaic floors and painted plaster walls, that ignored the earlier town planning. It looks like an elite reasserting and redefining themselves, individually adopting Roman ways.

Glanum III was a creation of the Augustan period: two forums, twin Imperial temples, a baths, a triumphal arch and probably an aqueduct – perhaps a theatre – all by AD 10. The basilica and curia came later in the first century, followed by the remodelled baths, but there is no evidence of any significant building activity in the second century. It implies a decline in prosperity which is supported by the poor quality pottery finds and the small number of coins. Third-century material is sealed below a metre-thick sediment brought down by torrential washes: the sewerage had broken down totally. Glanum appears to have been abandoned. Some evidence of fire has been interpreted as the work of barbarian invaders, but it was a town already living in reduced circumstances. There was a minor reoccupation on top of the old sanctuary in the fifth century AD, but since the fourth century the real late Roman centre had been the road-stop or villa on the new road alignment that was to become St Rémy.

Glanum site

Hours: Summer   9.00 a.m.–noon, 2.00–6.00 p.m.
        Winter   9.00 a.m.–noon, 2.00–5.00 p.m.

Glanum should be visited from the higher, southern end. Not only is it less exhausting taking your time coming down the slope, but it is also more logical, enabling you to see the earliest material first. It also takes you to the original *raison d'être* of the site – and the most evocative. Gallo-Greek and Gallo-Roman public buildings I distinguish from each other by lower and upper-case titles.

1   The sanctuary area

The rocks, the pale green grass, the smell of thyme, the birdsong all help to distance the modern world; it is a place to sit and feel the immediacy of the past – and perhaps people that vision.

The sanctuary

Steps on the west side of the road lead up to the terrace where a natural hole in the hillside had become the centre of the cult of Glan and his associates, the Glanicae. Two inscribed altars stand beside the steps. One, by the road, is in Greek script and is dedicated to the mother goddesses; the other, in a niche, records the thanks of a veteran of Legion XXI 'Rapax' (the greedy) to Glan, the Glanicae and Fortuna Redux, the personification of luck in getting home again.

Buildings to the south

The process of re-examining this section since Rolland's excavations has only just begun. Next to the niche and porter's lodge(?) at the foot of the sanctuary steps is a building that had a hypocaust. It was possibly a **small bathhouse** of Hellenistic date. Other buildings were houses which have re-used in their walls the **monolithic pillars** that had once been scattered on the hillside around the sanctuary.

The 'spring'

Opposite the sanctuary, a staircase, with one restored vault, leads down to an underground collecting basin. Beautifully cut large blocks epitomise the art of Hellenistic masonry. Proximity to the sanctuary and money found hidden in the crags below imply that this water source formed part of a cult, devoted to healing, common enough in Gaul. Also suggestive is the presence of temples on each side of the spring dedicated to the struggle against sickness.

TEMPLE OF HERCULES

A statue and inscribed base were discovered in this small square building. It records the thanks of C. P. Cornutus and a group of soldiers to Hercules

St Rémy-de-Provence

GLANUM:
1 Sanctuary Area

0   20m

N

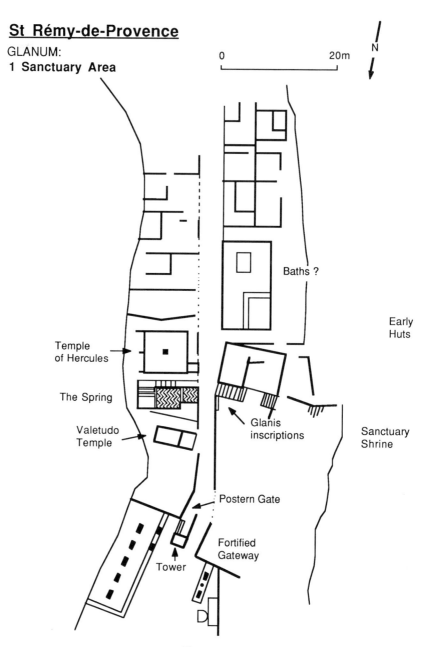

Baths ?

Early
Huts

Temple
of Hercules

The Spring

Glanis
inscriptions

Sanctuary
Shrine

Valetudo
Temple

Postern Gate

Fortified
Gateway

Tower

Figure 69

Victor for their safe return. Though we see him as a strong man hero, in the ancient world he was a protector in the broadest sense. A further five altars were found here.

Fortunately a section of the architrave of this attractive little temple with its three fluted columns has survived. It provides a dedication to 'Good Health' by Marcus Agrippa. It could date back to Agrippa's first visit to Provence in 39 BC, but more likely, now that the forum has been dated to the *c.* 20 BC, is that Augustus' son-in-law came to Glanum in 20–19 BC.

The fortified gateway

The gate isolates the sanctuary area from the rest of Glanum. Its walls close the defile and create a long passage for the road. Pedestrians could enter by a postern behind the tower on the eastern side of the road. Its Greek origin is clear: the large masonry, the rounded merlons that once topped the crenellation and the remains of gargoyles that drained water from the walls. Similar fortification is known at MARSEILLE and ST BLAISE.

2   *The monumental area*

More is known about this part of Glanum than any other, but it does not make it easy for the visitor to comprehend. The extensive excavation has revealed too many ravaged, overlapping buildings from different periods. The maps separate the two main phases, Gallo-Greek and Gallo-Roman, but intermediate Glanum II buildings appear on both.

The portico

Two Doric column bases of the portico survive, whilst five bases set in the middle of the building must have supported the roof. The dimensions and design of this building are very similar to those of the portico at Entremont (see AIX, pp. 133–4). Close by were found pillars with carved skull-shaped hollows, clearly dumped there at a later date. Was this portico also associated with the severed head cult or, as Rolland thought, was this a pilgrim's wash-room (note the basin here) and had the pillars been brought down from the sanctuary? Facing the portico on the west side of the gateway were **small chambers** for two seated warrior statues (see museum, p. 220). Did the portico perhaps become a wash-room only when the warriors were replaced by altars in the Roman period?

St Rémy-de-Provence

GLANUM

2 Monumental Area
   (a) Gallo-Greek

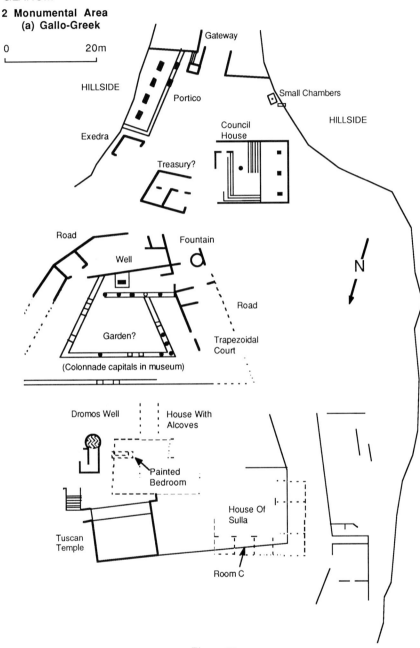

Figure 70

St Rémy-de-Provence

GLANUM

2 Monumental Area
(b) Gallo-Roman

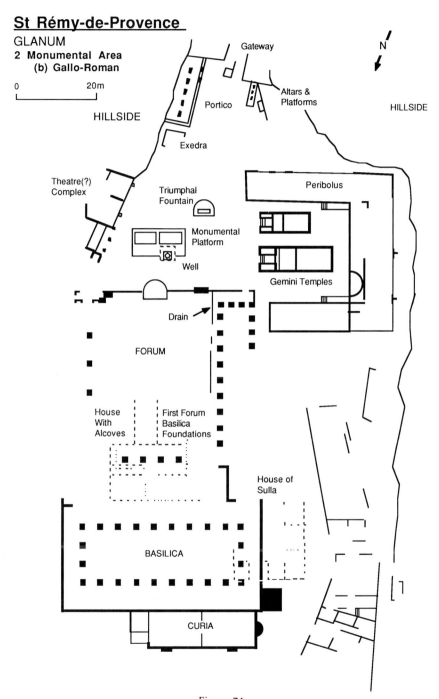

Figure 71

Although this certainly dates back to the Gallo-Greek period, the actual structure is late, the AD 70s or 80s. It is a decorative feature faced with white marble and provided with a stone bench. It seems to have been a good place for graffiti. When Rolland excavated the site, the outline of a Roman merchant ship was quite clear, now it is almost impossible to make out despite the protective glass.

THEATRE COMPLEX

Rolland excavated some porticoed buildings on the east of the site which appeared to him to suggest the rear structures of a theatre. Excavation in the 1990s should settle the matter.

Treasury and FOUNTAIN

The fragments of a small **double-roomed building** can be made out between the *exedra* and the council house. Tentatively identified as a town treasury, simply because Greek cities normally had them, in the Roman period it was pulled down. Behind this, there is the base of a **semi-circular fountain** decorated with reliefs of Roman victories over the Gauls (see Dépôt).

Council house

More than any other building this embodies Hellenism. A large rectangular room has stepped seats on three sides. In the centre there is a circular altar base. The *bouleuterion* has been found widely in the eastern Mediterranean and was the meeting-place of city councillors. It would have been in use from the second century BC, possibly into the first century AD when the southern gallery of the Gemini temples was constructed over half of the chamber. By then, the forum had been built in a more grandiose form and this small assembly room must have seemed out of date.

GEMINI TEMPLES

Despite the ruinous appearance (being restored in 1990s), it is obvious that the 'twins' and their surrounding gallery or *peribolus* formed an imposing sanctuary.

The temples are of the classic Roman type: high platform, steep steps at the front, a foyer or *pronaos* with six Corinthian columns and a rear *cella*. More of the small temple's platform has survived, but the quality of the masons' work on fluted columns, the floral decor and the beautiful *acroteria* suggests that both could have ranked with the Maison Carrée. The *peribolus* was equally well made. Partially cut into the rock itself, the foundations were buttressed with large semi-circular walls. The gallery with its open portico was reached by stairs in the rear corners. Architecturally it gave the temples unity.

Rolland believed they were dedicated like the Maison Carrée, to Lucius and Gaius, the adopted sons of Augustus. Current work points to slightly earlier construction. Gros argues that they are not twins and the style of the smaller temple is *c.* 30 BC, while the larger is better dated to *c.* 10 BC; the *peribolus* follows ten years after that. He suggests that they possibly started as temples to other gods (e.g., Sylvanus and Hercules), but were later adapted to emperor worship. It is still possible that the statue of a headless adolescent found by Rolland between the temples, and claimed by him as undoubtedly Lucius, could really be the unlucky youth. Restoration work may clarify their purpose.

Trapezoidal Court and MONUMENTAL PLATFORM

Some 25 m from the larger Gemini temple, large blocks were used to create a platform at the end of the first decade AD. It once carried some represen-tation of Roman power. It covers a **well**, possibly once sacred to the Gallo-Greek community of Glanum, and the traces of a large building. The well was the central feature in a series of rooms, the largest with mosaic and wall decor. The plan (rooms and 'garden') and the finds of food imply a house, but the superb figure-decorated capitals from the portico (see museum, p. 220) suggest a ceremonial role. Anne Roth-Congés has pro-posed that this was a *'prytaneum'* or symbolic home of the polis or state of Glanum, where magistrates and ambassadors would meet for state dinners.

FORUM

When the forum was built, older structures were levelled or Roman foun-dations driven into them to support the forum buildings.

Excavation has revealed remains down to near the bedrock, but at the cost of leaving what remains of the forum floor significantly above much of the current ground level.

There were two main phases of building: a simple forum early in the 20s BC and a grander rebuilding in the AD 10s with a large basilica at the northern end. A few years later, an annexe of rooms was added beyond the basilica. Development ended when the open southern end was closed off in the AD 70–80s.

The **southern enclosing wall** with its grandiose semi-circular *exedra* in the centre is well preserved. The interior court of the forum is non-existent, but a few sections of **side portico paving and gutter** survive. The basilica is represented best by the massive square **foundation pillars**.

Amongst the structures exposed below the forum is the square Hellenistic **Tuscan temple** with its two external side staircases, high podium and Tuscan-style capitals. But more exciting was the discovery in the 1980s of the unsuspected **Dromos well** with its three flights of stairs down the water-level. Like the spring in the sanctuary area it is likely to have been sacred, linked to the Tuscan temple. After the sack in the 90s BC it was broken but remained in use until the forum was built. In late Antiquity, when scavengers removed the best forum building stone, they used the well as a dump for less useful architectural statuary. Finds have included figures of soldiers, a head of Hercules and some dramatic *acroteria* theatre masks. Some have been left by the well and other pieces removed to the depot.

Though the best preserved Glanum II houses are under the forum, the **House with Alcoves** and **Sulla's House**, their remains give little idea of the reconstructions created on paper from the tiny fragments of painted plaster and mosaics found during excavation.

THE ANNEXE

On the northern side of the basilica is one of the finest looking buildings in Glanum, easily recognisable because of the great apse facing the main road. It would have been the meeting-place of the curia or town council and must have replaced the *bouleuterion*. It is likely to have been two storeyed as the narrow room at the eastern end should be a staircase. The large lower rooms could have housed the town archives and lock-up.

3   The residential area

Gallo-Greek large stonework is widespread and the Hellenistic peristyle house appears to have been a feature from Glanum I onwards, rather than appearing in the era of Augustus when it became fashionable. The buildings we see are what remained after they were abandoned in the third century AD, and representing some 400–500 years development. Note the traces of the drainage system and pedestrian pavement in the '**Rue des Thermes**'.

a   North-east quarter

House of the Capricorn and Hellenistic House

These two Glanum I houses survived into the Gallo-Roman era, but were eventually covered by the baths and the forum/curia. The remains are fragmentary. Two rooms in the first house have poorly preserved mosaics, covered by roofing. A capricorn at the centre of one gives the house its name.

St Rémy-de-Provence
GLANUM
3 Residential Area

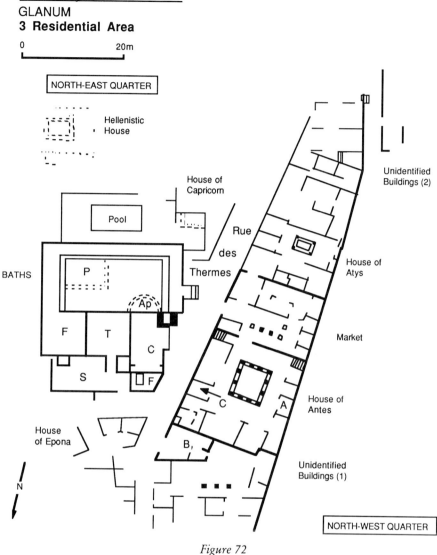

Figure 72

PUBLIC BATHS

Steps between square pilasters lead up from the road into the palaestra or
exercise yard. Here, a number of large paving stones have survived, but only
one portico column base. The palaestra and the swimming pool beyond,
with its **water god pipe**, were modifications made during the mid-first
century AD to a bath complex constructed before 25 BC. The extensions

213

involved covering in an earlier swimming pool – exposed now in the palaestra – and cutting off the apse of the *caldarium*. Behind the *frigidarium* and *tepidarium* is a service area for the slaves who worked the system. Note the stone water-pipes and the heat-affected red and black blocks next to the furnace.

House of Epona

Built over an earlier Gallo-Greek house, this was probably a series of workshops around a small court. One room contains a millstone. Its name is derived from an altar found here to the Gallic goddess Epona, the embodiment of prosperity as well as protection and fertility.

FOUNTAIN

The circular basin of a street fountain is the last excavated structure at the northern end of the site.

b   North-west quarter

Unidentified buildings 1

These partially excavated houses await further research.

House of Antes

This is the perfect Glanum peristyle house with its central court, pool and portico. Rooms face inwards on three sides, on the southern wall separating the house from the market. The fine ashlar blocks indicate the Hellenistic origins of the walling, though the peristyle is an Augustan rebuild. The dominant order is Doric with plain single piece columns, although Corinthian drum columns are used on the west side. These balanced the Corinthian pilasters by the west room (A) facing the pool that gave the house its name ('Anta': a classical building that uses another architectural order to create a contrast for a particular purpose). The stairs in the south-west corner show there was a second floor.

In the north-east corner there may have been a service area for keeping horses and chariots (B). A small room by the road (C) has some attractive tile and white marble oyster-design flooring.

Market

The original Gallo-Greek building is likely to have been a market. Opposite the entrance a row of four shops are clearly outlined by large Hellenistic blocks and door lintels. A gallery is distinguished by the square foundations and one column base.

When its market role came to an end in the Roman period, the northern section next to the House of the Antes became a back-door yard, whilst the southern section became a **cult centre** linked to the House of Atys by an entrance room next to the road. This contained a well (for sacred washing?). The main chamber was surrounded by a low bench for members of the cult. Two altars were found here: the larger, orientated north–south, is dedicated to the ears of the **Bona Dea** or Cybele, by her priestess Loreia. The other also records a priestess.

House of Atys

This house could be the home of the chief priestess/priest to the Cybele. It is another peristyle house with the mixed stonework of a Hellenistic and Roman heritage, though with fewer remains than the House of Antes. At the centre of the small pool with a four column portico (bases only) is the platform where the Atys relief was found (see depot, p. 221), after which the house was named.

Unidentified buildings 2

The aqueduct probably entered the town in this area.

Gallo-Roman quarries

Serious quarrying only ended in the twentieth century, but there is still evidence of ancient working.

Glanum site quarry

On the left by the path to the site entrance, disorganised and clumsy late Roman work took place.

Tor blanc and La Pyramide quarries

On the southern side of the Chemin des Carrières is an area of considerable quarrying. Finds show exploitation began in the Hellenistic period. In Tor blanc, 900 m from Les Antiques, Roman quarrymen left their marks ALTUM, CM or INC on the rock-face where they had stopped working because of faults. La Pyramide, 500 m from Les Antiques, is named after a dramatic, isolated pillar, 23 m high. It is believed this was left by Roman quarrymen to proclaim the depth and extent of their mining. It is mentioned in medieval texts. Stone from here was sent as far as Lyon.

'Les Antiques'

Binoculars will be useful.

The triumphal arch and mausoleum mark the point where, during the early Empire, the main Italy road met the road into Glanum. The mausoleum must have been the most prominent monument in the roadside cemetery, and the arch, like that at Orange, defined the sacred limit of the town.

Triumphal arch

Glanum arch is less than two-thirds the size of the arch at Orange, its small scale exaggerated by the single bay, the loss of the attic and the slanting eighteenth-century roofing tiles. It makes little impact today, though once it must have been over 11 m high and with statuary on top of that. The side panels have suffered particularly and the twin niches which probably held plaques or reliefs are empty. Only a few blocks remain of the architrave, and the winged victories with their laurel branches or banners can only just be made out.

The bay

The pilasters are plain, but the decorative work was by a master craftsman.

The **archivaults** are the outstanding masonry of the arch, embellished with a variety of flora and local fruits. On the eastern façade these seem to be youthful and spring-like; on the western façade they are fully flowered, even autumnal with misshapen grapes, as if pecked by birds.

The **impost frieze** illustrates a range of musical instruments including trumpets, cymbals and pipes; the thyrsus or staff carried by Bacchus; and various sacrificial objects. It might represent the tools of a thanksgiving ceremony.

The **vaulting** is in hexagonal coffers with flower blooms at the centre; twenty-eight different varieties have been identified.

The eastern façade reliefs (facing Glanum)

These are standard images of defeat: a bound man on the right and a woman on the left of fragmentary trophy tree-trunks. Their clothes define them as Gauls. Both ORANGE and CARPENTRAS have much better versions.

The western façade reliefs (facing St Rémy)

These are less conventional and more positively symbolic. The **south-west relief** shows a man stripped of all but his cloak beside a woman seated on a mound of military equipment; it is most likely that she represents Dea

St Rémy-de-Provence

TRIUMPHAL ARCH
Plan

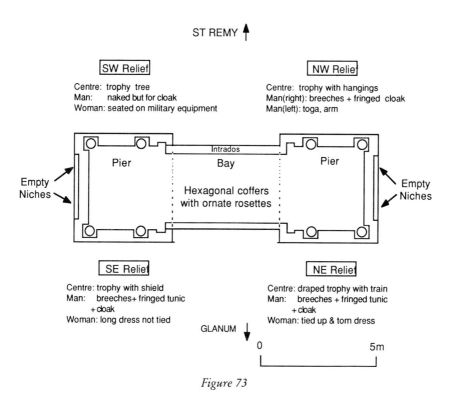

ST REMY ↑

SW Relief
Centre: trophy tree
Man: naked but for cloak
Woman: seated on military equipment

NW Relief
Centre: trophy with hangings
Man(right): breeches + fringed cloak
Man(left): toga, arm

Intrados

Pier   Bay   Pier

Empty Niches

Hexagonal coffers
with ornate rosettes

Empty Niches

SE Relief
Centre: trophy with shield
Man: breeches+ fringed tunic
          + cloak
Woman: long dress not tied

NE Relief
Centre: draped trophy with train
Man: breeches + fringed tunic
          + cloak
Woman: tied up & torn dress

GLANUM ↓

0   5m

Figure 73

Roma. It is not just defeat, but the triumph of Roman civilisation. In the **north-west relief** the figure on the right is the usual bound man, but on the left, a man, as his toga shows, places a hand on the prisoner's shoulder: surely an appeal for reconciliation and assimilation.

Date: Rolland linked it with one of Agrippa's visits. Gros and others have more recently argued that the style is Augustan/early Tiberian (AD 10–20) and part of a contemporary surge in arch building.

The mausoleum

This tall, elegant and well-proportioned structure consists of three elements: a podium base or socle decorated with pictorial reliefs on all sides; a four-sided or *quadrifrons* arch with an entablature above; and a circle of columns or tholos standing on a drum capped with a pointed roof. Whether it was a

217

real mausoleum or a cenotaph is uncertain. The podium has a hollow centre, but nothing to prove it was not just saving on construction work. More important is for whom it was built, and this has been a matter of major disagreement.

Two figures can be made out in the tholos, both male and wearing togas (with nineteenth-century restored heads). On close examination, the smaller and presumably younger figure seems to be carrying a locket, a symbol of adolescence. Even if the Gemini temples were not dedicated to the sons of Augustus could not this truly grand monument be theirs? Below them on the *quadrifrons* entablature appears the well-cut **inscription**:

SEX.L.M.IULIEI.C.F.PARENTIBUS.SUEIUS
('Sextus, Lucius, Marcus, sons of Caius, of the Julian family to their parents')

It contains the right names: Lucius and Caius and the Imperial family name Julii, though not in the appropriate combination! Even so, those who have wanted to argue for the Imperial connection have pointed out that two men cannot be identified as parents, therefore the inscription cannot anyway be accepted as a simple statement of the truth. However, I find more convincing Gros's reassertion that this is a local family claiming an elite position in Glanum. He sees the statues as those of a father and grandfather, who won Roman citizenship by their support of Caesar in the Gallic Wars (50s BC) and of Augustus in the civil wars (30s BC). The mausoleum is saying we won our citizenship by active support and personal grant; we carry the Imperial name, whilst the town as a whole obtained its 'Latin' status only through a general gift. Supporting evidence has been sought in the socle reliefs.

The east relief

In the centre a hero brandishes a sword and shield; a similar figure lies on the ground to the left of centre. On the far left a winged being reads from a scroll, a group around him listen. It has been seen as a heroic version of the almost contemporary deaths of the sons of Augustus: the death of one is announced whilst the other dies of his wounds. Gros sees instead heroic images of ancestors in the centre and to the right, while on the left there is an admiring – not sad – group listening to the announcement of citizenship.

The north relief

This is a conventional cavalry mêlée in which nothing clearly distinguishes friends and foes, though one figure has a strange double horned helmet. It could be a reference to warfare in Gaul as the costume is broadly Roman and the saddle on the dying horse is Gallic.

The west relief

Another battle scene, this time on foot. In the centre a group defend a naked figure lying on the ground. This is a conventional funerary scene, depicting the death of Patroclus, Achilles' friend, killed by Hector. The military equipment mixes Roman and foreign; especially impressive are the variety of helmet plumes.

The south relief

This has generally been taken to show two scenes. On the right, a kneeling figure is about to be attacked by a boar, but a horseman is poised to thrust with his lance. The scene is also taken to have a mythical origin. Heroes attempt to drive off a wild boar sent by Artemis to punish those who offended her (see Theseus raising his double-bladed axe). Traditionally the scene on the left has been taken to show the massacre of Niobe's children. She claimed her ability to produce children made her superior to a goddess: this was her punishment. Agonised and distraught figures fill the scene. Alternatively, the whole relief shows an accident-prone hunt put together from Hellenistic wall-painting sources.

The *quadrifrons*

The archivaults have floral decor with Medusa-like keystones. The architrave above has a series of sea-monsters, dragons, griffins and tritons. On three sides, the latter carry a disk or sun. This could embody an allegorical message: the passage of the noble soul through hostile seas to the night of death (the north has no sun). The 'Medusas' could be the four winds.

The tholos

The workmanship is poor here; not only do the capitals vary in size and the entablature and roof fit badly, but the columns are not grooved on the inner faces. It may have been rebuilt after lightning damage.

A mason's workshop

The mausoleum would have been made by a group of skilled craftsmen travelling round Narbonensis carrying out commissions. Similar workmanship has been identified in Lyon, Avignon and St Julien-les-Martigues (LA COURONNE). The team probably included Italians, bringing the fashion for a Hellenistic monument of this type, well known in the first century BC in central and southern Italy.

St Rémy town

Musée des Alpilles

Hôtel de Montdragon, Place Février.

Hours:	
July–August	10.00 a.m.–noon, 2.00–7.00 p.m.
April–June, September–October	10.00 a.m.–noon, 2.00–6.00 p.m.
November–December	10.00 a.m.–noon, 2.00–5.00 p.m.
January–March	closed

It is here that the most impressive pre-Roman sculpture from Glanum is displayed.

Cross-legged warrior

Two bases were found but only one badly worn and headless warrior. The tight tunic and rigid rectangular cloak is most like the warrior from Roquepertuse (see MARSEILLE, p. 176). He has a Celtic torc round his neck and a bracelet on his arm. Lacking forearms, it is impossible to tell if they once rested on severed heads.

Pillars and lintels

That the cult (see AIX, p. 129) did exist here is confirmed by architectural elements found on the wall above the portico by the Hellenistic gateway. The hollows are skull-shaped and intended to display heads. The lintel cavities still contain broken spikes.

Gallo-Greek capitals

These eight capitals from the **trapezoidal court** are a vigorous and intense, yet well-composed mix of classical and Gallic traditions, both technically and in subject-matter; they must be the product of one team working at the end of the second or early first century BC. Hellenistic lathe masonry is implied by the rings on top of the columns.

Each capital uses the basic Corinthian form with a ring of acanthus leaves at the base and four volutes forming corners. Between the volutes there are heads and, in one case, a bust. The ringed eyes, tight mouths, hair in parallel ribs or curls and the presence of torcs are typical Gallic features. Three capitals offer no obvious means of interpretation. Five have figures that are clearly gods or embody allegory. The most interesting include **Mercury or Hermes** with wings on his head, a broken-faced man with a torc and two fish on his forehead (a water-god?), a woman's head and a bearded man. Another includes **Apollo** with a crown of laurels together with a young man

220

wearing a Gallic torc. The identifying figures on the others are **Pan**, a **satyr** and **Africa**, the last recognised by the elephant-skin crown.

Dépôt Archéologique

Rue de Parage, Hôtel de Sade.
Hours: guided tours only

This Renaissance depot is little more than the storerooms for the rest of the material excavated at Glanum. However the guides are knowledgeable and patient.

The Gallic religious tradition is best represented by crude/charming altars of Sucellus and **Mercury with Rosmerta**. Though the latter twin altar seems Roman, the concept of Mercury with a consort is only found in Gaul. They both embody well-being, he with his bag of money, she with her cornucopia of plenty. Other altars have limbs incised on them, a feature of many water-associated sanctuaries in Gaul which obviously implies healing.

Official Gallo-Roman Glanum is well represented by high-quality **acroteria** from the Dromos well and the Valetudo and Gemini temples, but best of all by the two **female Imperial heads** found in a well by the Gemini temples where they must once have formed part of a group (see BEZIERS, p. 61). Both are young and have similar hairstyles. One has a round, open, almost chubby, face and has been identified as **Octavia**, the sister of Augustus, the other has a longer aristocratic face with high cheek-bones and is considered to be **Livia**, his wife. The headless toga figure, with a symbolic locket of youth, perhaps his adopted son Lucius, was found between the Gemini temples.

Amongst the rest of the material are early Gallo-Greek stelae, a very fine crystal ring, the **relief of Attis** (Atys), the Cybele's young, self-castrated, consort and the inscription recording the **Glanici Dendrophori** or 'tree-bearers', the college of local dignitaries who carried symbolic pine trees in a spring festival for the goddess.

In the backyard (visible but with no access) are the remains of **late Roman baths** associated with a villa or inn, later covered by the early medieval church of St Pierre and the Hôtel de Sade.

VAISON-LA-ROMAINE, Vaucluse

Michelin 81–2/3
IGN 60–B2
3,05/49,15gr
5°04/44°14

Major urban remains.

Roman Vaison is almost literally the re-creation of one man: the Canon

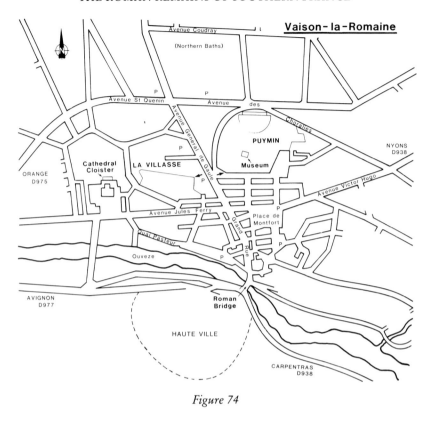

Figure 74

Joseph Sautel. From 1907 to 1955 Sautel organised excavations virtually every season. The result is that more Roman remains are exposed here than anywhere else in France, and little has been excavated without his overall direction. The extent of his achievement was recognised as early as 1929 when the town was designated 'La-Romaine'.

It is impossible not to feel a mixture of admiration and frustration when visiting Vaison. Sautel was driven by a passionate personal involvement and a belief (one I share) in the value of communicating a vision of Roman civilisation: the evocative ruins on the slopes of the two hills of Puymin and La Villasse seem justification enough for his work. Yet there has been a cost.

For Sautel, Roman civilisation was a static concept: the purpose of excavation was to reveal Vaison in its full flowering, not its evolution over time. He began his work in a period when little note was taken of stratigraphy, and he made few attempts subsequently to modify his techniques. He ruthlessly cleared material and the records he kept were often thin and imprecise. His reconstruction work certainly helps evoke a real sense of a past, but at the expense of understanding how the actual sites developed. Fortunately, since the 1970s, the outstanding re-excavation of the Dolphin

House by Christian Goudineau and the new work by Yves de Kisch has gone a long way to redeem this weakness.

Evolution of the Roman town

Rich agriculture and reasonable links with important trade routes, such as the Rhône and Durance valleys, suggest that during the Iron Age the Haute Ville hill was a major oppidum in the south-eastern corner of the region occupied by the Vocontii. Occasional Iron Age finds support this. The tribe probably represented a coalition of smaller tribal and clan groups which by the first century BC were led by a chief (praetor) and his advisers (senators) with their main political centre at Vaison.

Like most other southern Gaul tribes, the Vocontii were defeated in the campaigns of 125–118 BC and made part of the Transalpine province. The impact was minimal for the first fifty years, then in the 60s the tribe was formally allied to Rome, probably to prevent them being influenced by the less reliable Allobroges to the north. The effect was to transform the process of romanisation.

First Pompey, then Caesar, granted Roman citizenship to aristocratic tribal leaders; others became citizens by commanding the cavalry units demanded by Rome. By the time of Augustus Vaison had emerged as the political capital of the tribe or *civitas*. It soon produced some highly cultured men like the author Trogus Pompeius, the senator and consul (AD 56) Lucius Avitus, the commander of the praetorian guard and friend of Seneca, Sextus Burrus, and a case has been made that it was the home town of the great historian Tacitus.

Goudineau's study, published in 1978, at last made it possible to link this history, derived from literary sources, to Vaison's material remains. His precision excavations at the Dolphin House (see below, pp. 235–7, 242) revealed that there were three major forms of masonry: uneven and crudely made stonework; formally laid but still irregular courses, and *petit appareil*. The earliest building (50–30 BC) used Roman measurements and copied the fashionable peristyle design, but was built using poor local stoneworking techniques. These first houses were widely spread and little more than rather grand farms.

It was a haphazard and partial osmosis to Roman notions of urban living and helps explain why Sautel could not identify a regular city grid pattern. A second phase (AD 10–20), indicated by the better stonework, saw expansion with the addition of baths suggesting a conscious adoption of Roman ways. It no doubt also brought more people out of the old settlement and may have encouraged the construction of the theatre. The fully romanised town with regular streets, porticoes, central water supply and drainage and public facilities emerges under the Flavians. Now using *petit appareil*, wholesale house rebuilding takes place creating the typical noble *domus* found here.

Kisch's work has been particularly helpful in the Thès area, and has shown that there was widespread destruction in the later third century. However, evidence elsewhere is too fragmentary to say whether the destruction could be the result of barbarian attacks in the 280s. What is clear, though, is that rebuilding took place and occupation lasted here into the sixth century. Excavations by the cathedral and on the northern baths confirm other late Roman constructions. It fits the historical evidence of active bishops able to hold a Church Council in Vaison. Although the lower town was never entirely abandoned, it is likely that most people now sought the safety of the old oppidum site, which was to emerge subsequently as the medieval Haute Ville.

The great public buildings of cities like Nîmes and Arles have not been found here: their remains are hidden under the modern town or were destroyed in Antiquity. Vaison should be visited for the splendid houses and paradoxically for what Sautel helped to create: an atmosphere of Roman civilisation.

Plan on taking at least a day, with a rest between the two areas. This is a major centre that looks deceptively easy to cover quickly, but on a hot day drinks are essential and in France always enjoyable.

Puymin area

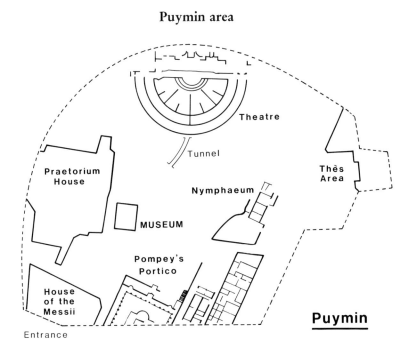

Figure 75

224

Hours: Tourist season   9.00 a.m.–12.30 p.m., 2.00–7.00 p.m. daily
       Spring and autumn   10.00 a.m.–12.30 p.m., 2.00–6.00 p.m.
       Winter   10.00 a.m.–4.00 p.m.

The lower slopes of the hill

Messii House

The main entrance to the house takes you down the steps into an open area, through a passage to the first reception court with a poorly preserved pool and mosaic surround. On the northern side Sautel identified a possible small **domestic cult room** for the Lares Familiares, the guardian spirits of the household. Behind it is the triclinium or dining-room with a perspective view, back across the court and its pool. The service area has a separate entrance to the street. In the **kitchen** there are two ovens and a wash-basin raised up over a drain. By the street there is a range of **lavatories** (extensively reconstructed) and a **small bath suite**. Along the northern wall of the house are a range of **'noble rooms'**, rooms intended to display wealth and status to outsiders. In room 9 is a head of Apollo that Sautel found on the premises (but mistook for Venus) and the two inscriptions that led to his name for the house. The dedication to Messia Alpina by two citizens was found at the entrance to the house. The other, a much finer carving, was found 6 km

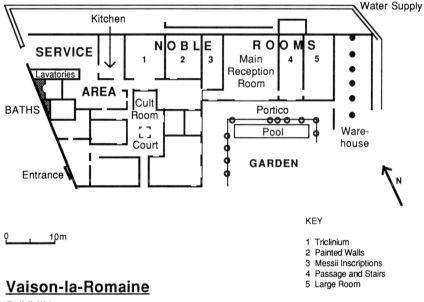

0 ____ 10m

Vaison-la-Romaine
PUYMIN
House of the Messii

Figure 76

225

away in the village of Faucon and was probably fixed to a statue base. It records a gift of the citizens of Vaison to L. Messius. It is likely that he was a leading figure of the community and one-time owner of the house; it is possible that Messia was a female relative.

Room 10 was once the grandest of all, covered with imported marble tiles in a red rectangular design. The long sill suggests how the door could be opened to provide a view over the pool and garden through the portico and its deliberately widely set columns. Undoubtedly this was the *tablinium*, the main reception room of the *domus*. A plinth in the rear of the room perhaps once held a statue of L. Messius himself.

Room 11 has stairs to a lavatory at the back. On the eastern side of the house is a naved room that Goudineau identifies as a **warehouse**.

Pompey's portico

This large garden may or may not have been public as the southern section is unknown and the walling to the north obscure. The major feature is the portico of Tuscan columns and a massive rear wall (heavily restored) with three niches. Each contains a statue cast: the classic athlete called Diadumenus (the original Roman copy of the Greek statue is in the British Museum), Sabina and Hadrian (see p. 232). None of the statues were excavated here – they were found in the theatre. Yet cities were filled with statuary and the effect humanises. Sautel had far less justification for naming the garden after Pompey; it is based on a fragmentary inscription to a woman Pompeia!

Tenement blocks

Two parallel roads running north–south create an area of small blocks: dwellings, shops and storerooms. Sautel had little evidence for identifying the *insula* as multi-storey units.

Nymphaeum

A confusing jumble of stones and walls with little obvious pattern is the remains of some structure with extensive water channels and piping (the long piece of lead-piping in the museum is from here). The large numbers of pillars, capitals and architectural fragments led Sautel to see a decorative fountain or grotto equipped with water-gods and nymphs.

Vaison-la-Romaine

PUYMIN AREA

Thès Quarter

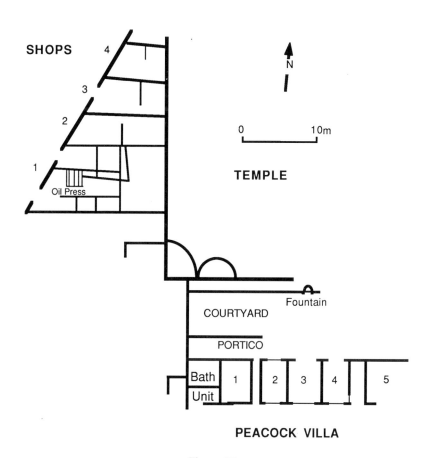

Figure 77

The Thès quarter

This is the most important area open to the public that has been excavated since Sautel's time, mainly by Yves de Kisch.

Peacock Villa

The best **mosaics** of Vaison were discovered here in the block of noble rooms dividing the garden and its surrounding structures from the northern portico and courtyard. The house dates from the Flavian period, but Kisch points out the similarities of the mosaics with those at St Romain (see VIENNE) and dates them to the end of the second century. The floor of room 11 is higher and stylistically different from the others, implying a third-century date.

Room 1: a black and white geometric design with small green and yellow flowers adding some colour.

Room 2: a geometric frame encloses eighteen squares; motifs include ducks and theatre masks but they were restored badly in antiquity. Eight motifs have been destroyed.

Room 3: the central room had the best perspectives through the wide doors marked by stone sills. This room has the **peacock mosaic**. Though named after the central emblem, the surrounding birds have survived much better than the peacock; there are ducks, partridges and parrots. Three of the spandrels were relaid in Antiquity with ornamental foliage, but one has an original splendid mythical beast: a panther with a twisting snake's tail ending in flower petals!

Room 4: like room 2 it uses eighteen medallions. They include still lifes, an octopus, a triton and a cupid riding a dolphin.

Room 5: stylistically rather different from the others and higher, this, the largest mosaic of all, is probably also a third-century addition. It has fifteen octagons with flowers, an eagle, a lion, etc.

The shops

The hillside was first terraced for building during the Augustan period. The shops now on view were constructed *c*. AD 60–80, probably contemporary with the road. Despite the triangular shape of the site, they all follow the same model: a front shop and a workshop/occupation room in the rear, maybe with simple second-floor garrets. During the third century the rear rooms were reduced to recesses and later the whole area was destroyed by fire. They were however cleared and reoccupied towards the end of the sixth century.

Shop 1: an oil supplier set up here after a fire burnt out the shop in the Hadrianic period. There are two large *dolia* and the base or *ara* of an oil press, used to drain off the oil from the *scourtins*, employing a simple direct press rather than the lever-type (see MOULIN DES BOUILLONS, p. 177).

Shop 2: loom-weights and needles discovered here suggest a textile or clothes shop.

Shop 4: the groove in the middle of the wide sill on to the road could be the base for a butcher's meat stall.

Temple

A well-preserved wall up to 1.8 m high and nearly 15 m long using irregular stonework marks a rectangular structure on a terrace north-east of the shops: it could be the base for an Augustan temple.

The theatre

In the mid-nineteenth century the steep hollow on the north of Puymin hill was turned into a 'hanging garden' by its owner, using two ancient windows, *'les lunettes'*, as architectural features; they were the only part of the theatre then exposed. Sautel chose this for his first major excavation in 1911–12. The rapid recognition of the site as a Roman theatre and the discovery of major ancient statuary established his fame.

The *cavea*

The thirty-two ranks of seats are reached by stairs up and down the *cavea* or by vomitoria from the sides and the top rear gallery.

The stage

The impact of stone robbing and nineteenth-century rail cuttings has been extensive. There are only traces of the stage foundations and little more than *'les lunettes'* of the side *versurae*. Behind the outline of the pulpitum wall and the twelve holes of the curtain lifting gear were found the remains of smashed statues and architectural elements that probably decorated the *frons scaenae*. In the summer, the theatre is used for concerts and the ancient stage is hidden by scaffolding and a wooden platform. Yet even without this, most of what the visitor sees today is not the theatre that Sautel excavated.

In 1932 Jean Formigé was invited by Sautel to come and restore the theatre. Wholesale reconstruction followed, subsequently defended on the grounds that the almost entirely new *cavea* seating and rear gallery were necessary because rapid disintegration was the only alternative. Looking at photographs of the exposed theatre as it was before 1932, the picture is one of rubble, in some places reduced to bare rock-cutting, in others some surviving seating; the 'covered' gallery was equally ruined and in places no more than a metre high. Fortunately even though the stone comes from the same source that was originally used, it looks new and is easy to distinguish from the original masonry. The theatre raises in a stark form the dilemma of recreating the past: how real is a reconstruction?

A tunnel behind the theatre through the top of Puymin hill is Gallo-Roman and niches for oil lamps can be seen.

Vaison-La-Romaine

PUYMIN
The Praetorium

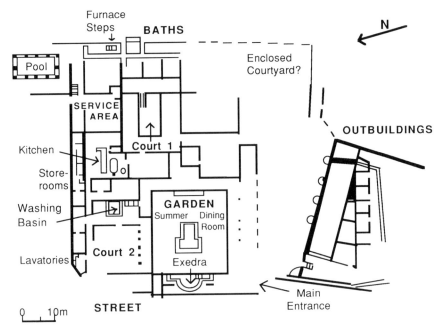

Figure 78

The western slopes

A path from the theatre curves round the Puymin hill to the museum. It passes above the so-called Praetorium house and some commercial buildings.

The 'Praetorium'

Sautel was uncertain about what he had found here, and when a friend suggested that this apparent mix of house and sanctuary might be the official residence of the praetor or magistrate of the *civitas*, he enthusiastically adopted the idea. Goudineau has shown that it is simply another grand *domus* and the 'sanctuary' the best preserved garden in Vaison.

Baths and pool: above the path are the remains of a water and baths system carved in the hillside itself. Rock-cut steps mark the access to feed the furnace. A large pool, also cut into the rock, surrounded by column bases could either be a swimming pool linked to the baths or a decorative reservoir for irrigating the orchard garden to the north of the house.

Passage: this allowed servants to move from the main service area to the bath complex.

First court: this is the centre of the original house, though poorly preserved and overgrown by weeds. All the rooms were grouped round the court's portico. In the north-west corner was the kitchen with its drain and oven.

Service area: when the house was enlarged to the north and west new rooms were added on to the kitchen. A room with a basin and *dolium* is followed by an open room with a large basin, probably for washing clothes. This in turn gives access to a large court with a passage on the south, lit by a series of windows whose sills survive. To the north a range of rooms were possibly storerooms or servants' living accommodation (these are now closed off to make a centre for the study of wall-painting).

Latrines: four seats are well preserved along with the drainage out to the sewer running beside the street below the house. It is possible that they might have been for public use as well.

Garden and noble rooms: the original house was turned into a grand *domus* in a distinctive way. A portico on raised foundations, built to bring it to the level of the old entrance to the original house, was constructed round three sides of a garden. The rooms to the east and south behind this portico are difficult to interpret and badly preserved, but the garden provides evidence of one of the finest perspectives in Vaison. Guests could look down over a fine summer dining-room – and no doubt sometimes be honoured with invitations to eat there – to the west wall with its *exedra* and fountains, in appearance a small *nymphaeum*. It was this and the summer triclinium that Sautel became convinced represented a ceremonial washing-place and an altar.

'Outbuildings'

To the south of the Praetorium, across the path with a few sarcophagi, is an east–west wall, buttressed with semi-circular alcoves. A small entrance and steps down perhaps suggest that the warehouse-like structure was an out-building. Architectural fragments are gathered here beside a memorial dedicated to the work of Sautel. Joined to it are rows of storerooms or shops.

Museum

Prior to 1911, virtually every find went to public and private collections outside Vaison; the Municipal Museum is very much Sautel's achievement. The display in the 1973 building is not very imaginative, but the atmosphere is pleasant.

Inscriptions and other stonework

There is a well-cut dedication to **Antistia Pia Quintilla** probably from a statue plinth. Her freedman records how she was a *flamenica* (a priestess of the Imperial cult) at St Paul-Trois-Châteaux. She is also remembered on an inscription at Arles. Her position and links with three places suggest that she was a patron and landowner in her own right with widespread holdings. Another inscription records the *utricularii*, a boatmen's guild and some rather poor altars. There are some fine **theatre masks** that decorated tombs and two excellent, delicate white disks or *oscilli*, used as wall ornaments.

Statues

The finest sculpture at Vaison is the collection of Imperial statues found in the theatre. They probably once embellished the theatre's *frons scaenae*, god-like figures dominating actors and audience, propagandist images of the Roman state.

Claudius (43–54)   The emperor is depicted with a draped toga over his bare upper figure. Despite the lack of one leg and a missing chest piece it is still an imposing statue. The cool, smooth finish, perhaps painted, is typically Julio-Claudian. He is portrayed here in a priestly role wearing an oak-leaf crown, sacred to Jupiter and Juno, the state gods. Oak leaves were also used for the *corona civica*, a military award for saving life given by the Senate; the symbolism is of course as saviour of his people.

Domitian (81–96)   Intelligent, morbid and cruel, Domitian was an able and effective emperor, particularly proud of his military achievements. He appears here wearing a fine commander-in-chief's breastplate. The head, though characteristic, is mediocre. The cuirass is excellent. It has a Medusa's head at the top to turn enemies to stone. Minerva, as goddess of war, and Pallas Athena, protectress of Rome, stands on a pedestal accompanied by dancing winged Victories. From the base of the cuirass hang scalloped tabs, each one with its own embossed decoration, recalling bronze models. The lower row is embellished with shields.

Hadrian (117–38)   Hadrian adopts the heroic pose based on the fourth-century BC ideal Greek hero, though with a crown to indicate his imperial dignity. He was the first Emperor shown with a beard. This in Greek theory was a symbol of ruler status and subsequent second-century Emperors copied Hadrian, gradually making their beards thicker. He is presented here in middle age with large open eyes and a tight mouth.

Sabina (117–36)   Hadrian was married at 24 to the 20-year-old Sabina, seventeen years before he became Emperor. Nakedness and a crown would certainly not have been adequate to embody the '*dignitas*' of a middle-aged Empress: her tunic covers all but her neck and forearms. Stately calm is embodied in the pose and the well-draped material: the true aristocratic lady. The only excess is the plaited hair heaped in two diadems above her brow.

The marriage was not happy. Sabina appears to have lacked sparkle and was married to a multi-talented intellectual, art-lover and traveller. Her friends were removed from court and she had no children, possibly not unconnected with Hadrian's attraction to young men. Here we only see contrasting public faces of an Emperor and his Empress.

Other finds

The **silver bust** found on La Villasse has some careful detail, but has neither high quality nor Gallic originality. The **three-spouted jugs**, on top of the sigillate case, are thought to have been used for Provençal lavender. Tiles from the workshop of Clarianus (note the unusual pig's trotter imprint!) and the lead water-pipe hint at industrial Vaison. The **ladies' pins** are a reminder of how necessary they were with hairstyles like Sabina's and how easy it must have been to lose them when visiting the baths, where most of these were found.

La Villasse area

Hours: see Puymin.

Vaison-la-Romaine
LA VILLASSE

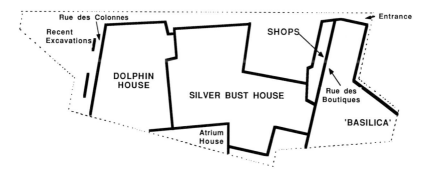

Figure 79

233

The street of shops

The road

The road surface on this steeply sloping hill has been significantly restored with many new polygonal paving stones. At the lower end of the road, the portico columns by the stepped pedestrian footway have of course been re-erected. On the eastern side, a large covered sewer drains down to the Ouvèze.

The 'basilica'

The fine arcade with incised, rectangular fluted columns and semi-circular arch is rebuilt. The break between old and modern *petit appareil* is clear, starting about half way up. The sections of original pilasters and arch are disappointingly small, but, as elsewhere, it does give the rare opportunity of gaining some idea of the elevation of Roman structures.

Not well dated but probably late first century AD, it was identified as a basilica by Sautel. Following the discovery of a *caldarium* under the post office and various sections of piping it is more likely that this was a public baths.

Silver Bust House site

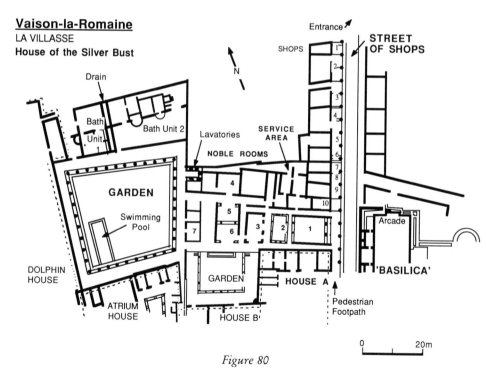

Figure 80

Silver Bust House

From the vestibule of the house, with a cast, not of the silver bust actually found here, but of a headless toga figure made from an original found in the theatre, the visitor moves into a peristyle garden with its fine fluted columns. The north-east quarter was probably a service area. The noble rooms look directly or indirectly on to the garden. **Room 4**, in which is placed a cast of the Domitian statue, has the best view and is probably the triclinium. It has a central perspective going through the columns of two courts, one open and one covered (5 and 6), into the rectangular garden.

Doorways end the east–west corridors and lead into a very large garden with a dual bath system on the northern side. It is in this garden that Sautel found the bust that led to his name for the house. As usual there are nuances to this identification! Goudineau notes that none of the noble rooms look out on the large garden and argues that the owner probably took over a public bath system when the 'basilica' baths were opened. Perhaps he simply wanted to impress, perhaps it was speculative, to make money from the baths, or perhaps he rented the baths out to a club or *collegium*, so extending his municipal influence. Hedges, flowers and grass have been replanted to evoke the garden/exercise area and bull-rushes mark the large swimming pool.

Atrium House

The northern tip of an early house built of irregular masonry has a room with a simple, poorly preserved mosiac looking out on a colonnaded garden.

Unnamed house

Only two rooms are exposed but with mosaics, plaster walls and a well.

Dolphin House site (see Figure 82, p. 242)

This was brilliantly re-excavated by C. Goudineau in the 1970s. The house is best approached by first looking at the street leading to the main entrance.

Column Street

A gravel street for pedestrians only (there are steps at the top), with a portico on the west side and shops on the east. It was constructed between AD 80 and 100. Behind the portico there are basins, possibly pools in an ornamental garden. This covered the outbuildings of the first Dolphin House and for this reason the garden might also have belonged to the *domus*. Excavation has not been completed in this area. Though one shop has a *dolium*, nothing was found in it and evidence of the businesses in the other shops is equally blank.

The house

Goudineau has conclusively demonstrated that this apparently perfect atrium house was the result only of a very late modification, in no way part of the original plan. The house started as a building round a central open court, then expanded using better masonry. In the late first century the house was pulled down and a new *petit appareil domus* put up, still employing some old walls as foundations. This *domus* was much bigger, having a second floor, a large garden and new entrance area, but was only converted into an atrium at least a century later.

The entrance and atrium: going down the steps, the visitor enters the atrium with its shallow, rectangular pool, a column at each corner. Where Sautel found the column drums is unknown, but not here. On the east side of the pool is a hole for a small fountain. Upright lion figures represent the remains of an ornamental stone table. Opposite the entrance is the *tablinium* where guests and clients could be welcomed. Originally the entrance area was an open space, the facing room was walled off and access to the peristyle was only via the corridor.

The service area: this part of the house is dominated by the enormous range of lavatories, twenty in all. Such a large number suggests, like the shops along Column Street, commercial exploitation of property. The kitchen is identified purely on the basis of proximity to the drain and a large 'noble' room that could be for banqueting.

The peristyle: the pavings of the pool still have metal clamps, and water was supplied by a pipe on the east and drained to the north-west. The pool and portico lack symmetry, revealing that the design was modified over time; no doubt it could be disguised by flowers and the play of the fountain. A large window would have looked out from the *triclinium* over the portico, but traces of painted plaster on the walls only hint at the room's former grandeur.

The north and east rooms: of these noble rooms, probably the main reception room was room 2 as it had the best perspective in the house. Behind room 3 is a small bath unit, first built on to the early house using improved irregular masonry; room 3 may have become the bath's vestibule. Note the use of irregular masonry for part of the walling here. Nothing in room 4 survived to allow anything more than a guess as to function – perhaps a library?

The southern garden: in the last phase of the house this must have been the centre of formal activity. A terrace with nine pillars overlooked a great pool with three decorative *exedrae* at the top of the garden. Typical of the house, despite appearances, nothing was ever quite right: room 5 overlooks an *exedra*, but in the corner; room 6 was converted into the major noble room, but the central *exedra* had to be enlarged to appear directly in front of the room's window, upsetting the pool's overall symmetry. The pool must have been filled with fish. Amphorae were buried in the flooring, a common method of providing a spawning place. The walls separating the end *exedrae* from the central basin were added late on; they probably became flower beds.

Other sites

The bridge

The single-arch bridge carried the road to Carpentras as well as providing a link with the old oppidum. It is 17 m wide and uses bronze clampons to secure the *grand appareil* stonework. The parapet was rebuilt in the nineteenth century and the bridge suffered again during the Second World War.

The cathedral cloister

Written sources show that Vaison was active as an episcopal see from as early as the fourth century. Epitaphs placed here record late Roman clergy: Floreintius and Vicentius of the fourth and Pentagathus and Eripius of the sixth centuries. The apse of the cathedral reuses many Roman columns and architectural pieces in its foundations, whilst the structure may be largely sixth century. The cathedral was certainly built on top of early Roman structures discovered but not identified in excavations during 1981–2.

Northern baths

Avenue Coudray.

These once magnificent public baths were fully excavated in the 1970s but are now completely overgrown. Eventually the site will be reopened to visitors.

VERNEGUES, Bouches-du-Rhône

Michelin 84–2
IGN 67–E1
3,18/48,54gr
5°12/43°41

Rural temple.

Vernègues

TEMPLE

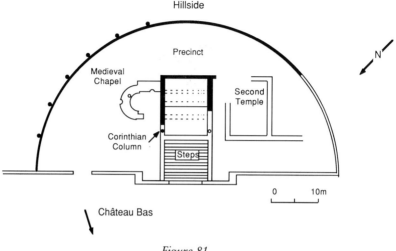

Figure 81

In the grounds of **Château Bas** by the D22, a turning left 27 km north-west of Aix-en-Provence by the N7.

The setting is idyllic: at the back of the château with its yellow and green tiles glinting in the sun, set at the foot of a hillside, the temple balances on the edge of wild and tamed countryside. At the back of the temple the stunted oaks, gorse and white rocks breaking through the thin orange soil; in front the small park with great trees swishing in the wind looking over to the private garden of the château and its swimming pool – or out to the vineyards that give the château its local popularity.

When Abbé Couture first recorded the ruins in the eighteenth century, it must have seemed the ideal folly: a genuine classical ruin. The front stairs and the heart of both the *cella* and the podium have been plundered and the east wall has a romantic dilapidated medieval chapel supporting its remains, but the west wall rises an amazing fifteen courses fronted by a fine pilaster. Most striking is the beautifully-proportioned lone Corinthian column and capital. The main excavations of the temple and its precinct were carried out by J. Formigé in the early twentieth century.

This type of temple is found all over the Empire: a staircase of nearly 8 m in length, a porch framed by four columns just over 6 m deep and a *cella* extending just under 7 m. The slope must have emphasised even more than usual the front-looking perspective of the temple. Little attempt was made to hollow out the rock and the cellars in the podium had little space at the back. Formigé argued that the Corinthian style was Augustan.

238

Enclosing the temple is a semi-circular precinct wall, still clearly visible, partly cut from the rock. When Formigé carried out his dig in the 1920s he found the foundations of a second building to the west of the temple. He argued that there must have been a third on the east side, removed when the chapel was constructed. He partly justified this on the grounds of symmetry, probably correctly. He also believed Vernègues was a rural *capitolium*, but unfortunately the altar and inscription evidence, some found in the château, is frustratingly elliptical.

Jupiter seems certain to have been one of the gods worshipped here: an altar found in the château records 'Jupiter the Thunderer'. Another inscription records Jupiter and Minerva, but combined with Neptune and Mercury, not Juno, the third member of the *capitolium* trinity. Even the Imperial cult is a possibility with an altar dedication to Rome and Augustus, though this could be associated with the local settlement remains identified by Formigé and confirmed by aerial photography during the 1980s.

Yet a rural site is more likely to have embodied Gallic conceptions; indeed the abundant local spring must have played a part in the selection of the site. Jupiter was widely adopted in Gaul, particularly in the south, but as a personification of the Celtic sky-god (see the altars in Nîmes Museum with Celtic wheels and Roman thunderbolts). A broken altar, found in the vicinity, un-named but identified as dedicated to Silvanus, suggests that perhaps this Roman woodland god, the embodiment of the fertility of nature in Gallic Provence, was also associated with a temple here. It is his spirit above all that pervades Vernègues.

* * *

OTHER SITES IN CENTRAL PROVENCE

Constantine, Bouches-du-Rhône

Michelin 84–2 or IGN 67–C1
3,11/48,37gr or 5°07/43°33

A fine oppidum site that looks south over the Etang de Berre, 1 km north-west of Château Calissanne on the D10. Occupied from the sixth century, it has a wall *c.* 350 m long with the remains of ten towers. The hill takes its name from the Emperor Constantine, whose gold statue was supposedly buried here.

Cucuron, Vaucluse

Michelin 84–3 or IGN 67–D2
3,45/48,65gr or 5°27/43°47

A small museum recently renovated, *c.* 12 km south-east from Apt. The

Gallo-Roman collection includes some good examples of bone carving found in a local noble family mausoleum.

Fontaine-de-Vaucluse, Vaucluse

Michelin 81–13 or IGN 67–B1
3,10/48,80gr or 5°08/43°55

Behind the remains of the modern Arches du Galas aqueduct on the D24 north-east roadside are traces of rock-cutting and the stonework channel of the Roman aqueduct that carried the Sorgue spring-water to Cavaillon. The ruined castle is on the site of a seventh-century BC oppidum with early Greek pottery and was fortified and reoccupied in the late Roman period.

Martigues, Bouches-du-Rhône

Michelin 84–12 or IGN 66–11D
48,23gr/3,02gr or 5°04/43°24

West of Marseille, astride the channel linking the Etang de Berre with the sea, Martigues is an attractive port and the site of important Iron Age discoveries. There are reconstructed and preserved houses *in situ* and a good modern museum display.

Mazan, Vaucluse

Michelin 81–13 or IGN 67–A1
3,10/48,95gr or 5°07/44°03

On the D942, 7 km east of Carpentras in the village cemetery by the church of Notre-Dame-de-Loup are sixty-two Roman sarcophagi. Occupation evidence found nearby suggests that there was a villa or a temple close to the site.

THE *DOMUS*: HOMES OF THE WEALTHY

The southern Gallo-Roman *domus* – 'noble house' – would not have been very impressive from the outside: flat walls, few windows and a strong door. Even walled towns knew the problem of robbers. Inside, the key design feature was the courtyard: some surrounded by porticoes, some paved, some as gardens. Most rooms overlooked one court or another. Two ways of demonstrating the wealth and cultivation of the owner were by the extent of the house and its internal decoration. Adding a new range of rooms round another court could show the owner's ability to buy up his neighbour's property and to increase the size of his household; the magnificence of the marble or mosaic floor and richly-painted wall decor could be a major feature in a society that used relatively little furniture.

The house would be filled with people, though not with lots of relatives: it was normal for sons to set up their own homes when they married. The paterfamilias was master of the household with extensive legal powers over its members. His wife was subordinate, but had the right to own property and, as it was usual to marry women some ten years younger, wealthy ladies could feature as 'masters' in their own right – for example Pia Antilla of Vaison. Early childhood was not a major concern for rich parents. After wet-nursing, probably by a young slave woman in the household or bought for the purpose, another nurse would take over care for infancy, gradually being replaced by a *paedagogus*, a person responsible for the general education and care of a child. Increasingly, the mother and father would take an interest to try and ensure the child grew up with the appropriate Roman virtues: Tacitus describes how Agricola, born in Fréjus, was tempted as an adolescent to take too much interest in philosophy, but was wisely corrected by his mother. The elite were born to the realities of domination, not contemplation.

The household servants were nearly all slaves, but the lucky were manumitted and made *liberti*, freedmen or women. Fondly remembered nurses or teachers were favoured in this way, but there were other leading figures in the household similarly rewarded: the steward who helped his master administer the estate, a fine cook or a chief banquet waiter. Amongst the property owned might be ships, apartments or shops (often next to a town house). Good slave merchants or shopkeepers who showed skills as businessmen were allowed to share the profits, freed and could become extremely wealthy, establishing large households of their own. They then merged with the master's free clients. Gallic society, like Roman, had a tribal background, with leaders and dependants. The leader protected his supporters, furthering their interests, expecting their support in return. Where once they had looked after his cattle and fought for him, now, whilst perhaps some might still be expected to look after his herds, most would provide the political support to further their patron's political aspirations, such as becoming a town magistrate.

241

Vaison-la-Romaine

LA VILLASSE

Dolphin house

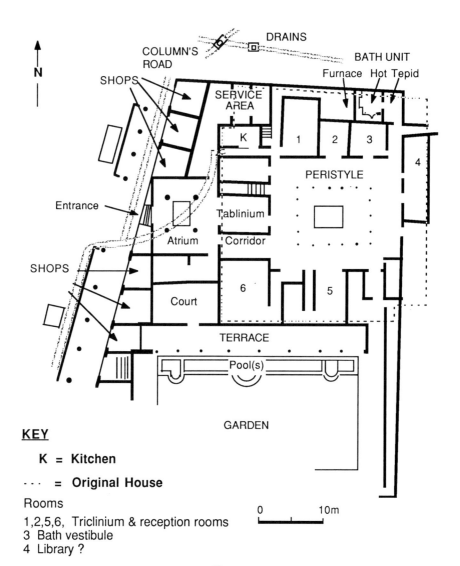

DRAINS

COLUMN'S ROAD

N

BATH UNIT

Furnace Hot Tepid

SHOPS

SERVICE AREA

K   1   2   3

4

PERISTYLE

Entrance

Tablinium

Atrium

Corridor

SHOPS

6   5

Court

TERRACE

Pool(s)

GARDEN

KEY

K = **Kitchen**

· · · = **Original House**

Rooms

1,2,5,6, Triclinium & reception rooms
3 Bath vestibule
4 Library ?

0   10m

Figure 82

The roles of patron and client helped define the way the house was built. As the Augustan architect Vitruvius reflected: 'Magnificent vestibules, alcoves and halls are not necessary to persons of common fortune, because they pay their respects by visiting among others and are not visited by others.'

The most important room in the house was the *tablinium* or reception room. Pre-eminently this was the master's room, where his chair once stood like a throne, ready for him to welcome his clients on their morning visit. They would wait at the gate or in the vestibule, an open court often replacing the Italian atrium, then come in to pay their respects and receive their gift, perhaps food if they were poor, perhaps a letter asking for a job or maybe the promise to become the patron of a guild or even to finance the rebuilding of an amphitheatre (see ARLES, p. 144). He would also dispense justice here. Close by would be the archives room, so that estate records could be checked with the steward.

Many large houses also had their own **baths**. The high costs of constructing and maintaining them would be recompensed by the admiration of friends invited to relax and enjoy the afternoon without the discomfort of mixing with the masses at the public baths.

The *triclinium* was the room in which family, friends, clients, *liberti* and even occasionally slaves banqueted. Like the other public rooms, this would be decorated to impress, generally with the best mosaic situated to allow guests to admire it from their couches and with a wide door to give a view, usually into a porticoed garden with fountains, sculpture and decorative alcoves. Normally there were three large couches with room for three people on each. In contrast to the Greeks, women took an equal share in banquets, though they were expected to sit rather than stretch out on the couch. Host and guests would wear flowers and perfumed oils, drink heavy wines watered to taste before eating heavily, entertained by music and dancing. Petronius' satire on Trimalcio, the Italian freedman's dinner with its drunken ostentation, was probably nearer Gallo-Roman reality than Plato's vision of an intellectual symposium, an ideal suggested by some Roman writers. Slaves might join a feast on the master's birthday, otherwise they ate the scraps.

Often a house would have two or more dining-rooms. This was not a public and private division, as Vitruvius makes clear: a true *domus* should have summer and winter triclinia, one minimising light and heat, the other maximising them. In fact the private section of the house was never totally separated from the rest, like a harem. The public rooms could be isolated from slave quarters, kitchens, children's rooms by curtains and wooden partitions covering open passages and doors. Servants could pass easily and they could be removed when not needed. Toilets, like the baths, would be a matter of pride, demonstrating the provision of running water from the aqueduct system (see NIMES, p. 103); normally chamber-pots were used.

Many of the smaller rooms in a *domus* are difficult to identify, but some must have been bedrooms. Privileged slaves would have their own, while personal slaves would sleep on the floor in the family's bedrooms; some slaves might be locked up. The flickering light of the tiny oil lamps and the occasional candelabra ensured life focused on the daytime. Hypocaust heating was rare outside the baths. Most windows lacked glass and although shutters could keep out the worst of the mistral, in winter people went to bed wearing their clothes and covered in animal skins.

Before romanisation, the typical house in southern Gaul had been a rectangular single room. People slept on the rafters and even cooked in the streets (see Entremont, AIX, p. 133). Gradually, there was an increase in size, and occasionally houses had three to four rooms, but it seems unlikely that status in this pre-Roman Gallic civilisation was significantly or widely embodied in houses. Personal display, especially bulky gold necklaces and arm bracelets, an aristocratic warrior statuary modelled on them, and of course their mass of dependants, seem to have been enough.

The Greek cities of Massalia, Nicea and Agatha must have had their **peristyle** houses, constructed round an open courtyard, often with an ornamental pool at the centre, surrounded by a portico, but no recognisable examples have been excavated. The second-century BC examples of this type of mansion found in Glanum are exceptional and no doubt reflect Greek rule. **Atrium** houses, in which there is a covered vestibule with a central open roof, usually with a shallow pool under the opening, probably featured in the early Roman colonies of Narbonne and Aix. An isolated example has been found in Ensérune, built at the beginning of the first century BC.

Throughout Narbonensis, it is during the second half of the first century BC that the *domus* house rapidly evolves, usually copying the peristyle model; it had become fashionable in Italy, though perhaps in Provence Hellenistic traditions were also a factor. Inevitably many *domus* remains are fragmentary, but at some places extensively excavated examples are visible, generally in their final late second- and early third-century AD forms (e.g. VIENNE, ST REMY and VAISON), and a growing trend is the reconstitution of Roman interiors (see NARBONNE, p. 90). The villa, or rural *domus*, is not well represented, though the small town of AMBRUSSUM has first-century AD farmhouses given a veneer of sophistication with modified yards. Fortunately at LOUPIAN there is an excellent example of the development of a medium-sized villa into the grandiose country *domus* of the late Roman period, reflected so well in its magnificent mosaics.

Eastern Provence

Major sites { Town ▣ / Rural ⊙

Sites { Town ▪ / Rural ●

Sites not covered in detail △

Autoroute ═══

0   30
kilometres

HAUTES - ALPES

LOWER
RHONE

△Gap

● Sisteron

△ Digne

ALPES DE HAUTE-PROVENCE

ALPES MARITIMES

Riez
▪

La Turbie

CENTRAL
PROVENCE

△
Gréoux-
les-
Bains

Mons ●

Nice
▣

⊙
Roquebrune-
Cap-Martin △

Fox-Amphoux
△

△Draguignan

▪ Antibes

▪ Aix

A8

△Taradeau

● Lérins Islands

A52

VAR

▣ Fréjus

Marseille
▣

A52

A50

Mediterranean Sea

● St Cyr-sur-
Mer

▪ Hyères

Figure 83

4

THE SITES OF EASTERN PROVENCE

ANTIBES, Alpes Maritimes

Michelin 84–9
IGN 68–B10
5,35/48,2gr
7°08/43°34

Museums and walls.

Despite the multiplication of hotels, the construction of wide boulevards and the linking of Antibes, Juan-les-Pins and most of Cap d'Antibes into one Riviera resort, the tiny streets of Vieil Antibes and the enclosed harbour of the Vieux Port still manage to give a sense of history beneath twentieth-century tourism. Such links with the past make it easier to imagine not only the medieval and Renaissance background, but also the Greek and Roman origins of Antibes.

Earlier writers interpreted 'Antipolis' as 'the town opposite' and presumed this referred to Nicea, the other Greek colony founded by Massalia on the Ligurian coast. However, the distance of about 18 km has always suggested some doubts, and current thinking is that -polis or town was added to a Ligurian name, describing 'le rocher', the 20 m cliff on the south of the *anse*. Excavation has revealed occupation began here during the Bronze Age in the tenth century BC.

The Côté d'Azur has few secure harbours: dangerous winds, violent currents and submerged rocks have helped make the coast a graveyard of ships, particularly those of Antiquity. Antibes is a typical choice as a Greek colony site: a low but steep rock site for an acropolis and a natural basin for a port. Even so, Antibes apparently remained relatively underdeveloped in the Greek period. There was trade with the Deciates, the local tribe, and pottery finds suggest plenty of coastal trade between Massalia and Italy, but the town remained largely huddled beside the port. Massalian domination must have limited opportunities and ensured a long history of conflict with the Ligurians. However, in the civil wars that led to the destruction of

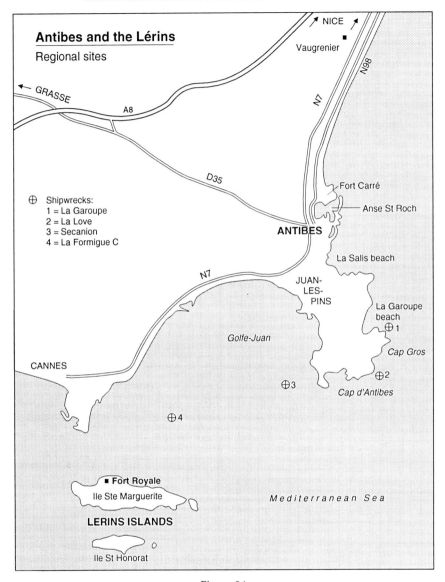

Figure 84

Massalian independence, Antibes probably made a wise choice in siding with Caesar; she was granted the status of an Italian colony in the 40s BC and rapidly emerged as a major coastal city.

Little has survived of Roman Antibes, but it clearly covered a significant area to the west of the old acropolis. No more than fragments are known and these are now hidden. The construction of Port Vauban yacht basin revealed

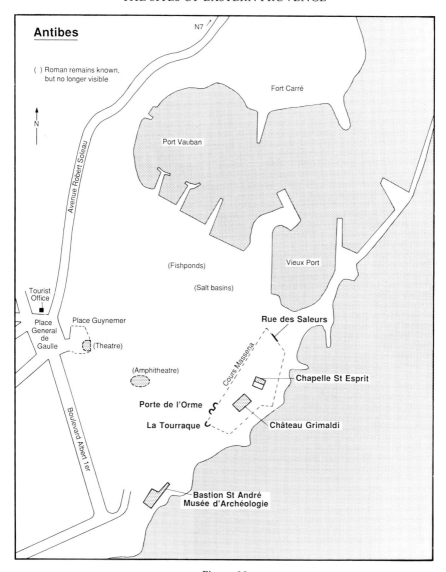

Figure 85

that Roman harbour installations surrounded the *anse* – a clear indication that Roman economic activity had outgrown the Greek 'Vieux Port'. No doubt part of this was due to the exploitation of olives (a mill has been excavated at Encourdoules) and also pines, the resin of which was used widely for lining wine amphorae. The first-century AD writers Martial and Pliny mention that Antibes was famed for its '*muria*', a variety of *garum*, the fermented fish liquor that for its weight was one of the most valuable

249

products in the Roman world. It was made from the guts of tuna – *garum* from Spain used the more prestigious mackerel – salted and exposed for days, then filtered and used as a highly seasoned condiment. Basins used in the process have been found along the southern shore of the *anse*.

   During the late Roman period the city declined. The city reverted to its Greek limits and new walls were built round the rock. The Constantinian treasure, found in the *anse* in 1971, reflects the importance of Arles, where so many of the coins were minted, rather than Antibes.

Late Roman walls

Rue Barque-en-Cannes.

La Tourraque, a massive corner tower with a solid core to resist battering rams and tunnelling. The *petit appareil* has been heavily modified with irregular stonework since the Roman period.

Rue de l'Esperon/Cours Massena.

Porte de l'Orme, a narrow gateway, through to the Rue de l'Orme. Grooves for a portcullis and the door-hinge holes survive. Nineteenth-century pebbling has been removed from the semi-circular towers.

Rue des Saleurs.

The *grand appareil* at the foot of the fortifications formed part of the **rampart** immediately above the Vieux Port. Since Antiquity, this side of the basin has been considerably filled in.

The coast side.

The sixteenth-century town walls were not pulled down here and so cover much of the late Roman material, but in front of the Grimaldi château a **rampart** section, about 5 m high, still stands.

Chapel le St Esprit

Crypt.

Excavations preserved *in situ* demonstrate occupation levels from the Bronze Age. There are also Roman cisterns under the cathedral and the château.

Château Grimaldi/Musée Picasso

Place du Barri.
Hours: Summer 10.00 a.m.–noon, 2.00–7.00 p.m., closed Tuesdays
         Winter 10.00 a.m.–noon, 2.00–6.00 p.m., closed all November

The old town museum still retains a small display of Greek and Roman finds. The most interesting material is in the inscription section. As well as the **child dancer's memorial** (see p. 47), there is a Greek lead curse, though only the name 'Damophanes' has been deciphered, and a cast (the original is in Paris) of the 'galet d'Antibes'. This large sea-washed stone, rather phallic in shape, is inscribed in a local dialect Greek, translated as 'I am Terpon, servant of Aphrodite, asking Cypris to favour those who put this here' (an appeal for children?). A Roman inscription records the *utricularii* of Antibes, perhaps river boatmen, but also possibly ferrymen to the LERINS ISLES where another dedication of theirs was found; it was a dangerous crossing and would need skilled local seamen.

Museé d'histoire et d'archaéologie

Bastion St André.
Hours: 9.00 a.m.–noon, 2.00–7.00 p.m.,   closed Tuesdays
   9.00 a.m.–noon, 2.00–6.00 p.m.,   closed all November

The two large windowless galleries provide a cool and well-lit setting for the underwater finds made in Antibes waters. One room is used for temporary exhibitions.

Over a dozen shipwrecks have been discovered in the Golfe de Juan, nearly all previously ransacked by treasure-hunters. Even so, the material presented here is only a sample of these. The **La Love** ship, named after an inlet in which it foundered, is one of the very few Etruscan ships known. It was carrying wine and drinking vessels, cups and jugs made of the distinctive black bucchero ware, thought to be from Vulci in southern Tuscany and probably heading for ST BLAISE.

The ship that was blown on to the **Garoupe** sands was a first-century AD Roman tanker! The hold was filled with massive *dolium* jars, some stamped with the central Italian firm's name 'Pirani'. They carried 25–30,000 litres of wine which was syphoned out: full jars were much too heavy to lift. The unyielding weight would have contributed to her sinking in a storm off the beach where she must have been sheltering. Other ships were carrying building tiles, copper ingots and even an attractive **Silenus**. The ships themselves are represented by the usual stone and metal anchors, and a less common lead **pump unit**.

Vaugrenier temple

4 km from Antibes by the N7 to Nice. On the northern side of the road in a public park, Villeneuve Loubet district.

The surviving remnant of this temple complex is the southern retaining wall of the precinct, with a wide opening in the centre where there was once a staircase, revealed by the contrast in the stonework between the exposed fine *petit appareil* and the once hidden rough finish work.

It is impossible for the visitor to visualise anything from the wall alone, but the excavators in the 1970s found enough other foundation traces to envisage the whole. The wall, with pavilions at each end, supported a portico with a rear *exedra*; a temple on a podium stood in the centre of the precinct.

Perhaps built near a local shrine when the coast road was completed in 13–12 BC, it was abandoned at the end of the first century AD.

FREJUS, Var

Michelin 84–8
IGN 68–B7
4,89/48,26gr
6°44/43°26

Major urban remains.

Approaching Fréjus, it is difficult not to recognise that this was once a Roman city. In the east the aqueduct, in the west the amphitheatre grandly proclaim quintessential Roman needs. Yet the narrow streets, the Place Formigé and the episcopal palace, cathedral and beautiful cloister, clustering in the centre, embody a different heritage. A tiny medieval community huddling in an area less than a quarter of the Roman site is not unusual; what might seem surprising is that Fréjus still had a population of only 6,000 as recently as the 1950s, probably significantly less than the Roman colony. The 1970s and 1980s, though, have been decades of rapid development. The new housing estates and supermarkets brought archaeological opportunities and crises, eventually stimulating the creation of a municipal archaeological service in 1982.

Until then, there had been a mixture of local indifference and passionate concern, the latter represented by the work of Texier and Aubenas in the nineteenth century and Donnadieu and Février in the twentieth. Donnadieu proclaimed Fréjus 'the Pompeii of Provence'. In reality, nothing here equals the remains at Arles or Orange, yet an aqueduct second only to that of Nîmes, the number of sites, some quite unusual, and the unpresuming feel of Fréjus, do make it one of the most attractive Roman centres in Provence.

Development

Excavation in Fréjus suggests that there was some occupation in the early Iron Age but this was small-scale and not continuous. Most Iron Age settlement in the region appears to have been walled hilltop sites, some very high. Agricultural sites in the plain have been found under the alluvium, but

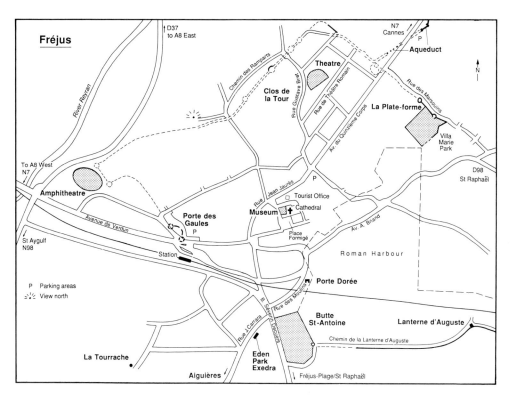

Figure 86

it is likely that the population was dominated by warring, pastoral communities. These Ligurians, by the late Iron Age, were perhaps part of the Salluvii Confederation (based on Entremont; see AIX, p. 127). Evidence of Massaliote influence is sparse.

The earliest Roman material found is pre-Augustan and a letter to Cicero mentions Forum Julii, suggesting there was a market town and harbour dedicated to Julius Caesar from at least the 40s BC. The relevance of a naval base in Gaul with an easy land link to Aix would have been apparent to Octavian, after his hard struggle with the ships of Sextus Pompey in the 30s BC. Following his triumph at Actium 31 BC, he transferred here a fleet of captured ships and construction work began on the port installations. However, before the harbour work began, Forum Julii became a colony for veterans from Legion VIII. Contemporary houses, found in the 1970s in the Clos de la Tour area, are small, though the discovery of mosaics and the superb Hermes (see p. 263) suggests more than one veteran invested his savings to embellish his home.

The port and its associated buildings were probably only completed by the end of the Augustan era. The shape of the harbour and the way it silted up imply that it was once an *étang*; probably the warships were at first beached or tied to wooden wharfs. The base included 1,000 m+ stone quays, two grandiose buildings overlooking the harbour at each end and many unidentified structures found below the town's harbour wall which no doubt included the dry docks, repair shops, provision stores necessary to an arsenal (a wet dock was discovered by the Porte Dorée in 1986 – now covered by a car park).

The fleet almost certainly had its barracks in the Villeneuve suburb. A baths, two probable barrack blocks and an enormous find of specially minted local coins together with pottery from Italy suggest military issues made in the 20s BC. Once the Empire was firmly established and the threat of civil war receded, Forum Julii's strategic role declined. Misenum in Italy took over the role of fleet base in the western Mediterranean, but it is clear from Tacitus that Fréjus continued to be used as a subsidiary naval station and was again significant in the civil wars following Nero's removal (AD 68–9). However, the archaeological material at the barrack site ends at about this time and there is no further literary reference.

It has so far proved impossible to identify any of the central Roman public buildings securely, even though they must have been in an area near the cathedral square. However, excavations at the Clos de la Tour site have provided a continuous picture of a residential neighbourhood where occupation was uninterrupted until the end of the fourth century.

All the best-known post-Augustan buildings (amphitheatre, theatre, aqueduct) are poorly dated, but opinion now favours the first century. Yet there are hints that Fréjus did not expand in a way that the first Roman settlers might have expected. During the 1980s, excavations in the Place Formigé revealed beautifully painted houses of the early first century AD, but none here or in the Clos area develop along the lines of houses in VIENNE or VAISON. The land beyond the theatre, but within the ramparts, appears to have been used for cultivation. The many rescue excavations outside the ramparts have revealed potteries and cemeteries, but little of residential suburbs. During the first and second centuries AD on the north-east of the town, the high-quality clay was used to manufacture amphorae and fine ware.

There were of course villas near to the city, such as that found at Villepey: perhaps one of them was the home of Forum Julii's most famous citizen, Gnaeus Julius **Agricola**. Born in AD 40, firmly educated here by his mother Julia Procilla and allowed to absorb only a limited dose of soft Greek learning in Massalia, he went on to a career that culminated with his governorship of Britain and victory over the Caledonians of Scotland at the battle of Mons Graupius. Agricola was a model for those in the local elites who committed themselves to the Roman Imperial order: promotion to the top was possible. His parents owned estates in Gaul and Italy and both sides had achieved senatorial status; his father important enough to be murdered by Caligula. Julia Procilla is described by Tacitus as a 'paragon of feminine virtue' – perhaps as much because she too was to be murdered (AD 69), in her case defending family property in Italy against Otho's troops.

Fréjus did not play a leading part in late Roman southern Gaul, though it did manage to become the centre of an episcopal diocese with its first known bishop in 374. Most housing was clustered around the cathedral with little more than hovels elsewhere: in the northern Pauvadou cemetery the walls were used to build lean-to huts. At least the city, or rather its bishop, was able to attract leading masons to construct a fine baptistery, much of which still stands.

Visiting the sites

To visit everything will take at least a day and if you decide you want to see the remains of the aqueduct outside Fréjus (which I so enjoyed), then they alone will take half a day or more, depending on how much you decide to walk and where you choose to eat.

The aqueduct

Avenue du Quinzième Corps. Parking area on south side of road.

The remains stretch along the N7 between the Avenue des Aqueducs and the D437 roundabout.

The pillars are massive and their height striking. They have been repaired, some rather excessively. The builders used red and green sandstone from different local quarries for the facing blocks, whilst the arches, better preserved nearer the roundabout, are outlined with longer blocks of brown sandstone. These are in turn enclosed by a row of small, square, *petit appareil*. Some pillars are strengthened with buttresses. The holes in the pillars were left by the Gallo-Roman workers when they used them to carry their wooden scaffolding.

When the aqueduct reached the town rampart it turned sharply north, using the walls as support for the channel. The rampart forms the south-western boundary of the parkland.

Gate and ramparts

Northern side of Avenue du Quinzième Corps.

The gate: little survives of the rare oval courtyard gateway explored by Donnadieu in the 1930s. A single pillar marks the rear gateway, built of *grand appareil* and now decorated with a cross. The aqueduct crossed the top of the north tower.

The rampart: the gate design, the high, but thin, curtain wall (2.35 m thick), the mix of round and semi-circular towers, help date this to the time of Augustus. The aqueduct obviously makes a mockery of the ramparts as even minimal military defences.

The north-east section: made of red sandstone plus largely green sandstone aqueduct additions, it is easy to follow, despite its dilapidation. The wall followed the ground topography, but the aqueduct had to remain level, therefore as well as having arches across two tower interiors, extra walls had to be made in places to carry the channel, whilst at others the channel cut into the top of the wall. Amongst the cypress and oak trees, the aqueduct cuts the north-east corner rejoining the rampart on the northern side.

The north rampart: this long and heavily restored section of walling and aqueduct can be followed to the few fragments after the Porte de l'Agachon/ Chemin de Pauvadou. The main interest is the **large semi-circular tower**. It rises above second-storey height where the upper windows mark the parapet level; it must have originally risen to *c.* 15 m, but the walling is only 1.2 m thick. The lower green sandstone restoration work helps explain why the other towers along this section of walling have collapsed and are only marked by traces of foundation walling. The last scraps of the Porte de l'Agachon were destroyed in 1955.

Clos de la Tour

Excavated by Février, this important Roman residential area has not been built on, but has become entirely overgrown.

The theatre

Rue du Théâtre Romain. Well signposted, but kept locked. The key is available from Hôtel de Ville, Services Culturels.

The theatre is very ruined and has not been heavily restored, but with scaffolding added it is used for summer performances.

Little remains of the stage area. Four drums of a column and a piece of architrave have been re-erected. The *cavea* is represented by the radial stone ribs that once supported the vaulting. The absence of lower seating around the orchestra implies that it may have been wooden.

La Plate-forme

Rue des Marsouins. Signposted south-east from Porte de Rome, *c.* 350 m.

After passing the Pourcin stadium, the road begins to fall steeply, leaving a grass and tree-covered outcrop on the right. This hides a section of rampart with two circular towers, subsiding outwards under the weight of La Plate-forme above. A track goes through the undergrowth behind the

Fréjus

LA PLATE-FORME

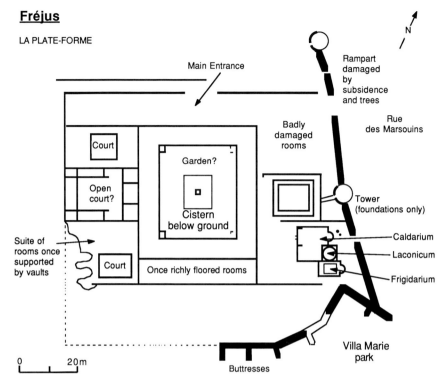

Figure 87

embankment. Although still not properly cared for, the main features of the site can be distinguished and there is **a splendid cistern**.

'The platform' is on an outcrop that overlooked the Roman port. The hillock was surrounded by walling and then filled with rubble to create a flat surface for what must have been an impressive building. Février's work (1960–3) did most to clarify its history. It was occupied from the AD 10s until at least the late second century and probably longer. This was not a bastion or a redoubt: the wall on the flat northern approach was thin, but note the section of reticular or diamond pattern block work. Février thought it was a mason having fun! Like La Butte St Antoine (see p. 258) it is best interpreted as the residence of an important official. Perhaps one belonged originally to the commander (prefect) of the fleet whilst the other was used by the provincial governor.

The site

The residency was built round a central courtyard with a pool made of now fragmentary tiles and concrete. Four corner holes and a central drain took rain into a cistern of 13 × 11 m. A modern staircase leads down into the three barrel-vaulted galleries, separated by arcades. The only drawback is modern rubbish.

It is possible to distinguish the circular room of the bath complex on the domestic side of the court, less easy to make sense of the rooms on the formal western side which has been more damaged by subsidence. The south-west corner gives a view over the town and dried up harbour area.

The impressive south and west sides are best seen from the exterior. Descend to the **Villa Marie public park**. The massive southern platform support walling rises 8 m and was reinforced with buttresses to resist the outward pressure of the earth and rubble. Three of the four eastern buttresses survive. The west side is equally striking with seven arcaded vaults, possibly used not simply as structural supports for the platform but as warehouses.

La Porte Dorée

Rue des Moulins, by the junction with Avenue Aristide Briand on the slope above the railway track.

This very impressive structure is not a gate, but the surviving arched section of a *frigidarium* belonging to a bath complex, originally recognised as such by Texier, above the north-west quay of the Roman port. The extensive use of brick is a relatively late technique and in 1988 it was dated to the late second century, rather earlier than the similar baths at Nice.

La Butte St Antoine

Boulevard Séverin Decuers.

Parking off Rue des Moulins immediately after railway bridge.

This mound marks the western end of the arc round the northern side of the Roman port. It too was surrounded by a buttressed wall to create a flat surface on which a large courtyard building could be constructed (see La Plate-forme, pp. 256–7).

Beside the Boulevard Séverin Decuers/de la Mer there is a 145 m section of **fine enclosing walling** sitting on some exposed sandstone bedrock. To obtain the strength needed to contain the sand and earth mix on top of the rock, a series of semi-circular niches were constructed. These were then faced with a thin cover of *petit appareil* stonework. In many places the facing has disintegrated or been removed, leaving the niches exposed. A large entrance at the southern end may be original.

The site is neglected and even more overgrown than La Plate-forme. Traces of wall do little more than indicate the Augustan residence on the

Fréjus

LA BUTTE ST ANTOINE

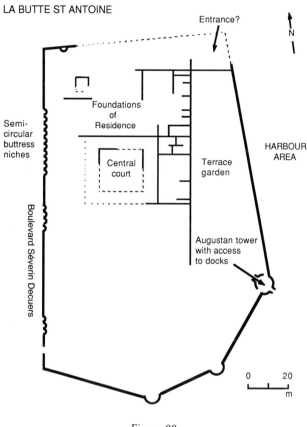

Figure 88

western side. No buildings were found on the side overlooking the harbour: perhaps this was a garden. The south-eastern corner has extensive remains of a large Augustan round tower, modified subsequently. Texier, without any evidence, identified it as a harbour lighthouse. By the tower are remains of the small seventeenth-century chapel that gave La Butte its full name. It is possible to reach the Chemin de la Lanterne Auguste via the tower, possible part of the original design providing direct access to the harbour.

The Roman port and La Lanterne d'Auguste

Chemin de la Lanterne d'Auguste.

The best view of the Roman port has always been from the road running along on top of what was the **southern quay**, 4 m wide and some 500 m long, and from the Rue du Port Romain, still marked by the original harbour walling. In spite of the railway track through the middle, the luxuriant allotments have helped to distinguish the harbour basin. Development threatens the area and a clear sense of the Roman past may disappear. New research work is also planned. Hopefully it will still be possible to imagine the triremes and biremes by the quay, rarely ever called on to do any fighting but often carrying out escort duties for provincial governors and others.

They would have rowed out past the 'lantern', a solid tower topped with a six-sided pyramid, still surviving to its full height of 10 m. During the nineteenth century it was heavily restored, but the eastern face is the most original. It was probably a marker for the harbour entrance. Traces on the other side of the canal suggest it had a companion there. Donnadieu saw these lanterns as poles to hold a chain for defending the harbour, but the design does not seem really appropriate.

The *exedra* burial chamber

Rue Jean Carrara, Eden Park estate, *c.* 100 m from the junction with Boulevard Séverin Decuers.

The south-west cemetery has been known for many years, but unlike Pauvadou and St Lambert has not had any co-ordinated excavation; paradoxically two monuments have survived here.

The alcove or *exedra* is not *in situ*. To be preserved it was painstakingly dismantled and re-erected 20 m from the find site. The *exedra* contained a memorial altar placed on fine marble flooring, forming part of a much larger room, about the size and shape of a triclinium. In Italy there are many examples of such funerary rooms where the family of the deceased would hold commemoration dinners in his/her honour; this could be a founder colonist's tomb where the family celebrated '*parentalia*'.

La Tourrache

Rue de la Tourrache, near Villeneuve school.

This large circular mausoleum is now a weathered concrete mass, the exterior *grand appareil* blocks having all been removed. It too has an Italian model in the '*columbaria*'. Inside it has four small and one large niche, where urns and sarcophagi rested.

Villeneuve baths/Aiguières

The well-preserved walls of the large bath complex are still visible as part of a wine merchant's. The twin baths were perhaps for officers and men, linked to the early barracks found on the Aiguières estate (nothing preserved). Equally the baths could be a more conventional male/female system associated with a suburb, hinted at by later buildings on top of the barracks.

The amphitheatre

Entrance Rue Henri Vadon, off the Avenue de Verdun.
Hours: 1 April–30 September   9.30–11.45 a.m., 2.00–6.15 p.m.
        1 October–31 March   9.00–11.45 a.m., 2.00–4.15 p.m.

Approaching the entrance, the scale of the great radiating *cavea* walls still proclaim that this was a Roman amphitheatre, but it has not been lucky. It has suffered from both geological weakness and human mistreatment. The sandstone rock, from which the northern side was carved, crumbled away over the centuries. The terrible flood of 1959, when the Malpasset dam broke and killed 420 people, swept the loose remains from the interior and left the arena water and silt-filled for months – but did little else. The destruction of the exterior façade is thought to have been a deliberate act by the townspeople to prevent Saracen raiders using it as a fortress in the Middle Ages. A final regret, on my part at least, is the heavy restoration in some parts of the building, first in the later nineteenth century using brown *petit appareil* and then even more excessively during the 1960s and 1970s using fresh green sandstone.

Charles Texier's work published in 1849 is still the fundamental study, only slightly modified by later archaeological research.

The arena

This is almost as large as those at Nîmes and Arles. The main entrances were on the long axis, the western entrance still having its stone flooring. On the southern side there was a small entrance that was probably used by scene-changers and other amphitheatre officials. Now hidden by the modern arena floor is a cruciform cellar; only 2 m deep it may have been used for water rather than the usual 'surprise' appearances; a channel found on the north side could have supplied the water.

The cavea

Much smaller than Nîmes or Arles, the capacity can have been no more than *c.* 12,000. The northern side was partly cut from the hillside and is unimpressive. The south is much better preserved. Here there was a ground floor, first floor and attic with galleries and vomitoria for access. However, as Donnadieu demonstrated, there was no external gallery. Spectators entered direct through the façade, either by a passage to the main internal gallery (heavily restored) where they could enter the lower seating, or used the alternating staircases to reach the upper rows. Most of the stairs have gone, but lines of sloping double bricks along the radiating walls, above which the vaulted ceilings began, indicate which were staircases or passages.

Dating is uncertain. A design utilising the hill and the absence of an external gallery suggests an early date, AD 40s–60s, the use of brickwork (original – or renovation?) a late second-century date.

Porte des Gaules

Corner of Avenue de Verdun and Rue Martin Bidoure, below the Place Agricola (parking).

The construction of the Place Agricola in the mid-nineteenth century, 6.5 m above the ancient ground level, turned the Roman gateway into a containing wall, though managing to preserve its Augustan outlines.

The central gate and its two side passages, the old stonework easily distinguished from the new wall, were guarded by two semi-circular towers, shown by base courses of *grand appareil*. At first circular towers were intended, and one is exposed to the left of the gateway, but the plan was changed before more than the foundations were built. Curving *petit appareil* walls formed a courtyard that once had round towers at the corners: the reconstructed northern tower clearly bears no resemblance to the Roman original.

Place Formigé, cathedral and baptistery

During the 1980s, isolated digs were possible. The most important discovery was an Augustan house under the Place Formigé (1988 and immediately filled in), made special because plastered and painted walls survived to a metre high. It implies the expected early Empire public buildings must have developed elsewhere.

The baptistery

The medieval walling on the corner of the cathedral building encloses the fifth-century baptistery. J. Formigé restored it sensitively in the 1920s. Original material figures in all the structure up to the octagon, above is speculative. Février has argued that an external pointed polygonal top is more likely than Formigé's guess of a round tower. Inside, the niches are separated by Corinthian columns. The northern and western pairs are both reused: respectively second and fourth century AD. The south and east were both carved when the baptistery was constructed, the eastern showing a markedly 'medieval' trend to individual features. The octagon reuses a

Roman sculpture for one pier. The pool is largely rebuilt and the canopy very much an idea of Formigé's.

The cathedral

Largely medieval, late Roman walling and part of a mosaic were found during repairs. They could have formed part of a fifth-century church.

Fréjus museum

Hours:	Summer	9.00 a.m.–7.00 p.m. daily
	Winter	9.00 a.m.–noon, 2.00–5.00 p.m., except Tuesday

By the twelfth-century cloisters there is a two-room museum with a small collection of the material from Forum Julii. For a number of years, the room containing monumental stonework and tombstones has been kept locked and the outstanding Hermes has only been displayed as a replica, the original hidden somewhere else – naughtily not admitted to on the label.

The **double-headed Hermes** is a beautiful example of classic art, found in the Clos de la Tour area in 1970. The faces are very similar, almost expressionless, but not the same. They are both young men with richly decorated hair. One has a long, pointed beard, evocative of early Greek gods, but his moustache ends in second-century AD twirls, like the waves of his beard. It suggests Hermes, the rather immoral messenger of the gods. The other has a shorter curly beard and on the forehead the worn, slight, horns of a goat: this is Pan, Hermes' son. Both are identified with virility and fertility and normally might have stood in a young men's association room or a baths. The soft sophisticated Gallo-Roman image makes a sharp contrast with the stark, sinister Gallic double-head found at Roquepertuse (see MARSEILLE, p. 176).

St Raphaël Archaeological Museum

Rue des Templiers, next to the church above the junction of the Avenue Leclerc, Rue M. Allongue and Avenue de Valescure.

Hours:	15 June–15 September	10.00 a.m.–noon; 3.00–6.00 p.m., except Tuesday
	16 September–14 June	11.00 a.m.–noon; 2.00–5.00 p.m., except Sunday

Despite having a good small collection of Roman underwater discoveries, the museum has the feel of a place for a rainy day seaside outing. Both the shipwrecks represented and the sub-aqua archaeological equipment displayed date from the early 1960s; sadly the presentation appears to have remained unaltered since then (for more complete and up-to-date exhibitions of shipwreck material see MARSEILLE, pp. 171, 175, and AGDE, p. 52).

The two main cargoes represented here were from ships that sank off the Cap du Dramont, 6 km east of St Raphaël. In the garden, ranks of amphorae have been stacked to suggest how they would have been carried on **Dramont A** in the first century BC. A reconstructed anchor shows how the lead and wooden parts fit together and help make sense of widely differing sizes and weights of other Roman lead anchor arms on display.

Inside the museum there is material from **Dramont D**. When it went down in the first century AD, its load was pottery mortars – pelves – and amphorae. The stamped mortars show they were made by a business in central Italy. Dates and figs once filled the amphorae, probably from the eastern Mediterranean. The crew are most poignantly represented by the water pump, little use to them when the ship foundered.

Le Pont des Esclapes

Roman bridge.

West of Fréjus, 2.25 km along the N7. Opposite Les Esclapes industrial estate take the minor road south over the level crossing and 75 m further on. It is about 15 m west of a modern concrete bridge.

Amongst the reeds of the drainage channel the three arches of the bridge can just be discerned; these are decorated with double rows of long and small blocks, like the aqueduct. The semi-circular buttresses are even harder to see. The bridge carried the road to the bay of St Tropez across a stream in what was then marshland.

The aqueduct outside Fréjus

This description covers most of the visible remains between the D437 roundabout and the site of the Malpasset dam, a distance of about 8 km in a straight line, markedly longer by road and track. The course of the aqueduct is sometimes obscure, not simply because sections have been destroyed, but where possible the Romans buried the channel. Most of the sites are within minimal walking distance from places where it is possible to park a car. The aqueduct was 40 km long; for its beginnings, see MONS (p. 276).

Château Aurélien public park

Junction of N7 and D437/Avenue André Léotard.

For about 500 m there are remains of pillars and arches gradually getting

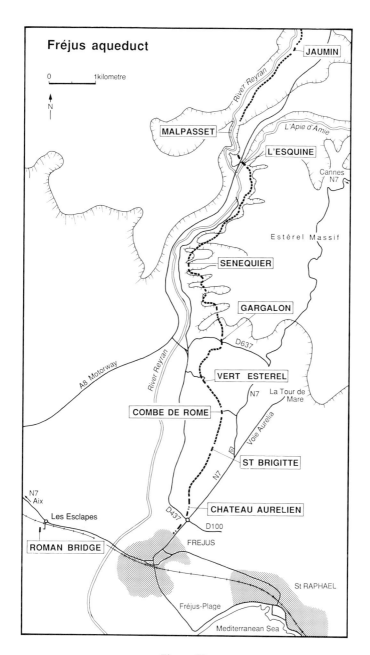

Figure 89

lower as the ground rises, until it finally disappears at the fence marking the limits of the park and the youth hostel beyond. The pinkish stonework has been restored without excess.

St Brigitte

Park in the left turning, shortly after the N7 swings away from the Voie Aurélia to La Tour de Mare.

The 'Mur de Ste Brigitte' is a low wall 37 m long that carried the aqueduct channel in the open land c. 200 m behind the campsite. The wall and channel are 1–1.5 m high and filled with vegetation, though it is planned to clear this. Turning north, the channel goes underground.

Combe de Rome

Take turning on left c. 600 m beyond Europa camp site at La Combe de Rome into La Pinède Romane housing estate.

The 'Arcs Bonnet' cross a small ravine in the centre of the estate by the Avenue du Pont Romain. Squat pillars, consolidated to preserve them, support a channel in which the water-resistant concrete lining is clearly visible.

Vert Estérel estate

It is not possible currently to walk direct from the Combe de Rome to here. By car, this can only be approached by turning east off the D37, some 300 m from the A8 *péage*. It might be more convenient to visit the Gargalon arches first.

The 'arcs Bérenguier' are on the Avenue de Val des Arches, c. 100 m from the D37. At the southern end the channel emerges from a conduit and is carried on small arches across the narrow valley.

Gargalon arches

On the D637, just over 1 km from the junction with the N7.

The road passes under a massive arch, one of the last of an arcade of fourteen that crossed the attractive valley setting of the Gargalon River, bending sharply into the hillside. One collapsed as recently as 1967, whilst some of the arches and pillars on the other side of the river are largely supported by trees and ivy. The arch is 15 m high and it is not surprising that it has supporting buttresses.

Le Reyran valley sites

The D637 joins the D37 at the *péage* for the motorway. Follow the D37 up the eastern side of the valley. The final ridges of the Estérel massif form tiny valleys round which the aqueduct winds. Most of the course is hidden, but where the builders decided to cross a valley and arcades were constructed, evidence still survives and is now being kept clear of gorse.

Sénéquier arches

The aqueduct has two channels here, as elsewhere. Possibly the sharp turns on the twisting route had led to frequent blockages. Inaccessible valleys must have made maintenance difficult. A double channel would have enabled repairs to be carried out without cutting off the supply to Forum Julii. It rises 20 m above the valley floor and is made of red porphyry, quarried only 100 m away.

L'Esquine arches in l'Apié d'Amic valley

The motorway crosses the Reyran to follow a ridge on the eastern side. The l'Apié d'Amic trickles down here in the summer. Follow one of the pathways north *c.* 200 m, east of both the motorway and stream. About 100 m below the motorway are five twin arches, no longer overgrown, but still set in romantic woodland. The aqueduct bends quite sharply here; thick deposits are still clearly visible in the channel.

The D37 track comes to a virtual end at the motorway. It is a difficult walk (1 km) from here to the Malpasset dam, site of the 1959 disaster, and even more intimidating (another 2.5 km) to the single arch, again double channel, leaping the **Jaumin** valley.

HYERES, Var

Michelin 84–17
IGN 68–D2
4,22/47,90gr
6°08/43°07

Greek town remains.

5 km to the south of Hyères (take the N559), in the suburb of L'Almanarre on the shore opposite Giens, are the ruins of a small Greek and Roman town. They lie partially exposed in a fenced area next to Pomponiana hospital, soon after the road turns sharply westwards at its junction with a minor road down a causeway to what was once the island of Giens, now linked to the mainland by sand-dunes and salt-beds.

Hyères

THE SITE OF OLBIA

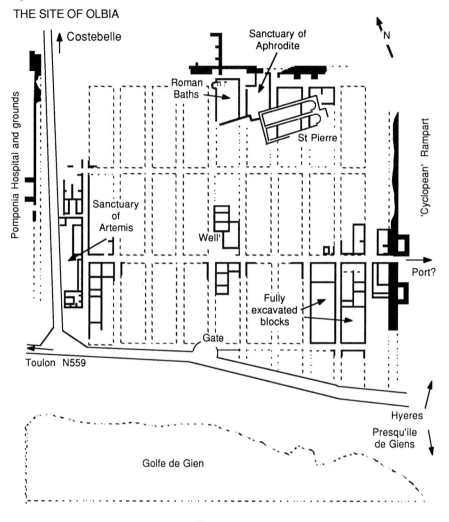

Figure 90

The first ancient remains were found in the mid-nineteenth century and immediately identified as 'Pomponiana', a place mentioned on early Roman itineraries in roughly this area. However, in 1909 a Latin inscription was found dedicated to the Genius or guardian spirit of Olbia, a Massaliote settlement mentioned by Strabo. Jacques Coupry devoted a lifetime to working here and showed that this was indeed a Greek town founded in the mid-fourth century BC.

Coupry revealed a small, formally constructed square settlement with sides of 160 m (= 600 Greek feet). Inside were forty rectangular blocks split in half by a main street running east–west from the sanctuary of Artemis to the town gate. It is a design in the spirit of Hippodamus, the Greek architect associated with the development of grid-iron cities, but equally the small blocks are barrack-like, divided into tiny living units; with its wall and towers, it strongly suggests a fort with accommodation for a *speira* or battalion of *c.* 200–250 men and their households.

Massalia may have decided to found this sub-colony to protect the sea-route to Italy. Local relations must have developed well: Costebelle oppidum is only 2.5 km to the north and Greek centuriation has been found in the area. Olbia clearly settled down as a farming and trading settlement in its own right; by mid-second century BC domestic dwellings within the blocks had been expanded. Occupation was continuous until the sixth century AD, though the lack of any significant Roman public buildings suggests that it was never an important centre. Since Antiquity, the sea's incursions have destroyed the southern rampart and the adjoining house-blocks.

The most recent work has been associated with Giens 'island'. At **L'Acapte** on the northern shoreline, Coupry and Mme Giffault have excavated a rural sanctuary to Aristaeus, the son of Apollo and the nymph Cyrene. The sherds of an estimated 650 vases were found, many inscribed, some simply to the god, others almost making poems. Eighty per cent have Greek names. It was used until the early first century AD.

Off-shore from **La Madrague**, underwater archaeologists led by A. Tchernia and P. Pomey excavated a large Roman ship with a capacity of *c.* 400 tonnes – more than most ships until the eighteenth century! The cargo was mixed: wine amphorae and glazed ware from Terracina in central Italy. It sank in the 70s BC. Many amphorae had been removed, not by modern treasure-hunters, but by ancient rescue divers using heavy stones to propel themselves to the bottom. No doubt the load was valuable and the ship not too deep. The prohibitive costs of constructing a special sealed chamber (see MARSEILLE, p. 175) meant it was left once again.

The Olbia remains

The main gate

This led to the port, now covered by the airport. Best preserved is the **northern tower**, built using regular rectangular drystone walling. A much more irregular type, that Coupry identifies as 'Cyclopean', is found in the **eastern rampart** to the north of the tower where two courses of facing stones have survived.

Excavated blocks

Numbers 2, 6 and parts of 1 and 5, just inside the gate, show an area that changed little in outline over 500 years. Despite internal room changes, the external block walls remained virtually unaltered. Street paving survives and there is a drainage gully in the centre of the road.

Main road

The central crossroads are marked by a well. Most of the blocks here are either overgrown or unexcavated.

Sanctuary of Artemis

The precinct covering blocks 38 and 39 makes it the largest building on the site. Coupry found niches for offerings near the entrance and dedications to Artemis, Massalia's protecting goddess.

The north-east corner

The most recent excavations have been carried out here. Block 20 is covered by a **small Roman bath complex**, whilst block 16, based on the interpretation of a small altar, was probably the site of an Aphrodite temple. In the Middle Ages the convent of **St Pierre de l'Almanarre** and its cemetery covered much of this area.

Museum

Place Théodore Lefebvre, Hyèrçs.
Hours: 10.00 a.m.–noon, 3.00–6.00 p.m. Monday, Wednesday, Thursday, Friday
3.00–6.00 p.m. Saturdays, Sundays for special exhibitions

This is a small top-floor museum in an almost domestic setting used to display some of the finds from Olbia.

LA TURBIE, Alpes-Maritimes

Michelin 84–10
IGN 61–D9
5,63/48,61gr
7°24/43°44

Roman victory monument.

La Turbie

Restoration

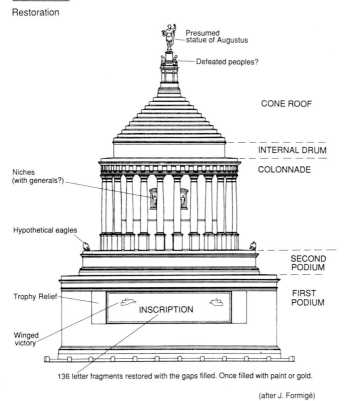

Presumed statue of Augustus

Defeated peoples?

CONE ROOF

INTERNAL DRUM

COLONNADE

Niches
(with generals?)

Hypothetical eagles

SECOND PODIUM

FIRST PODIUM

Trophy Relief

INSCRIPTION

Winged victory

136 letter fragments restored with the gaps filled. Once filled with paint or gold.

(after J. Formigé)

Figure 91

The village of La Turbie is 6 km from Monte Carlo, 18 km from Nice and 13 km from Menton.

The Alps plunge steeply down to the coast above Monaco. When the Romans began to survey and mark out their new coast road to Gaul in 13 BC, they took the easiest route, crossing the highest ridge of Mt Agel where there was a natural depression forming a break 500 m up; they called it 'Summa Alpe' – the alpine summit. The view from here looks far into Italy and on to the Estérel beyond Antibes. It was the perfect site for a victory monument; all who lived or travelled through the area would see it, as long as it was imposing enough. Augustus made sure it was: his 'Tropaeum' or trophy was originally 50 m high. It still stands 35 m and dominates the village. Most evocative is the approach from the east. The D2564 follows the Via Julia Augusta and every twisting corner presents the trophy, the white limestone and marble faces gleaming, its size giving an illusory nearness.

271

The trophy

Hours: Tourist season   9.00 a.m.–7.00 p.m. daily
        Out of season   9.00 a.m.–noon, 2.00–5.00 p.m. daily

Binoculars useful.

The summer entry price is high, but as you will be assured, it also includes a hunting and exotic bird sanctuary with, in the afternoons, a display.

The splendid modern appearance of the trophy is not a fortuitous survival but superb restoration work, based on the money of a wealthy American, Dr Edward Tuck, and the brilliance of the Formigés, inspired by the commitment of Philippe Casimir, a local archaeologist. During the early Middle Ages the monument suffered seriously from barbarians, including Christians who perceived it as dedicated to the pagan Apollo. Inevitably its position and ready-made structure led to its conversion into a castle (thirteenth century), whilst the houses that clustered around it used the rubble remains for their walls. Until 1860 it lay outside France and in an earlier war (1705) a French general had attempted to blow it up – fortunately its loose solidity enabled it to survive this assault. Just before it was handed over to the French, the Savoy royal family ordered its first restoration, largely a matter of preventing further decay.

Little more was done until Casimir began excavations in the 1900s and attracted the interest of the Formigés and Tuck. Perhaps the greatest contribution came from Jules Formigé, who worked out the basic unit – 4 Roman feet – and the principles of proportion used by the designers. (These might have embodied more for the Romans than architectural principles: Picard argued that they were thought to have magical significance, reinforcing the expression of power implicit in the structure.) A single unit was embodied in the length of the *grand appareil* used in the base. Other measurements were multiples of this: the diameter of the circular inner core, the length of each side, the height of the two podiums and the estimated overall height. Close examination of the stonework combined with Formigé's deductions enabled the excavator–rebuilders to complete their work by 1934.

The precinct

A wide area around the trophy has clearly been levelled. For the Romans it was more than the necessary preliminary to building, it created a temple-like precinct; this was almost a place of worship.

The west face

This face is nearest the entrance and is the most complete. The Roman road passed by this side.

At the foot of the trophy is a pavement separating the building from the precinct, twelve short pillars on each side mark its edge.

The first podium: two courses of massive blocks form the foundations for the rest of the slightly recessed plinth and cornice. On this face are two trophy reliefs; two winged Victories and an enormous inscription. All are reconstructed from fragments.

The inscription: the beautifully cut stone letters were like an incomplete jigsaw. Fortunately Pliny gave the full inscription when concluding his description of Italy. J. Formigé was able to use it to sort out the original words and fill in the gaps with new stonework.

It opens in letters over a foot high:

> To the Emperor Augustus, son of the Sanctified Caesar, supreme pontiff, in his fourteenth year of holding imperial power and seventeenth year of tribunician power, [erected by] the Senate and People of Rome.

It continues in small script:

> To commemorate that under his leadership and auspices all the Alpine peoples stretching from the Adriatic Sea to the Mediterranean were brought under the dominion of the Roman people. The Alpine people conquered . . . [there follows a list of forty-five different tribes].

The practice, however hollow it was becoming, of the Senate granting powers to Augustus, makes it possible to date the completion of the monument to 7 or 6 BC. At that time the Roman Imperial dream seemed to have no limit. With the uncertainties of alpine supply lines overcome by 14 BC, the Roman armies had been sweeping over the German plains as far as the Elbe and through the mountains of the Balkans and out into the Danube basin. Though the dream ended with revolt in the Balkans (AD 6) and a disastrous defeat in Germany (AD 9), making Augustus and his successors face the limitations posed by the defence of an already vast empire, the alpine tribes never again presented any threat to the Roman order. The last fifteen names are thought to have been tribes of the Alpes-Maritimes area.

The reliefs: whilst the small winged Victories present their crowns to Augustus, the two larger trophy reliefs seem to have been typical portrayals of chained captives kneeling by the T-shaped wooden post on which hang the tunics, shields and military equipment of defeated enemies. The position of the 'Victories' is a guess and the reconstruction of the 'trophy' fragments, ninety-eight on the left but only sixty-three on the right, is very much based on the later versions at ORANGE.

The second podium: also square, this is recessed behind the first forming a terrace. It too has a base (difficult to see), plinth and cornice. The corners certainly had statuary of some kind; Formigé thought they would have been eagles.

The circular colonnade: only four of twenty-four columns survive complete. The bases and capitals are of marble, the order is Doric; the frieze is decorated with reliefs of military symbols. Behind them it is possible to make out the remains of niches, originally twelve, perhaps filled with statues of Augustan generals.

The cone roof: behind and above the colonnade, the central drum continues to rise three courses, then the roofing begins. It has been possible to restore a few stones of the first four rows, but most of the drum still shows the medieval modifications made to create a crenellated battlement. On top of the cone there would certainly have been a statue, perhaps a trophy – probably Augustus. There might even have been a light on top of that; if so, La Turbie would have been visible at night far along the coast and out to sea.

The south face

This face had an entrance leading to the two interior staircases; the threshold and the pediment are largely original, the bronze doors are arbitrary recreations. The staircases as such have not survived, but the space for them is quite apparent. They finished with spiral staircases to the top of the second square podium. From there a passage led into the drum where a spiral staircase went up into the cone.

The east and north faces

It has not been possible to restore much on either of these sides as the depravations of the past have been too great. However, it does leave exposed the internal structure: the twenty-four spurs made of large blocks, filled in between with irregular small blocks.

The museum

On site. Opened 1934, it has a rather bleak and dated atmosphere.

There are milestones from the Via Julia; unassigned architectural pieces; clamps, stamped AUGUS or AU, used on the first two courses; a reconstruction model like a wedding cake; and interesting photographs of the Alpium Tropaeum before reconstruction.

Quarries

The marble was brought from Carrara in Italy, probably landed at Cap Martin rather than Monaco as the road climbed at a lower gradient from here.

The limestone came from nearby. The **Mont des Justices** quarry is *c.*

700 m east of La Turbie. Unfinished drums and blocks, left due to faults, still lie abandoned. A second quarry at **Giram**, *c.* 750 m north on the western flank of the Mt Agel ridge, has steps created by the quarry-workers cutting out a series of blocks.

LERINS ISLANDS, Alpes-Maritimes

Michelin 84–9
IGN 68–B9
5,25/48,35gr
7°03/43°32

Greek and Roman remains (see Figure 84).

The two Lérins islands lie close to the coast. Boat trips from Cannes to Ile Ste Marguerite and St Honorat take respectively only 15 and 30 minutes. Excursions are also possible from Antibes, Golfe-Juan, La Napoule and Nice.

Both islands were occupied in Antiquity. The overall name can be traced back to Strabo's Lero and Lerina, whilst their modern names derive from the fifth-century founders of a monastery and a convent. Ile Ste Marguerite is of course much more famous for the seventeenth-century Fort Royal where the 'Man in the Iron Mask' was held.

Ile Ste Marguerite

Traces of the Roman port and baths

These were found by J. Formigé in 1937 to the west of the modern port by the Etang Bataiguier.

Fort Royal

Hours: Summer   10.30 a.m.–noon, 2.00–5.30 p.m.
        Winter   10.00 a.m.–noon, 2.00–4.30 p.m.

North-west quarter: the remains can be viewed from above. The excavations here seem to confirm Pliny in saying that there had been an oppidum on the island and the Greek sanctuary described by Strabo was probably close to this site. The lowest levels belong to the fourth century BC. Italian influence, rather than Greek, predominates from early on and the mosaic flooring could be mid-first-century BC Roman settler housing. A massive rampart and its buttresses could be part of a Roman rebuilding of the sanctuary precinct. Other walls are interpreted as the remains of a portico and *cryptoporticus* (see ARLES, p. 145) constructed after an earthquake.

Vaulted cisterns: in other parts of the fort, four Roman cisterns have been identified and cleared of seventeenth-century rubble.

Ile St Honorat

After the collapse of Roman power in the north of Gaul, many officials fled south, including ecclesiastics like Honoratus. He chose the relative security and isolation of Lerina to create a monastic community, but one that still enabled him to keep in contact with other Christian leaders like Cassian in Marseille. He died in 430, having spent the last two years of his life as Bishop of Arles.

In the **old cloister** and the **museum** Greek and Roman architectural elements, broken inscriptions and sarcophagi show how the monks reused earlier material; a Constantinian milestone was even brought from the mainland as a ready-made column. The most interesting survivals are an inscription recording the *utricularii* or boatmen, who must have ferried people to the island, and a large *priapus* – no doubt avoiding destruction only because it was found relatively recently.

MONS, Var

Michelin 84–8
IGN 68–A7
4,87/48,55gr
6°43/43°42

Aqueduct cutting.

Mons is a quiet mountain village in the alpine foothills with a splendid view over the valley of the Siagnole, looking south towards the coast, across tree-covered hills and gorges. The main road, the D563, comes south 12.5 km from the N85 (Grasse–Castellane) or north 18.5 km from the D562 (Draguignan–Grasse) via Fayence. Its significance is as the **source** of the Fréjus aqueduct. A spring below Mons supplying the Siagnole was tapped with a channel following the course of the stream on the left bank, then after 200 m switching to the right. Large blocks in the stream bed are the relics of the aqueduct's beginnings.

The Roche Taillée

This dramatic cutting, made to carry the aqueduct on the western rock-face of the Siagnole valley, is only 2 km from the village, but by the D56 it is about 7.5 km. It is signposted, but is hidden from view below the road. 150 m above the river, the builders first cut a ledge round the cliff, but it was faulted and must have crashed into the valley. To get a secure base, the Romans dug this 50 m long, 20 m deep cutting. They would have used hand drills and wedges, then fire to heat and water to quench, so splitting the stone, but it would have done no more than slightly reduce the amount of back-breaking chisel work.

The path of the aqueduct can be followed downstream with ease for some distance. The atmosphere is secluded, even mysterious. It looks empty of human habitation and apart from the swine-herds and woodmen, it must have been so in Roman times.

NICE, Alpes-Maritimes

Michelin 84–19
IGN 61–D9
5,49/48,55gr
7°17/43°43

Amphitheatre and baths.

The Scottish novelist Tobias Smollett visited Nice in 1765 and saw 'a rich mine of Antiquities'. It was not in the old town or on the colline du château, where the recently destroyed fortifications had left exposed the foundations of a medieval cathedral, but 3 km above Nice in the vineyards and olive groves of Cimiez, next to the monastery. Two ruins helped identify the 'mine' for the treasure hunters: fragments of an amphitheatre and a 'Temple of Apollo', its massive walls then filled with a farmhouse.

In 1943, when Nice was under Italian control, P. M. Duval undertook a brilliant excavation of the amphitheatre and surveyed the whole area, setting the archaeological agenda for the next thirty years. F. Benoit then painstakingly carried this through, with the same passion he showed in his work for Arles. The new Cimiez site museum and research centre, opened 1989, marks a renewed impetus.

Development

Nice derived its name from the Greek Massaliote colony, but Nikaia has proved to be elusive. It once seemed obvious: the name itself, a variant on the word Nike or 'victory', declared a defeat of the local Ligurians and the establishment of an acropolis on the steep **colline du château**, by the mouth of the Paillon River and overlooking the port on the east. Now an attractive park, in all likelihood it was a native oppidum with no more Greek influence than elsewhere in Liguria. Where then was the Greek colony? Current thinking suggests Vieux Nice, west of the hill. The Paillon then had a branch joining the sea at the Promenade des Anglais, leaving a wide beach suitable

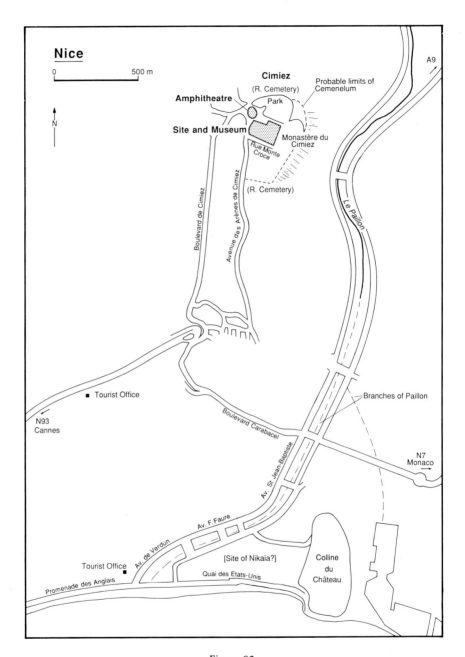

Figure 92

for unloading small ships. Unfortunately, no traces of it have yet been found.

Nikaia could only have been settled with the approval of the local tribe, the Vediantii, nor does the evidence suggest that their abandonment of their main oppidum in Cimiez followed conquest. Rampart walling of large polygonal blocks in the **Jardin du Monastère** are the sole exposed remains. Pottery thought to be from here suggests Cemenelum had a growing importance from the third century BC onwards with a strong element of imported Italian wares. The prehistoric track from Gaul to Italy came by the spur, giving it strategic significance. In 154 BC when the Romans came to help Massalia defend Antipolis and Nikaia from Ligurian attack, the Vediantii are not mentioned as foes, nor do they appear on the list at La Turbie. Roman Cemenelum developed as a town on the slopes around and below the tribal centre.

The new province of ALPES MARITIMAE only emerged during the latter first century AD – the date is still uncertain, but from 14 BC Cemenelum was its regional centre, at first with a military controller, then a procurator governor. Inscriptions show a locally raised regiment, the Cohors I Ligurum, and a regiment of cavalry from the borders of the Sahara desert, the Cohors Gaetulorum. They were no doubt used to patrol the main roads and recruit troops for frontier service. There was also a Cohors Nautici, presumably a naval detachment from Fréjus, which must have been based down in Nikaia.

The cemeteries suggest a town at its maximum of 20–25 ha, but it was never walled. It had neither the prestige of a great city nor was it seriously threatened until the later fourth century AD. No army fort, no forum, no temples, nor any other public buildings have been found except the amphitheatre and three public baths.

Cemenelum apparently peaked under the Emperors Severus and his son Caracalla, AD 193–217, when all three baths were built and the amphitheatre altered. Quite why this should be so is unclear. Perhaps they were built on Imperial initiative, but it was more usual for public buildings to be paid for by local patrons. What could have stimulated their sudden wealth? Perhaps the profits of coastal trade or the export of herbs and dye plants, or new rich seams found in lead- /silver-mining? Why the stress on leisure and entertainment? Was it linked to the road and an upsurge in travellers between Gaul and Italy?

In the late fourth century, when the barbarians finally passed through (the burning level is so widespread it could hardly be anything else), the transformation of the town was dramatic. Streets were still used and water was still supplied (indeed water still flowed in sections of the Mouraille aqueduct in 1974!). Even so, all the baths went out of use: one had poorly built houses, another was perhaps made a strongpoint. The third was converted into a cathedral for the Bishop of Cimiez. During the fifth century the site degenerated further, to be finally abandoned when the bishop admitted defeat in his battle with the Bishop of Nikaia; Nice was to grow from the settlement clustered around the cathedral on the colline du château, not Cimiez.

Amphitheatre

3 km north from the city centre at the junction of Boulevard de Cimiez and Avenue des Arènes.

This amphitheatre makes none of the impact that Nîmes or Arles achieve. It is not simply less well-preserved, it was also markedly smaller: the two-tier *cavea* held only 5,000 spectators.

The arena: carved from the rock it was about two-thirds that of Arles. The size, the lack of a cellar and the absence of service rooms in the *cavea* must have restricted the performances possible. Gladiators would have fought here, but animal hunts would have been very difficult. Perhaps mimes and shows more frequently found in theatres were presented. The remains of the podium wall have been stripped of marble facing.

The cavea: Duval showed that this must have been built in two major stages as the inner and outer rings supporting the seating are quite different. The inner two ovals are made of rectangular blocks filled with embanking to support the seats (apart from the rock on the north-east). These he dated to the Augustan period. In contrast the exterior wall and its radiating arms use *petit appareil* alternating with two–three brick courses in a thick mortar, best seen from outside on the northern side where the corbels have also survived best. The vaults of the arms are constructed using concrete alone, in some places the timber frame mould marks are still visible. This outer ring was a Severan addition.

Duval convincingly showed that the first amphitheatre was tiny, holding *c.* 500–600 with wooden seats initially. A tiny amphitheatre makes sense as a military building, mixing training work and visiting gladiators, and later examples are found in Germany and Britain (e.g., at Caerleon in Wales).

The main site and museum

Rue Monte-Croce, about 150 m south-east of amphitheatre.
Hours: 1 May–30 September   10.00 a.m.–noon, 2.00–6.00 p.m.,
                                                   closed Monday and Sunday mornings
              1 October–30 April   10.00 a.m.–noon, 2.00–5.00 p.m.,
                                                   closed as above

The Cimiez archaeological site covers over 1 ha of the north-east corner of the town. Not all of the enclosed area has yet been exposed. The museum on the west of the site has been built on sterile ground. The mansion housing the Musée Matisse probably covers the Mourielle aqueduct water distribution point. Two well-made east–west roads, Decumanus I and II, and one poorly defined north–south *cardo* define three *insula* each with a bath complex as its central building, all using the same floor plan. The best starting point is the northern *insula* where the so-called 'Temple of Apollo' still rises far above the rest of the remains.

Insula I

Decumanus I and the buttressed wall

A central sewer runs down the road to be joined by side drains and then run under pavings on the southern side of the road. On the north is a thick wall with buttresses 3 m apart dated to the later first century AD. Too small to be shops, perhaps purely decorative, but probably carrying an aqueduct through the town.

Northern baths

The baths filled a natural alcove, the terrace above, then 3 m higher, secured by embankment walls. There are **two entrances**, in the first of which there is still a door sill with jamb holes and a herring-bone brick pattern called *opus spicatum*, widely found in all three baths. The second has fragmentary paving and is beside the **latrines**, in which two hollowed lavatory seats still perch over the gully for running water. Behind them stretch reservoirs for collecting water and the annexe rooms, perhaps used for hanging clothes and by workers in the baths.

The **swimming pool** was once lined with marble. Only the chalk rubble base survives. One re-erected white limestone column symbolises the colonnade built round three sides of the pool.

A monumental entrance surrounded by another colonnade, of which only the base survives, once led to the *frigidarium*, known from the Middle Ages as the 'Temple of Apollo'. Well-cut stone and triple courses of brick rise all of 10 m. White marble thresholds and massive lintels (middle blocks missing), with semi-circular arches above, define the two entrances. The windows were once filled with glass (see examples from the eastern baths in the museum). The roof was vaulted using T-shaped brick ribs to secure tiles between them. Polychrome marble facing covered the floor, walls and oval plunge bath. In the niches were statues, shattered fragments of which were found in the bath, along with the almost complete figure of Antonia (see p. 286).

Here, even if the decor has disappeared, it is still possible to imagine the richness of the experience of visiting a bath in Antiquity. It was the leisure centre dream palace of the time: open to all and noisy, with slaves who applied the oil and scraped it off with their strigils, masseurs at work,

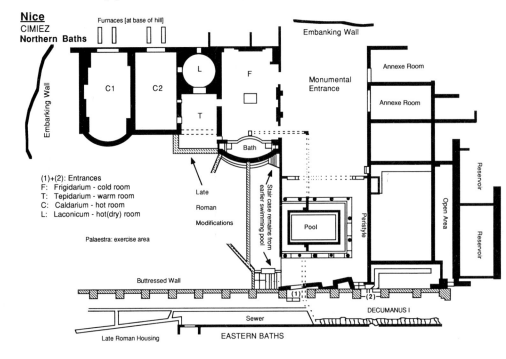

Figure 93

salesmen wandering around and the customers lounging and chatting, moving on to or returning from the various hot rooms beyond.

The other rooms are comparatively poorly preserved with collapsed floors and many of the hypocaust bricks removed. The **tepidarium**, as the western exterior wall of the *frigidarium* shows, was once vaulted in the same way. The two *caldaria* beyond were converted to houses in the late Roman period and the furnaces supplying them lie ruined. Originally there was one circular **laconicum** or dry heat room; this was too near the steam rooms and was replaced by two new *laconica* at the north end of the *frigidarium*.

Insula II

Eastern baths

Built on unidentified earlier buildings, this complex was probably constructed after the northern baths. The entrance from Decumanus II leads from the palaestra or exercise area to a pool set parallel to the road and surrounded with a herring-bone brick pavement. Behind the niche wall looking over the pool, alas without any decor, lay the service area. The furnace for the second *caldarium* has some stairs beside it, no doubt to

282

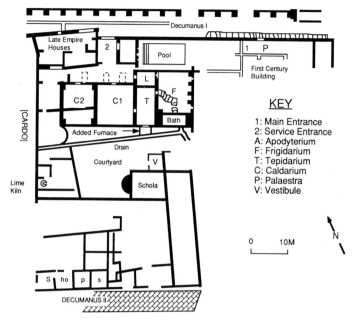

Figure 94

enable slaves to fill the boiler tank with water to supply steam in the baths. Part of the area has typical late Empire houses, one with a *dolium* storage jar. None of the rooms are particularly well preserved, though the first *caldarium* has the best hypocaust on the site.

Southern quarter

The small apsed structure set at the end of a long corridor, perhaps belonging to a public building of some kind, was a **schola**. This was a meeting-place for an artisans' guild or collegium, identified by the dedication found here set up by the patron of the *utricularii*, the river boat- and ferrymen of the town. They would have met and perhaps feasted here at their patron's expense in return for giving their political support.

Decumanus II is an exceptionally well-preserved example of town roadway made of polygonal pavings. By the *cardo* there is a late Roman lime kiln for making mortar.

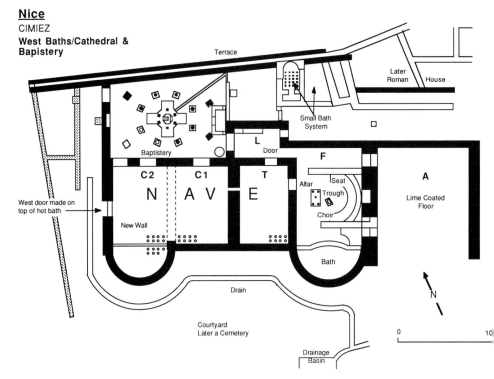

Nice
CIMIEZ
**West Baths/Cathedral &
Bapistery**

Figure 95

Insula III

Western baths and late Antiquity church

This complex is believed to be the last constructed, perhaps solely for women; the drains were filled with hairpins and ear-rings. As the fifth-century church simply converted the existing buildings they are best described together.

The two furnaces have been pulled down to create the space for a **baptistery**, but the two arches for the hot air to enter the *caldaria* are still visible. The baptismal pool is six-sided and made of pink concrete. A canopy was suspended over the pool on six small columns; three bases survive. The central cupola in the roof was supported by eight marble columns, two of which have been re-erected. The roof was supported by four thick square pilasters, the eastern pair frame a small raised area or podium.

The **church** nave was created by pulling down the walls separating the *caldaria* and *tepidarium* and the choir built in the *frigidarium* with a new west-facing apse and presbytery bench set along the edge. By the ruined altar base is a trough; it could have held an early saint's relics. The oval bath was filled in to make a sacristy.

The *laconicum* perhaps became a changing room. Baptism in this period involved the convert being immersed, helped by officials standing on the triangular pool steps, whilst receiving the bishop's blessing from his podium, then, in a special white tunic, entering the church to pray.

For Benoit, the small baths were used by the convert before baptism; a more recent and cynical interpretation is that they belonged to the partially excavated house, probably the bishop's!

The museum

New, white and rather stark, but embodying some imaginative effects.

Section I–III

The donated material was largely collected in Italy and therefore provides a fine art picture of Etruscan, Greek (mainly made in Italy) and Italian pottery; there are a few Etruscan bronzes. In addition there is a display of third- and fourth-century AD African red-slip ware from Tunisia. However, considerably more striking are the **La Formigue 'C' bronzes**.

La Formigue 'C' sank between 80 and 60 BC in the Golfe-Juan (see Figure 84) after hitting an underwater reef. As well as the usual cargo of amphorae, she was also carrying a banqueting suite of couches and drinking equipment; a few superb bronze fittings have survived water, time and robbery.

Couch fittings: the most important are three couch fulcrums. These are curved bronze pieces that fitted on the side of the armrest against which the guest would lounge at dinner. One is shaped like a duck, another ends as a horse, a third a donkey (often associated with Dionysus).

Silenus: one of two decorating the handle of a wine bucket or *situla* (its pair disappeared after discovery). The splendid confidence of line and the distant but knowing face make it one of the finest examples found anywhere. It was inlaid with copper to give a gold effect.

Sections IV–VI

Pre-Roman oppida material and milestones from the Via Julia, including an Augustan example from when the road was built.

Sections VII–XI

Roman Cimiez through the products of daily life. For me the most evocative are: the incense bottles fused on the funerary pyre; a bronzeworker's collection – for sale or to melt down? – including a dancing faun copied from a Pompeiian version; and the silver trident, only survivor of a statuette of Neptune or Triton.

The most interesting evidence of municipal life in Cimiez is provided by the guild inscriptions: for example, that of C. Cassius Paternus, patron of the three colleges of the *utricularii* (the river boatmen), the *fabrii*, usually carpenters, and the *centonarii*, the fabric- or sail-makers. Combined guilds were only permitted from Caracalla's time. Though the main role was to ensure decent burial, the combination could have provided a fire-fighting service which the number of furnaces in the baths would have made important (see also ALBA, p. 20).

Caracalla himself is represented by the curly hair and intense eyes of a broken portrait head. Almost complete is the statue of **Antonia**. She died in AD 37, four years before her son Claudius became Emperor and declared her divine, here indicated by her diadem. After her husband Drusus died, she lived many years in Rome, an embodiment of Roman rectitude.

Sections XII–XIII in the basement

A successful attempt to evoke the cemeteries around Cimiez is made here with subdued lighting and large mural panels. An artificial floor level allows various types of graves to be 'buried' but visible in glass cases. The tombstones of the auxiliary soldiers are set up here, and there is a selection of sarcophagi, though none of great artistic merit.

It is a pity that the harsh daily life of early Christian Cimiez and the transfer to Nikaia could not have been more imaginatively demonstrated than through cases of ceramics and lamps.

RIEZ, Alpes de Haute-Provence

Michelin 84–5
IGN 60–D9
4,15/48,68gr
6°06/43°48

Temple and baptistery.

Riez has never been a very important town. Its small-scale success has been based on the rich soil of the Colostre valley and the crossroads of useful but secondary routes in the mountains of Haute-Provence, reinforced in the past by its religious vitality. Today, it is a quiet, gently attractive place, not far from the wild beauty of the Gorges du Verdon, with the long-term potential of becoming a major archaeological centre.

A short distance to the north-east of Riez rises Mt St Maxime, once the hillfort capital of the Reii, a Celto-Ligurian tribe. Roman conquest resulted in a new valley floor settlement that became Colonia Julia Augusta Apollinaris Reiorum. During the early Empire the town seems to have been prosperous, excavations revealing richly decorated buildings, both public and private. A field with the nineteenth-century name, 'les Arènes', may hide the remains of an amphitheatre. Little is known of Riez in the late Empire – the evidence so far suggesting a serious decline – but by the fifth century new building was taking place both in Riez and on St Maxime's hill. It marked a dynamic era when the town was able to play a regional role.

In the early Middle Ages, the focus of the town itself moved gradually to steeper land to the north, caused probably by a rising river level. Much of Roman Riez was covered by a thick layer of alluvium from the Colostre and its tributary the Auvestre. Modern building is still rare in the southern section, but only a fraction has been excavated.

The temple

Visible from the junction of main roads D952 and D11, 100 m north–west of the baptistery. Open all the time.

By clearing the thick deposits of alluvium, H. Rolland in 1955 and then G. Barroul in the 1960s made clear that the four long-known columns belonged to a temple. The polished granite pillars, 6 m high, are impressive and have fine marble capitals and architrave. Smaller, broken columns surround the temple. The front staircase and the rear of the podium were removed in Antiquity.

The size of the building and the costly materials point to this being the Temple of Apollo that gave the town its full name. 200 m away is a spring with evidence of ancient foundations around it and an inscription with a dedication to Aesculapius, the son of Apollo and the greatest of the classical healing gods. It seems that this was a large temple complex attracting a clientele like a modern spa, such as nearby GREOUX-LES-BAINS (see p. 291). The foundations of rich baths excavated by the baptistery (no visible remains) are likely to have been linked to the temple.

The cathedral site

Barroul also explored the vicinity of the baptistery for remains of the early cathedral. He revealed a fifth-century structure with three naves and a large apse, parts of which are still visible today in the field across the road, east of the baptistery. The ruins are complex because he found the cathedral had been constructed on top of a much larger, but unidentified, first- to second-century AD public building. Other walls are the remains of later medieval churches.

The baptistery

The exterior is a 10 m square and in the fifth century was surrounded by a 4 m wide gallery as well as having a corridor to the cathedral. The interior uses eight granite columns, robbed from an earlier Roman building, to form an octagon of apses. In the middle was a large baptismal pool. It is one of the earliest known baptisteries in all France, an explicit symbol of the activities of Bishop Maxime, 434–60, and his successor Faustus, 461–93, whose dynamism helped ensure the leading cultural role of the church in the era of romanised barbarians. The sanctification of Maxime helped maintain Riez's status as a healing town. Even in the nineteenth century, the 'blessed' water attracted the faithful locally.

It has, of course, been restored frequently. The cupola is Romanesque and only the overall design of the lower portions is original.

Museum

At present housed in the baptistery, but purpose-built premises are planned for Riez.

The current display is small, dusty and without labels. Of interest are the *taurobolium* altar (the hole was cut for fountain water when it stood in a garden, not for pouring the bull's blood as the locals will tell you), the altar to Silvanus and the tiny votive lamps.

SISTERON, Alpes de Haute-Provence

Michelin 81–6
IGN 60–B8
4,02/49,10gr
5°57/44°12

Rock-cut inscription.

Going 10 km east-north-east out of Sisteron by the D3 to St Geniez and Authon, the road winds up into the mountains and reaches a long ravine in which runs the wild winter torrent, Riou de Jabron. The gorge is called the 'Pierre Ecrite' and is named after the seventeen-line inscription. On the southern side of the road, cut into a rock about 4 m above road level, protected from dripping water and minor rock falls by a modern weather-board, it has survived remarkably well and is easily accessible.

In 410 the world was collapsing. Rome itself fell to Alaric's Visigoths, an almost unbelievable image of destruction for all civilised people. The power-less Emperor Honorius could only hide his court in Ravenna. In northern and central Gaul, barbarians roamed freely. In Arles, the usurper Constantine III had set up court. He had come from Britain bringing many of its troops; Honorius, when appealed to by the Britons for help against Saxon invaders, could only write telling them to look after themselves. Yet there were still loyal officials with a belief in both the Roman Empire and

Honorius: one of the most important was Cl(audius) Postumus Dardanus.

The **inscription** begins with his full name. The cognomen, Dardanus, suggests his family came from the Balkans. It is followed by a list of all the official posts that he had held, ending with his most important, Praef(ecto) Pret(orio) Gall(iarum) – praetorian prefect of the Gauls, the top late Roman civil governorship for the whole of Gaul. He then names his wife Nevia Galla (line 6): clearly she was born more locally. Towards the end of the inscription (line 13), Dardanus also mentions his brother Cl(audius) Lepidus and the important posts that he had held. The inscription commemorates the construction of the road through the gorge and the creation on his estate of a walled strongpoint called Theopolis (lines 8–11). It appears traditional enough: the great man records his titles and generosity to the community, but it embodies the growing unreality of the Imperial Order and the search for survival in Christian isolation. It is undated but is probably 414–30.

Certainly Dardanus was proud of the status that he achieved by his loyal service, but what kind of role did he actually play? As praetorian prefect from 409 to 414, he must have tried to collect taxes and dispense justice, but power was in the hands of barbarians and usurpers much of the time. The moment Constantine III was destroyed in 411, another usurper arose. Jovinus was a local nominee of barbarians and a group of central Gallo-Roman nobles. He too was put down and, on the orders of Honorius, Dardanus personally killed Jovinus. What kind of Imperial authority was restored? The Visigoths who had sacked Rome provided the forces for crushing the usurpers, and though these had withdrawn from Gaul they remained a major force in Roman Spain and were soon to return to Gaul; the Franks had moved into northern Gaul and Roman authority in Britain was even more shadowy. If Dardanus was satisfied with his achievements in 414, he does not seem to have had a hopeful political vision: it is simply a mountainous and personal redoubt.

Where others sought the security of islands, like St Honorat (see LERINS, p. 276), Dardanaus used his estate hidden away in the Alps. Letters from both St Jerome in Palestine and St Augustine in Africa (414 and 417) show that he was deliberately rejecting the political life: he had been newly baptised and had apparently become a committed Christian. Like St Augustine's 'Civitas Dei', embodied in the book he was writing at the time, Dardanus' Theopolis or 'City of God' can only be found far away from the disintegrating real world.

However, the walls and towers of Theopolis remain a puzzle. Most likely is that it lies under St Geniez, though the name 'Theon' for an old farmhouse is suggestive. So far no Gallo-Roman remains have been identified at either site. More interesting is **Notre-Dame de Dromon**. This small chapel clinging to the side of the 1,290 m high Rocher de Dromon is approached by a track 2.5 km from St Geniez.

The chapel itself is not ancient, but the small crypt with its attractively carved capitals is considered to be eighth or early ninth century. F. Benoit has argued that this is perhaps an early restoration of the tombs of Dardanus and his wife, turned into a place of local pilgrimage in memory of their status and sanctity. If so, the reputation of Dardanus in central Gaul was not so high. Sidonius Apollinaris writing in the 450s claimed Dardanus had been a monster with all the vices, but then the bishop recognised different realities. Unlike Dardanus he did not see loyalty to a Roman Emperor as meaningful, but he wished to retain a Roman lifestyle and that meant actively working with the local barbarians. Dardanus lived by the standards of a disappearing world, Sidonius by those of the new environment. Indeed, before Sidonius died, the last Emperor of the west had been deposed in 476.

* * *

OTHER SITES IN EASTERN PROVENCE

Digne, Alpes de Haute-Provence

Michelin 81–17 or IGN 60–C10
4,32/48,98gr or 6°15/44°06

Dinia was the tribal capital of the Bodiontici and in the regional museum there is a small collection of local finds, the most attractive of which is a sculpture of Silenus.

Draguignan, Var

Michelin 84–7 or IGN 68–B5
4,60/48,37gr or 6°28/43°33

The Musée-Bibliothèque has a collection including material from nearby St Hermentaire, where a cemetery and a major bath complex attached to a villa were found, the settlement at Flayosc and the sanctuary site of Fox-Amphoux.

Fox-Amphoux, Var

Michelin 84–5 or IGN 68–A2
4,18/48,44gr or 6°07/43°36

Below the tiny hilltop village and its very pleasant restaurant are the overgrown remains of an Augustan sanctuary; traces of the portico wall, column bases and paving are still visible though overgrown. At the D13–D32 junction, by the first farm on the D32 east of the minor road leading from Le Logis to Grand Rougiers.

Gap, Hautes-Alpes

Michelin 77–16 or IGN 60–A9
4,15/49,50gr or 6°05,44°35

Roman city of Vapincum and capital of Aventici tribe. It owed its importance as a road junction through the Alps. Late Roman walling visible and in
the museum a regional collection is newly displayed. It includes rich finds
from the sanctuary sites of St Laurent-du-Gros and Mons Seleucus.

Gréoux-les-Bains, Alpes de Haute-Provence

Michelin 81–15 or IGN 67–D4
3,95/48,63gr or 5°54/43°45

East of Gréoux, a modern establishment has grown up on the site of the
Roman hot spring healing baths, dedicated to the nymphs of 'Griseliae'. Fine
remains of a swimming pool and other buildings have been discovered in
recent excavations. The prestige of the second-century baths is indicated by
the visit of Anna Faustina, a relative of Marcus Aurelius, later murdered by
Commodus. There is an inscription in the main hall. The future of the pool
was uncertain at time of writing.

Roquebrune–Cap-Martin, Alpes Maritimes

Michelin 84–10 or IGN 61–D10
5,72/48,63gr or 7°28/43°46

Below Roquebrune on the N7, take the Cap-Martin turning. At the junction
of the Avenue Paul Dowmer and Avenue Bedoux by what was the Via Julia
is a large and elaborately decorated mausoleum, possibly first century BC.

St Cyr-sur-Mer, Var

Michelin 84–14 or IGN 67–J3
3,72/47,97gr or 5°42/43°10

On the Route de la Mardrague, in Les Lecques by the bay of La Ciotat are
the remains of a grand and luxurious villa, misidentified as part of the town
Tauroentum. Remains include mosaics, part of a peristyle, a reconstructed
mausoleum and a small collection in the museum.

Taradeau, Var

Michelin 84–6 or IGN 68–B5
4,55/48,28gr or 6°26/43°27

A fine second- and first-century BC Iron Age oppidum, perhaps originally built by the Salyens against the Romans, reoccupied in the late Empire. 4 km north of Vidauban, overlooking the village of Taradeau. Subject to major recent excavations. Extensive ramparts and house remains have been exposed. Finds include evidence of an oil press.

GLOSSARY

acanthus: Prickly plant whose foliage and leaf design was copied in decoration.

acroteria: Blocks with statuary set at the corners of a roof pediment.

amphora: A large two-handled storage vessel for containing foodstuffs (e.g., oil, wine, *garum*). The wide variations in shape and size have been catalogued and numbered by Dressel.

appareil: Masonry.

'grand appareil' consists of large rectangular blocks.

'petit appareil' refers to the small regular blockwork, 10–15 cm long, often used as facing for a rubble core.

appliqué: Decorative addition in one material added to another.

architrave: The lower entablature (see NIMES, Maison Carrée, Figure 32, p. 97).

Arretine: Early red gloss sigillata pottery made in Arezzo, first century BC and early first century AD.

ashlar: High-quality large blockwork, particularly used by Greek masons.

atrium: Reception hall or vestibule of traditional Roman house, usually with a pool and central open roof.

ballista: Large crossbow-like catapult machine.

balteus: Wall (see THE ROMAN THEATRE, Figure 16, pp. 46–7).

bouleterion: Greek council chamber.

bucrania: Ox-skulls, often used as decoration on temples and tombstones recalling ritual sacrifices.

caldarium: The hot, wet-heat, room of a bath system.

Campanian ware: Black gloss pottery manufactured in southern and central Italy during the last three centuries BC.

capital: The carved crowning block on top of a column.

capitolium: A triple temple dedicated to Jupiter 'Best and Greatest', Juno and Minerva. They guaranteed the Roman state.

cardo: The main road running north–south in a town. See *decumanus*.

caryatid: A column in the form of a draped female figure.

castrum: A Roman fort; in France often used when referring to a late

293

Roman structure, forming a castle-like refuge.

cavea: The seating area of a theatre or amphitheatre.

cella: The cult room inside a temple.

cinerary urn: The jar holding cremation ashes.

cisalpine Gaul: Northern Italy between the Apennines and the Alps. At the end of the fifth century the area was settled by Celtic peoples, called 'Gauls' by the Romans. Though they sacked Rome in 390 BC, they were ultimately absorbed both culturally and politically by Rome. The area was then also known as 'Gallia Togata', equally distinguishing it from the un-Italicised Transalpine Gaul, across the Alps.

civitas: The 'community of citizens', seen ideally by the Romans as a self-governing unit, based on a city with its surrounding, supporting countryside. The Gallic tribes were recognised and organised as *civitas*, despite varying traditions and levels of urbanisation. All *civitates* had administrative centres, some developed urban features so rapidly that they were granted city status (*municipium*) or even given the prestigious title of colony.

corbel: A projecting block.

Corinthian (Order): Most decorative of the Greek architectural styles with its acanthus-based capitals, particularly popular in the Roman period.

cornice: The upper entablature (see NIMES, Maison Carrée, Figure 32, p. 97).

cornucopia: The horn of plenty, symbol of abundance and peace.

corporation: A guild bringing together groups of craft workers, merchants or artists. Corporations also functioned as burial clubs or as cult associations.

crater: A large Greek bowl for mixing wine with a wide mouth and double handles.

crenellation: Alternating high and low portions of battlements.

cryptoporticus: Semi-subterranean vaulted corridors, often under a forum.

curia: Meeting-place of a Roman town council.

cut-water: A projecting pier designed to break the force of a river current.

decumanus: The main road running east–west through a town. See *cardo*.

diocese: Late Roman administrative division made up from small provinces. The governor was called a vicar.

Dionysus: Also known as Bacchus, the Greek god of wine and ecstasy. His semi-divine male and female followers were known as Bacchi and Bacchae.

dolium: A large globular jar with a wide mouth, particularly associated with storing olive oil.

domus: A rich house (see pp. 241–4).

Doric (Order): Simplest of Greek architectural styles with a plain capital.

duplex knot: A mosaic design compounding two knots. Also called lover's knot.

engaged column: A column attached to a wall.

entablature: The part of an architectural order above the columns and below the roof (see NIMES, Maison Carrée, Figure 32, p. 97).

equites: Originally those who fought as cavalry, it became the name of the second rank in Roman society, after the senators. Based on wealth, it gave many provincials the opportunity to gain status and prestige in their communities or follow a career in the Roman army and administration.

euripus: The decorated walls around which raced circus chariots.

exedra: A semi-circular or rectangular recess in a wall or colonnade.

fanum: A Romano-Celtic temple, typically of square design with a *cella* and surrounding portico.

forum: A central open space surrounded by public buildings.

frieze: The middle entablature (see NIMES, Maison Carrée, Figure 32, p. 97).

frigidarium: The cold water room in a bath system.

frons scaenae: The facing of the building behind the stage. Often highly decorated (see pp. 46–7 and ORANGE, pp. 187–8).

Greek key: A simple repeated geometric pattern particularly used in mosaics.

groma: The Roman surveyor's instrument for taking bearings.

Hellenistic: Greek, especially the third and second centuries BC.

hypocaust: A floor supported by small columns to allow hot air to circulate below. The air was heated by an external furnace and escaped via box flues in the walls of the room.

imbrex: A tile. See *tegula*.

impost: Projecting section of walling on which an arch rests.

in situ: Used by archaeologists to describe (a) artefacts found in their place of original use, or (b) artefacts left in the place where they were discovered.

insula: The normally rectangular street block into which towns were divided.

Ionic (Order): An architectural style using capitals decorated with scrolls or volutes.

itineraries: Diagrammatic maps listing stations on routes. The Antonine Itinerary is probably third century AD.

laconicum: Dry hot room in bath system.

lapidary: Concerned with stones.

lyre: A plucked string instrument used to accompany lyric poetry.

mansio: Post-inn where the Imperial messengers changed horses.

mausoleum: A grand tomb.

medallion: Used for a featured panel in a mosaic.

metopes: Carved or plain slabs between triglyphs in a Doric frieze.

mortaria: Earthenware mixing bowl with a gritty inside surface.

necropolis: Cemetery.

nymphaeum: A decorative shrine associated with water nymphs.

Octavian/Augustus: Up to the age of 19, before his posthumous adoption by Julius Caesar, he was called by his family name, **Octavius**. Subsequently, he changed his name to Octavianus (44 BC). From 27 BC he took the title of **Augustus**.

obol: A small silver Greek coin. Massalia produced its own.

odeon: Small theatre, traditionally used for literary readings.

oppidum: A general Latin name for a settlement that said nothing about its status. Used by archaeologists to define large non-Roman settlements with a range of urban features such as walls, streets or industrial processing going on. During the Iron Age, many in Gaul were hillforts.

opus signinum: Concrete floor with crushed brick or stone finish.

ordo: The council of a *civitas*.

oscillum: Engraved marble disc used as decoration in a portico.

palaestra: Exercise courtyard often linked with a public baths.

patera: Saucer-shaped bowl used for religious offerings.

pediment: Triangular gable above entablature of building.

peribolus: Enclosing wall of a temple precinct or *temenos*.

peristyle: A garden or court surrounded by a portico inside a building.

Phocea: The Greek city in Turkey from which came the settlers of Massalia/Marseille.

Phrygia: Western Central Turkey particularly associated with a type of hat.

pilaster: Rectangular column projecting slightly from a wall.

pisé: Clay or mud laid directly on a wall, sometimes dried with temporary wooden shutters holding it in place.

podium: High platform on which Roman temples were built.

portico: Covered colonnade.

postern: Small doorway in a rampart wall.

prefect/praefectus: Title used for Imperial officials of widely differing status and powers.

Priapus: Male god of fertility symbolised by the phallus.

proconsul: The status of the governor in Narbonensis who was appointed for one year by the Senate. It indicated the *imperium* or power delegated to him as of a chief magistrate's type (consular). The governor of Alpes Maritimae was a prefect appointed by the Emperor.

pronaos: Porch in front of a temple *cella*.

pulpitum: Timber stage for actors fronted by a decorative wall.

RF: Abbreviation used here for a Roman foot. This was usually 29.6 cm or 11.6 inches.

Romanesque/'Romane': The medieval revival of some features of Roman art during the eleventh and twelfth centuries.

sarcophagus: A decorated stone coffin.

scaena: Stage building (see pp. 46–7).

sevir: Priest of the Imperial cult; generally a wealthy freedman.

sherd: A broken fragment of pottery.

(Terra) Sigillata: The most widely found fine ware in the Empire. A glossy red to pink pottery called Samian in Britain. First made in Italy and called Arretine, then manufactured on a large scale in France, particularly at La

Graufesenque (Aveyron) but also at smaller sites in Languedoc.

Silenus: A demi-god, depicted as a wise but drunken old man and often therefore linked with Dionysus.

sondages: Test-holes investigating a restricted area of a site. Usually sampling to establish answers to specific questions about a site.

spandrels: The triangular section created by the springing of an arch.

spina: The name used in late Antiquity for the *euripus* (see p. 33–4).

stela(e): An upright stone block, often inscribed and generally a tombstone.

stratigraphy: Analysing and placing in chronological sequence the levels or deposits found in archaeological excavation.

strigil: A curved metal tool used in the bath to scrape sweat, dirt and soap off the body.

stylobate: A base on which columns have been set.

tablinium: Main reception room in the *domus*.

taurobolium: A ceremony when a bull was sacrificed to the goddess Cybele. The bull's blood was scattered over the dedicant.

tegula: A flat roof tile with ridges on each side. The **imbrex**, a curved tile, fitted over two adjacent tegula ridges.

tepidarium: Warm room in a bath system.

tesserae: The tiny blocks used to make a mosaic.

toga: Formal male Roman dress.

torc/torque: An open-ended neck-ring, sometimes twisted, made of gold or bronze. Particularly popular in the late Iron Age Celtic world.

Transalpine Gaul: 'Gaul across the Alps' was the name used for southern France in the Republican period, contrasting it with northern Italy, then known as Cisalpine Gaul.

tribune: A title used for an officer in the army and usually a stepping stone for a wealthy man on the path to senatorial rank. Augustus held 'tribunician power'. This was based on his claim to represent the people in the way that the Republican tribunes of the plebs had limited the power of patrician magistrates.

triclinium: The dining-room of a Roman house.

triglyph: Blocks with vertical grooves separating the metopes on a Doric frieze.

triton: A merman.

Tuscan (Order): Simplified version of Doric order.

versurae: Projecting buildings on each end of theatre stage (see pp. 47).

vicus: The smallest unit of self-government in the Roman provinces, they were villages and small towns with their own magistrates. During the later Empire some *vici* became *civitates*.

volute: Scroll placed on the side of an Ionic or Corinthian capital.

vomitorium: Tunnel entrance into a (amphi)theatre.

votive: Offering left for god(s).

voussoir: Wedge-shaped block on the underside of an arch.

SELECT BIBLIOGRAPHY

It should be noted that many of the texts are only available in specialist libraries.

MAJOR ORIGINAL SOURCES MENTIONED IN TEXT

Julius Caesar, *The Battle for Gaul*, translated A. and P. Wiseman, London, 1980
Frontinus, *Strategems and Aqueducts*, translated C. E. Bennett, Loeb, London, 1925
Pliny, *Natural History*, vols I–X, translated H. Rackham, Loeb, London, 1958
Sidonius, *Poems and Letters*, vols I–II, translated B. Anderson, Loeb, London, 1956
Strabo, *The Geography*, vols I–VIII, translated H. L. Jones, Loeb, London, 1969
Suetonius, *The Twelve Caesars*, translated R. Graves, Penguin, Harmondsworth, 1957
Tacitus, *Histories/Annals*, translated M. Grant, Penguin, Harmondsworth, 1956
—— *On Britain and Germany (Agricola and Germania)*, translated H. Mattingly, Penguin, Harmondsworth, 1948
Unknown, *Lives of the Later Caesars*, translated A. Birley, Penguin, Harmondsworth, 1976

GALLO-ROMAN STUDIES

Archéologie de la France: 30 ans de découvertes (1989), (Exposition organisée par la Réunion des musées nationaux, la Direction du Patrimoine, et la Direction des musées de France, 1989), Paris
Archéologie sous-marine: vingt ans de recherche sur les côtes de la France (c. 1988), (Exposition à Nantes, Oleron, Perros-Guirec et Nice, 1985–8?), Catalogue for the exhibition at Nice, Nice
Barbet, A. (1988), *Recueil général des peintures murales de la Gaule. I. Province de Narbonnaise*, Paris
Bedon, R., Chevallier, R. and Pinon, P. (1988), *Architecture et urbanisme en Gaule Romaine*, books I and II, Paris
Blanc, A. (1966), 'Ponts gallo-romains et très anciens de l'Ardèche et la Drôme', *Gallia*, 24, 1: 77–96
Brogan, O. (1953), *Roman Gaul*, London
Carte archéologique de la Gaule romaine: the volumes are I: *Alpes Maritimes* (1931); II: *Var* (1932); V: *Bouches-du-Rhône* (1936); VI: *Basses Alpes* (now Alpes de Haute-Provence); VII: *Vaucluse* (1939); VIII: *Gard* (1941); X: *Hérault* (1946);

XI: *Drôme* (1957); XII: *Aude* (1959); *Ardèche* (1975), Paris

Chevallier, R. (1982), *Provincia*, Paris

Coulon, G. (1985), *Les Gallo-Romains: au carrefour de deux nations*, Paris

Cryptoportiques dans l'architecture romaine, Les (1973) (Conference, 19–23 April 1972), Ecole Française de Rome, Paris

Cunliffe, B. (1988), *Greeks, Romans and Barbarians*, London

Duval, P. M. (1976), *Les Dieux de la Gaule*, 2nd edn, Paris

Esperandieu, E. (1907–66) *Recueil général des bas reliefs, statues et bustes de la Gaule romaine*, Paris

Février, P. A. (1980), *La Ville antique* (= L'Histoire de la France Urbaine, I), Paris

Golvin, J.-C. *et al.* (1987), 'Les amphithéâtres de la Gaule', *Dossiers histoire et archéologie*, 116: 6–55

Goudineau, C. (ed), (1976), *Sites de l'Age du Fer et Gallo-Romains de la région de Nice*, USIPP Livret-Guides B3, Nice

—— (1983), 'Marseille, Rome and Gaul from the third century to the first century BC', in P. Garnsey, K. Hopkins and C. R. Whittaker (eds), *Trade in the Ancient Economy*, London

Grenier, A. (1931–60) *Manuel d'archéologie gallo-romaine*, vols I–IV, Paris

Gros, P. (1979), 'Pour une chronologie des arcs de triomphe de Gaule narbonnaise', *Gallia*, 37: 55–83

—— (1991), *La France gallo-romaine*, Paris

Hatt, J. J. (1989), *Mythes et dieux de la Gaule*, Paris

King, A. (1990), *Roman Gaul and Germany*, London

Landes, C. *et al.* (1989), 'Les théâtres de la Gaule', *Dossiers histoire et archéologie*, 134: 6–45

Lavagne, H. (1979), *Recueil général des mosaïques de la Gaule. III. Province de Narbonnaise*, Paris.

Lerat, L. (1986), *La Gaule romaine*, 2nd edn, Paris

MacKendrick, P. (1971), *Roman France*, London

Nerzic, C. (1989), *La Sculpture en Gaule romaine*, Paris

Pelletier, A. (1989), *Histoire et archéologie de la France ancienne Rhône-Alpes*, Le Coteau-Roanne

Pobé, M. and Roubier, J. (1961), *The Art of Roman Gaul*, London

Rivet, A. L. F. (1988), *Gallia Narbonensis*, London

Salviat, F. (1979), 'La sculpture pré-romaine en Provence', *Dossiers de l'archéologie*, 35: 31–51

Salvait, F. and Barroul, G. (eds) (1976), *Provence et Languedoc Mediterranéen sites: protohistoriques et Gallo-Romains*, USIPP Livret-Guides C3, Nice

Turcan, R. (1972), *Les Religions de l'Asie dans la vallée du Rhône*, Leiden

SITE BIBLIOGRAPHY

The journal *Gallia* provides a fairly regular survey of all the current work taking place at these and other sites in the southern departments.

Agde

Clavel, M. (1970), *Béziers et son territoire dans l'antiquité*, Paris

Jully, J., Fonquerle, D., Aris, R. and Adge, M. (1978), *Agde antique*, Pézenas

Aix-en-Provence

Ambard, R. (1984), *Aix romaine*, Aix-en-Provence

Coutagne, D. (1987), *Archéologie d'Entremont au Musée Granet*, Aix-en-Provence

Alba

Lauxerois, R. (1983), *Le Bas Viverais à l'époque romaine*, Paris

Lauxerois, R., André, P. and Jourdan, G. (1985), *Alba* (Guides archéologiques de la France, 5), Paris

Ambrussum

Fiches, J.-L. (1980), 'Ambrussum et la voie Domitienne', *Rivista di Studi Liguri*, 46: 132–57

—— (1986), *Les maisons gallo-romaines d'Ambrussum*, Paris

Antibes

Rogors, G. and Olivier, A. (1978), 'Le monument romain de Vaugrenier', *Revue archéologique de Narbonnaise*, 11: 143–94

Violino, J.-P. (1983), 'Antibes', *Archéologie du Midi mediterranéen*, 8: 9–88

Apt

Barroul, G. and Dumoulin, A. (1965), 'Le théâtre romain d'Apt', *Revue archéologique de Narbonnaise*, 1: 159–200

Arles

Benoit, F. (1969), *Arles*, Collection Alpina

Rouquette, J.-M. and Sintes, C. (1989), *Arles antique* (Guides archéologiques de la France, 17), Paris

Avignon

Gagnière, S. and Granier, J. (1970), *Avignon de la préhistoire à la papauté*, Avignon

Barbégal

Benoit, F. (1940), 'L'usine de meunerie hydrolique de Barbégal (Arles)', *Revue archéologique*, 15: 42–80

Hodge, A. Trevor (1990), 'A Roman factory', *Scientific American* (November): 58–64

Sagui, C. L. (1948), 'La Meunerie de Barbégal (France) et les roues hydroliques chez les anciens et au moyen âge', *ISIS*, 38 (February): 225–31

Sellin, R. H. J. (1983), 'The large Roman watermill at Barbegal', *History of Technology*, 8: 91–109

Beaucaire

Bessac, J.-C. *et al.* (1987), *Ugernum: Beaucaire et le Beaucairois à l'époque romaine*, Caveirac

Béziers

Clavel, M. (1970), *Béziers et son territoire dans l'antiquité*, Paris
Colin, M.-G., Feugere, M. and Laurens, A. F. (1986), 'Le trésor d'argenterie antique de Béziers', *Archéologia*, 210: 26–34

Bourg-Saint-Andéol

Lauxerois, R. (1983), *Le Bas Viverais à l'époque romaine*, Paris
Walters, V. J. (1974), *The Cult of Mithras in the Roman Province of Gaul*, Leiden

Carcassonne

Johnson, S. (1983), *Late Roman Fortifications*, London
Viollet-le-Duc, E. (1983), *La Cité de Carcassonne* (reproduction of 1888 edition), Paris

Château-Roussillon

Barroul, G. (ed), (1980), *Ruscino: Château-Roussillon*, Paris
Marichal, R. (1983), 'Ruscino, capitale du Roussillon antique', *Archéologia*, 183: 34–41

Die

Desaye, H. (1985), *Die, Musée d'Histoire et d'Archéologie*, Die

Ensérune

Gallet de Santerre, H. (1962), 'Ensérune', *Archaeology*, 15: 163–71
—— (1980), *Ensérune: les silos de la terrace est*, Paris

Fréjus

Février, P-A. (1977), *Fréjus (Forum Julii)*, 2nd edn, Cuneo.

Hyères

Coupry, J. (1981), 'Les fouilles d'Olbia', *Dossiers histoire et archéologie*, 57: 29–31

Istres

Liou, B. (1987), 'Les découvertes archéologiques du Golfe de Fos et les traces du littoral antique', in *Déplacements des lignes de rivage en Mediterranée* (Colloques de CNRS, Aix-en-Provence, 1985), Paris

La Couronne

Bedon, R. (1984), *Les Carrières et les carriers de la Gaule romaine*, Paris

Lattes

Arnal, J., Majurel, R. and Prades, H. (1974), *Le Port de Lattera*, Bordighera/ Montpellier
Unnamed (1987), 'Le complex archéologique de Lattes', *Archéologia*, 220: 46–54

La Turbie

Formigé, J. (1949), *La Trophée des Alpes*, Paris
Mouchot, D. (forthcoming), *Une guide de La Turbie*

Le Pont Julien

Barruol, G. and Martel, P. (1962), 'La voie romaine de Cavaillon à Sisteron', *Revue d'études Ligures*, 28: 125–202

Lérins Islands

Fletcher, Lord (1980), 'The monastery at Lérins', *Journal of the British Archaeological Association*, 17: 17–29
Vindry, G. (1981), 'L'Acropole de Lero à l'Ile Sainte Marguerite', *Dossiers histoire et archéologie*, 57: 62–6

Les Cluses

Grau, R. (1978), 'Un fort romain à sauver: le Castell dels Moros de l'Ecluse', *Archéologia*, 124: 64–70

Loupian

Lavagne, H., Prudholme, R. and Rouquette, D. (1976), 'La Villa gallo-romaine des Prés-Bas à Loupian', *Gallia*, 34: 215–35

Marseille

Escalon de Fonton, M. *et al.* (1979), *Naissance d'une ville: Marseille*, Aix-en-Provence
Jacob, J.-P. and Morel, J.-P. *et al.* (1990), 'Marseille dans le monde antique', *Les dossiers d'archéologie*, 154: 2–96

Moulin des Bouillons

Brun, J.-P. (1986), *L'Oléiculture antique en Provence*, Paris
Le Moulin des Bouillons, uncredited and undated local pamphlet, Gordes

Narbonne

Gayraud, M. (1981), *Narbonne antique: des origines à la fin du III siècle*, Paris
Solier, Y. (1986), *Narbonne* (Guides archéologiques de la France, 8), Paris

Nice

Benoit, F. (1977), *Le Cimiez antique*, Paris
Mouchot, D. (1989), *Nice-Cimiez, Le Musée d'Archéologie*, Nice

Nîmes

Amy, R. and Gros, P. (1979), *La Maison Carrée*, Paris
Musée Archéologique (1990), *Archéologie à Nîmes 1950–1990*, Nîmes

Orange

Amy, R. (1962), *L'Arc d'Orange*, Paris
Bellet, M.-E. (1991), *Orange antique* (Guides archéologiques de la France, 23), Paris

Pont du Gard

Hauck, G. (1988), *The Aqueduct of Nemausus*, Jefferson, North Carolina

Riez

Barroul, G. (1968), 'Un centre administratif et religieux des Alpes du Sud: Riez', *Archéologia*, 21: 20–7

Roquepertuse

Eydoux, H.-P. (1963), *Révélations de l'archéologie*, Paris

St Blaise

Bouloumié, B. (1980), *Guide archéologique de St Blaise*, Rognes-Marseille
—— (1984), 'Un oppidum Gauloise à St Blaise en Provence', *Dossiers histoire et archéologie*, 84: 6–96

St Chamas

Lafran, P. and Roth-Congés, A. (1989), *Le Pont-Flavien de St-Chamas*, St Chamas

St Rémy-de-Provence

Bessac, J.-C. and Lambert, N. *et al.* (1989), 'Glanum', *Les dossiers d'archéologie*, 140: 2–83

Salviat, F. (1990), *Glanum* (Guides archéologiques de la France, 19), Paris

Sisteron

Benoit, F. (1951), 'La crypte en triconque de Theopolis', *Rivista di Archeologia Cristiana*, 27: 69–89

Eydoux, H.-P. (1964), *Realités et énigmes de l'archéologie*, Paris

Vaison-la-Romaine

Goudineau, C. (1979), *Les Fouilles de la Maison au Dauphin*, Paris

Goudineau, C. and de Kisch, Y. (1984), *Vaison-la-Romaine* (Guides archéologiques de la France, 1), Vaison

Valence

Blanc, A. (1953), *Valence romaine*, Valence

—— (1980), *La Cité de Valence à la fin de l'antiquité*, Paris

Vienne

Laroche, C. and Savay-Guerraz, H. (1984), *St Romain-en-Gal* (Guides archéologiques de la France, 2), Paris

Pelletier, A. (1980), *Vienne antique*, Roanne

INDEX